Pay Attention to
DANIEL'S
PROPHECY!

First Printing in English:
5,000,000 Copies

Unless otherwise indicated, Scripture quotations
are from the modern-language
New World Translation of the Holy Scriptures—With References

Pay Attention to Daniel's Prophecy!
English (*dp*-E)

Made in the United States of America

CONTENTS

CHAPTER ONE

THE BOOK OF DANIEL AND YOU

A POWERFUL king threatens to execute his wise men because they are not able to reveal and interpret his puzzling dream. Three young men who refuse to worship a towering image are thrown into a superheated furnace, yet they survive. In the midst of a festive celebration, hundreds behold a hand that is writing mysterious words on a palace wall. Evil conspirators have an elderly man thrown into a pit of lions, but he emerges without a scratch. A prophet of God sees four beasts in a vision, and their significance stretches millenniums into the future.

[2] These are just some of the accounts found in the Bible book of Daniel. Do they merit serious consideration? What possible relevance could this age-old book have for our day? Why should we be concerned about events that occurred some 2,600 years ago?

DANIEL—AN ANCIENT BOOK FOR MODERN TIMES

[3] Much of the book of Daniel focuses on the theme of world rulership, a subject that is of paramount concern today. Almost everyone will agree that we live in difficult times. On a daily basis, news reports bombard us with grim reminders that human society is sinking into

---

1, 2. (a) What are some of the unusual situations presented in the Bible book of Daniel? (b) In our modern times, what questions arise regarding the book of Daniel?

3, 4. Why are many people justifiably concerned about the future of mankind?

a quagmire of perplexing problems—and this despite remarkable achievements in science and technology.

⁴ Consider this: Man has walked on the moon, but in many places he cannot stroll on the streets of his own planet without fear. He can furnish a home with all sorts of modern conveniences, but he cannot stem the tide of broken families. And he can bring about the information age, but he cannot teach people to live together peacefully. Hugh Thomas, a professor of history, once wrote: "The spread of knowledge and education has taught mankind little in the way of self-control and less in the art of living with other men."

⁵ In an attempt to establish a measure of order in society, men have organized themselves under a wide variety of governments. None of them, though, have been exempt from the truthfulness of King Solomon's observation: "Man has dominated man to his injury." (Ecclesiastes 4:1; 8:9) Of course, some rulers have had noble ideals. Nevertheless, no king, president, or dictator can eradicate sickness and death. No human can restore our earth to the Paradise that God purposed it to be.

⁶ Yet, the Creator is both willing and able to do such things. He does not need the permission of human governments to accomplish his purpose, for to him "the nations are as a drop from a bucket; and as the film of dust on the scales they have been accounted." (Isaiah 40: 15) Yes, Jehovah is Sovereign Ruler of the universe. As such, he has authority far above that of human governments. It is God's Kingdom that will replace all human rulerships, to mankind's eternal blessing. Perhaps no-

---

5. For the most part, what has been the result of man's rulership?
6. Why does Jehovah not need the cooperation of human rulerships to accomplish his will?

where is this made clearer than in the Bible book of Daniel.

DANIEL—GREATLY BELOVED BY GOD

[7] Jehovah God had great affection for Daniel, who served as his prophet for many years. Indeed, God's angel described Daniel as "someone very desirable." (Daniel 9:23) The original Hebrew term translated "someone very desirable" can mean "greatly beloved," "highly esteemed," even "a favorite." Daniel was especially precious in God's sight.

[8] Let us briefly consider the unique circumstances of this beloved prophet. In 618 B.C.E., Babylonian King Nebuchadnezzar besieged Jerusalem. (Daniel 1:1) Shortly thereafter, certain well-educated Jewish youths were forcibly taken into exile in Babylon. Daniel was among them. At the time, he was probably in his teens.

[9] Daniel and his companions Hananiah, Mishael, and Azariah were among the Hebrews selected to receive three years of training in "the writing and the tongue of the Chaldeans." (Daniel 1:3, 4) Some scholars note that this was likely more than just a language course. For instance, Professor C. F. Keil states: "Daniel and his companions were to be educated in the wisdom of the Chaldean priests and learned men, which was taught in the schools of Babylon." So Daniel and his companions were being specially trained for government service.

[10] What a drastic change of circumstance this was for Daniel and his associates! In Judah they had lived among

---

7. Who was Daniel, and how did Jehovah view him?
8. How did Daniel come to be in Babylon?
9. What training was given to Daniel and his Hebrew companions?
10, 11. What challenges did Daniel and his companions face, and what help did Jehovah give them?

worshipers of Jehovah. Now they were surrounded by a
people who worshiped mythological gods and goddesses. Nevertheless, young Daniel, Hananiah, Mishael, and
Azariah were not intimidated. They were determined
—despite this faith-challenging situation—to hold fast to
true worship.

11 This would not be easy. King Nebuchadnezzar was a
zealous devotee of Marduk, the chief deity of Babylon.
The king's demands were at times totally unacceptable to
a worshiper of Jehovah. (For example, see Daniel 3:1-7.)
Yet, Daniel and his companions had Jehovah's unfail-
ing guidance. During their three years of training, they
were blessed by God with "knowledge and insight in all
writing and wisdom." In addition, Daniel was given the
ability to understand the meaning of visions and dreams.
Later when the king made an examination of these four
young men, he found them to be "ten times better than
all the magic-practicing priests and the conjurers that
were in all his royal realm."—Daniel 1:17, 20.

PROCLAIMING GOD'S MESSAGES

12 Throughout the many years he spent in Babylon, Daniel served as God's messenger to such men
as Kings Nebuchadnezzar and Belshazzar. Daniel's
assignment was a crucial one. Jehovah had allowed Nebuchadnezzar to destroy Jerusalem, using him as His
instrument. In time, Babylon too would be destroyed.
Truly, the book of Daniel magnifies Jehovah God as the
Most High and as Ruler in "the kingdom of mankind."
—Daniel 4:17.

13 Daniel continued in court service some seven decades, until the fall of Babylon. He lived to see many

12. What special assignment did Daniel have?
13, 14. What happened to Daniel after Babylon's fall?

Jews returning to their homeland in 537 B.C.E., though the Bible does not state that he accompanied them. He was very active until at least the third year of the reign of King Cyrus, the founder of the Persian Empire. By that time, Daniel must have been close to 100 years of age!

¹⁴ After the fall of Babylon, Daniel put the most significant events of his life down in writing. His document is now a remarkable part of the Holy Bible and is known as the book of Daniel. But why should we pay attention to this ancient book?

TWO THREADS, ONE MESSAGE

¹⁵ The unique book of Daniel contains two very different threads—one is narrative, the other is prophetic. Both aspects of Daniel's book can build our faith. How? The narrative portions—among the most vivid in the Bible—show us that Jehovah God will bless and care for those who keep their integrity to him. Daniel and his three companions remained steadfast in the face of life-threatening trials. Today, all who want to remain loyal to Jehovah will be strengthened by a close consideration of their example.

¹⁶ The prophetic portions of Daniel build faith by showing that Jehovah knows the course of history centuries—even millenniums—in advance. For example, Daniel provides details concerning the rise and fall of world powers from the time of ancient Babylon right down to "the time of the end." (Daniel 12:4) Daniel directs our attention to the Kingdom of God in the hands of His appointed King and associate "holy ones," pointing to it as the government that will endure forever. This

---

15. (a) What two threads are contained in the Bible book of Daniel? (b) How can the narrative portion of Daniel benefit us?
16. What lesson do we learn from the prophetic portions of Daniel?

government will fully accomplish Jehovah's purpose for our earth and will result in the blessing of all those who want to serve God.—Daniel 2:44; 7:13, 14, 22.

[17] Thankfully, Jehovah does not keep knowledge of future events to himself. Rather, he is the "Revealer of secrets." (Daniel 2:28) As we consider the fulfillment of the prophecies recorded in the book of Daniel, our faith in God's promises will be strengthened. We will come to feel ever more sure that God will accomplish his purpose at the exact time and in the precise manner that he chooses.

[18] All who study the Bible book of Daniel with a receptive heart will grow in faith. Before embarking on an in-depth examination of this book, however, we need to consider evidence as to whether this book is truly authentic. Some critics have attacked the book of Daniel, saying that its prophecies were actually written after their fulfillment. Are the claims of skeptics justified? The next chapter will address this matter.

17, 18. (a) How will our faith be strengthened by a close examination of the book of Daniel? (b) What matter needs to be addressed before we embark on a study of this prophetic Bible book?

WHAT DID YOU DISCERN?

- Why is Daniel a book for modern times?

- How did Daniel and his companions come to enter Babylonian governmental service?

- What was Daniel's special assignment in Babylon?

- Why should we pay attention to Daniel's prophecy?

CHAPTER TWO

DANIEL—A BOOK ON TRIAL

IMAGINE yourself in a court of law, attending an important trial. A man stands accused of fraud. The prosecuting attorney insists that the man is guilty. Yet, the accused has a long-standing reputation for integrity. Would you not be interested in hearing the evidence for the defense?

² You are in a similar situation when it comes to the Bible book of Daniel. Its writer was a man renowned for integrity. The book that bears his name has been highly regarded for thousands of years. It presents itself as authentic history, written by Daniel, a Hebrew prophet who lived during the seventh and sixth centuries B.C.E. Accurate Biblical chronology shows that his book covers the period extending from about 618 to 536 B.C.E. and was completed by the latter date. But the book stands accused. Some encyclopedias and other reference works imply or assert outright that it is a fraud.

³ For example, *The New Encyclopædia Britannica* acknowledges that the book of Daniel was once "generally considered to be true history, containing genuine prophecy." The *Britannica* claims that in reality, however, Daniel "was written in a later time of national crisis —when the Jews were suffering severe persecution under [Syrian King] Antiochus IV Epiphanes." The encyclopedia dates the book between 167 and 164 B.C.E. This same work asserts that the writer of the book of Daniel

---

1, 2. In what sense does the book of Daniel stand accused, and why do you think it is important to consider evidence in its defense?
3. What does *The New Encyclopædia Britannica* say regarding the authenticity of the book of Daniel?

does not prophesy the future but simply presents "events that are past history to him as prophecies of future happenings."

⁴ Where do such ideas originate? Criticism of the book of Daniel is not new. It started back in the third century C.E. with a philosopher named Porphyry. Like many in the Roman Empire, he felt threatened by the influence of Christianity. He wrote 15 books to undermine this "new" religion. The 12th was directed against the book of Daniel. Porphyry pronounced the book a forgery, written by a Jew in the second century B.C.E. Similar attacks came in the 18th and 19th centuries. In the view of higher critics and rationalists, prophecy—the foretelling of future events—is impossible. Daniel became a favorite target. In effect, he and his book were put on trial in court. Critics claimed to have ample proof that the book was written, not by Daniel during the Jewish exile in Babylon, but by someone else centuries later.* Such attacks became so profuse that one author even wrote a defense called *Daniel in the Critics' Den.*

⁵ Is there proof behind the confident assertions of the critics? Or does the evidence back the defense? A lot is at stake here. It is not just the reputation of this ancient book but also our future that is involved. If the book of

---

* Some critics try to temper the charge of forgery by saying that the writer used Daniel as a pseudonym, just as some ancient noncanonical books were written under assumed names. However, the Bible critic Ferdinand Hitzig held: "The case of the book of Daniel, if it is assigned to any other [writer], is different. Then it becomes a forged writing, and the intention was to deceive his immediate readers, though for their good."

---

4. When did criticism of the book of Daniel begin, and what fueled similar criticism in more recent centuries?
5. Why is the question of the authenticity of Daniel an important one?

Daniel is a fraud, its promises for mankind's future are just hollow words at best. But if it contains genuine prophecies, doubtless you will be eager to learn what these mean for us today. With that in mind, let us examine some of the attacks upon Daniel.

⁶ Take, for example, the charge made in *The Encyclopedia Americana:* "Many historical details of the earlier periods [such as that of the Babylonian exile] have been badly garbled" in Daniel. Is this really so? Let us consider three alleged mistakes, one at a time.

THE CASE OF THE MISSING MONARCH

⁷ Daniel wrote that Belshazzar, a "son" of Nebuchadnezzar, was ruling as king in Babylon when the city was overthrown. (Daniel 5:1, 11, 18, 22, 30) Critics long assailed this point, for Belshazzar's name was nowhere to be found outside the Bible. Instead, ancient historians identified Nabonidus, a successor to Nebuchadnezzar, as the last of the Babylonian kings. Thus, in 1850, Ferdinand Hitzig said that Belshazzar was obviously a figment of the writer's imagination. But does not Hitzig's opinion strike you as a bit rash? After all, would the absence of any mention of this king—especially in a period about which historical records were admittedly scanty—really *prove* that he never existed? At any rate, in 1854 some small clay cylinders were unearthed in the ruins of the ancient Babylonian city of Ur in what is now southern Iraq. These cuneiform documents from King Nabonidus included a prayer for "Bel-sar-ussur, my eldest son." Even critics had to agree: This was the Belshazzar of the book of Daniel.

---

6. What charge is sometimes made regarding the history in Daniel?
7. (a) Why did Daniel's references to Belshazzar long delight critics of the Bible? (b) What happened to the notion that Belshazzar was merely a fictitious character?

⁸ Yet, critics were not satisfied. "This proves nothing," wrote one named H. F. Talbot. He charged that the son in the inscription might have been a mere child, whereas Daniel presents him as a reigning king. Just a year after Talbot's remarks were published, though, more cuneiform tablets were unearthed that referred to Belshazzar as having secretaries and a household staff. No child, this! Finally, other tablets clinched the matter, reporting that Nabonidus was away from Babylon for years at a time. These tablets also showed that during these periods, he *"entrusted the kingship"* of Babylon to his eldest son (Belshazzar). At such times, Belshazzar was, in effect, king—a coregent with his father.*

⁹ Still unsatisfied, some critics complain that the Bible calls Belshazzar, not the son of Nabonidus, but the son of Nebuchadnezzar. Some insist that Daniel does not even hint at the existence of Nabonidus. However, both objections collapse upon examination. Nabonidus, it seems, married the daughter of Nebuchadnezzar. That would make Belshazzar the grandson of Nebuchadnezzar. Neither the Hebrew nor the Aramaic language has words for "grandfather" or "grandson"; "son of" can mean "grandson of" or even "descendant of." (Compare Matthew 1:1.) Further, the Bible account does allow for Belshazzar to be identified as the son of Nabonidus. When terrified by the ominous handwriting on the wall, the desperate Belshaz-

---

* Nabonidus was away when Babylon fell. Thus, Belshazzar is rightly described as king at that time. Critics quibble that secular records do not give Belshazzar the official title of king. Nevertheless, ancient evidence suggests that even a governor may have been spoken of as king by the people in those days.

---

8. How has Daniel's description of Belshazzar as a reigning king been proved true?
9. (a) In what sense may Daniel have meant that Belshazzar was the son of Nebuchadnezzar? (b) Why are critics wrong to assert that Daniel does not even hint at the existence of Nabonidus?

zar offers the *third* place in the kingdom to anyone who can decipher the words. (Daniel 5:7) Why third and not second? This offer implies that the first and second places were already occupied. In fact, they were—by Nabonidus and by his son, Belshazzar.

[10] So Daniel's mention of Belshazzar is not evidence of "badly garbled" history. On the contrary, Daniel—although not writing a history of Babylon—offers us a more detailed view of the Babylonian monarchy than such ancient secular historians as Herodotus, Xenophon, and Berossus. Why was Daniel able to record facts that they missed? Because he was there in Babylon. His book is the work of an eyewitness, not of an impostor of later centuries.

WHO WAS DARIUS THE MEDE?

[11] Daniel reports that when Babylon was overthrown, a king named "Darius the Mede" began to rule. (Daniel 5:31) Darius the Mede has not yet been found by name in secular or archaeological sources. Thus, *The New Encyclopædia Britannica* asserts that this Darius is "a fictitious character."

[12] Some scholars have been more cautious. After all, critics once labeled Belshazzar "fictitious" as well. Undoubtedly, the case of Darius will prove similar. Already, cuneiform tablets have revealed that Cyrus the Persian did not assume the title "King of Babylon" immediately after the conquest. One researcher suggests: "Whoever

---

10. Why is Daniel's account of the Babylonian monarchy more detailed than that of other ancient historians?
11. According to Daniel, who was Darius the Mede, but what has been said of him?
12. (a) Why should Bible critics know better than to state categorically that Darius the Mede never existed? (b) What is one possibility regarding the identity of Darius the Mede, and what evidence indicates this?

bore the title of 'King of Babylon' was a vassal king under Cyrus, not Cyrus himself." Could Darius have been the ruling name, or title, of a powerful Median official left in charge of Babylon? Some suggest that Darius may have been a man named Gubaru. Cyrus installed Gubaru as governor in Babylon, and secular records confirm that he ruled with considerable power. One cuneiform tablet says that he appointed subgovernors over Babylon. Interestingly, Daniel notes that Darius appointed 120 satraps to govern the kingdom of Babylon.—Daniel 6:1.

[13] In time, more direct evidence of the precise identity of this king may come to light. In any case, the seeming silence of archaeology in this regard is hardly grounds to label Darius "fictitious," much less to dismiss the entire book of Daniel as fraudulent. It is far more reasonable to see Daniel's account as eyewitness testimony that is more detailed than surviving secular records.

THE REIGN OF JEHOIAKIM

[14] Daniel 1:1 reads: "In the third year of the kingship of Jehoiakim the king of Judah, Nebuchadnezzar the king of Babylon came to Jerusalem and proceeded to lay siege to it." Critics have found fault with this scripture because it does not seem to agree with Jeremiah, who says that the *fourth* year of Jehoiakim was the *first* year of Nebuchadnezzar. (Jeremiah 25:1; 46:2) Was Daniel contradicting Jeremiah? With more information, the matter is readily clarified. When first made king in 628 B.C.E. by Pharaoh Necho, Jehoiakim became a mere puppet of that Egyptian ruler. This was about three years before Nebu-

13. What is a logical reason why Darius the Mede is mentioned in the book of Daniel but not in secular records?
14. Why is there no discrepancy between Daniel and Jeremiah regarding the years of King Jehoiakim's reign?

chadnezzar succeeded his father to the throne of Babylon, in 624 B.C.E. Soon thereafter (in 620 B.C.E.), Nebuchadnezzar invaded Judah and made Jehoiakim a vassal king under Babylon. (2 Kings 23:34; 24:1) To a Jew living in Babylon, Jehoiakim's "third year" would have been the third year of that king's vassal service to Babylon. Daniel wrote from that perspective. Jeremiah, however, wrote from the perspective of the Jews living right in Jerusalem. So he referred to Jehoiakim's kingship as starting when Pharaoh Necho made him king.

[15] Really, then, this alleged discrepancy only bolsters the evidence that Daniel wrote his book in Babylon while among Jewish exiles. But there is another gaping hole in this argument against the book of Daniel. Remember that the writer of Daniel clearly had the book of Jeremiah available and even referred to it. (Daniel 9:2) If the writer of Daniel were a clever forger, as the critics claim, would he risk contradicting so respected a source as Jeremiah—and in the very first verse of his book at that? Of course not!

TELLING DETAILS

[16] Let us now turn our attention from the negative to the positive. Consider some other details in the book of Daniel indicating that the writer had firsthand knowledge of the times he wrote about.

[17] Daniel's familiarity with subtle details about ancient Babylon is compelling evidence of the authenticity of his account. For instance, Daniel 3:1-6 reports that Nebuchadnezzar set up a giant image for all the people to

---

15. Why is it a weak argument to attack the dating found in Daniel 1:1?
16, 17. How has archaeological evidence supported Daniel's account of (a) Nebuchadnezzar's setting up a religious image for all his people to worship? (b) Nebuchadnezzar's boastful attitude about his construction projects in Babylon?

(Below)
Babylonian temple cylinder names King Nabonidus and his son Belshazzar

(Above) This inscription contains the boasting of Nebuchadnezzar regarding his construction projects

worship. Archaeologists have found other evidence that this monarch sought to get his people more involved in nationalistic and religious practices. Similarly, Daniel records Nebuchadnezzar's boastful attitude about his many construction projects. (Daniel 4:30) Not until modern times have archaeologists confirmed that Nebuchadnezzar was indeed behind a great deal of the building done in Babylon. As to boastfulness—why, the man had his name stamped on the very bricks! Daniel's critics cannot explain how their supposed forger of Maccabean times (167-63 B.C.E.) could have known of such construction projects—some four centuries after the fact and long before archaeologists brought them to light.

¹⁸ The book of Daniel also reveals some key differences

18. How does Daniel's account of the different forms of punishment under Babylonian rule and Persian rule reflect accuracy?

According to the Nabonidus Chronicle, Cyrus' army entered Babylon without a fight

between Babylonian and Medo-Persian law. For example, under Babylonian law Daniel's three companions were thrown into a fiery furnace for refusing to obey the king's command. Decades later, Daniel was thrown into a pit of lions for refusing to obey a Persian law that violated his conscience. (Daniel 3:6; 6:7-9) Some have tried to dismiss the fiery furnace account as legend, but archaeologists have found an actual letter from ancient Babylon that specifically mentions this form of punishment. To the Medes and the Persians, however, fire was sacred. So they turned to other vicious forms of punishment. Hence, the pit of lions comes as no surprise.

[19] Another contrast emerges. Daniel shows that Nebuchadnezzar could enact and change laws on a whim.

19. What contrast between the Babylonian and the Medo-Persian legal systems does the book of Daniel make clear?

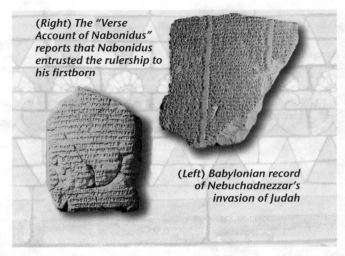

(Right) The "Verse Account of Nabonidus" reports that Nabonidus entrusted the rulership to his firstborn

(Left) Babylonian record of Nebuchadnezzar's invasion of Judah

Darius could do nothing to change 'the laws of the Medes and the Persians'—even those he himself had enacted! (Daniel 2:5, 6, 24, 46-49; 3:10, 11, 29; 6:12-16) Historian John C. Whitcomb writes: "Ancient history substantiates this difference between Babylon, where the law was subject to the king, and Medo-Persia, where the king was subject to the law."

20 The thrilling account of Belshazzar's feast, which is recorded in Daniel chapter 5, is rich in detail. Apparently, it began with lighthearted eating and plenty of drinking, for there are several references to wine. (Daniel 5:1, 2, 4) In fact, relief carvings of similar feasts show only wine being consumed. Evidently, then, wine was extremely important at such festivities. Daniel also mentions that women were present at this banquet—the king's

---

20. What details regarding Belshazzar's feast reflect Daniel's first-hand knowledge of Babylonian customs?

secondary wives and his concubines. (Daniel 5:3, 23) Archaeology supports this detail of Babylonian custom. The notion of wives joining men at a feast was objectionable to Jews and Greeks in the Maccabean era. Perhaps that is why early versions of the Greek Septuagint translation of Daniel omit the mention of these women.* Yet, the alleged forger of Daniel would have lived in the same Hellenized (Greek) culture, and perhaps even during the same general era, that produced the *Septuagint!*

²¹ In view of such details, it seems almost incredible that *Britannica* could describe the author of the book of Daniel as having only a "sketchy and inaccurate" knowledge of the exilic times. How could any forger of later centuries have been so intimately familiar with ancient Babylonian and Persian customs? Remember, too, that both empires had gone into decline long before the second century B.C.E. There were evidently no archaeologists back then; nor did the Jews of that time pride themselves on knowledge of foreign cultures and history. Only Daniel the prophet, an eyewitness of the times and events he described, could have written the Bible book bearing his name.

DO EXTERNAL FACTORS
PROVE DANIEL A FORGERY?

²² One of the most common arguments against the book of Daniel involves its place in the canon of the Hebrew Scriptures. The ancient rabbis arranged the

---

* Hebrew scholar C. F. Keil writes of Daniel 5:3: "The LXX. have here, and also at ver. 23, omitted mention of the women, according to the custom of the Macedonians, Greeks, and Romans."

---

21. What is the most reasonable explanation of Daniel's having intimate knowledge of the times and customs of the Babylonian exile?
22. What claim do critics make regarding the place of Daniel in the canon of the Hebrew Scriptures?

books of the Hebrew Scriptures in three groups: the
Law, the Prophets, and the Writings. They listed Daniel,
not among the Prophets, but among the Writings. This
means, the critics argue, that the book must have been
unknown at the time when the works of the other prophets were collected. It is grouped among the Writings
supposedly because these were collected later.

²³ Nevertheless, not all Bible researchers agree that the
ancient rabbis divided the canon in such a rigid manner
or that they excluded Daniel from the Prophets. But even
if the rabbis did list Daniel among the Writings, would
this prove that it was written at a later date? No. Repu-
table scholars have suggested a number of reasons why
the rabbis might have excluded Daniel from the Prophets. For instance, they may have done so because the book
offended them or because they viewed Daniel himself as
distinct from other prophets in that he held secular office
in a foreign land. In any case, what really matters is this:
The ancient Jews had deep regard for the book of Daniel
and held it to be canonical. Moreover, the evidence suggests that the canon of the Hebrew Scriptures was closed
long before the second century B.C.E. Later additions
were simply not allowed, including some books written
during the second century B.C.E.

²⁴ Ironically, one of these rejected later works has been
used as an argument against the book of Daniel. The
apocryphal book Ecclesiasticus, by Jesus Ben Sirach, was
evidently composed about 180 B.C.E. Critics like to point
out that Daniel is omitted from the book's long list of
righteous men. They reason that Daniel must have been
unknown at the time. This argument is widely accept-

23. How did the ancient Jews view the book of Daniel, and how do
we know this?
24. How has the apocryphal book Ecclesiasticus been used against
the book of Daniel, and what shows this reasoning to be faulty?

ed among scholars. But consider this: The same list omits Ezra and Mordecai (both of whom were great heroes in the eyes of postexilic Jews), good King Jehoshaphat, and the upright man Job; of all the judges, it names only Samuel.* Because such men are omitted from a list that makes no claim to be exhaustive, occurring in a noncanonical book, must we dismiss all of them as fictitious? The very notion is preposterous.

OUTSIDE TESTIMONY IN FAVOR OF DANIEL

²⁵ Let us move again to the positive. It has been suggested that no other book of the Hebrew Scriptures is as well attested to as Daniel. To illustrate: The famous Jewish historian Josephus attests to its authenticity. He says that Alexander the Great, during his war against Persia in the fourth century B.C.E., came to Jerusalem, where the priests showed him a copy of the book of Daniel. Alexander himself concluded that the words of Daniel's prophecy that were pointed out to him referred to his own military campaign involving Persia.# This would have been about a century and a half before the "forgery" as proposed by critics. Of course, critics have assailed

---

* The apostle Paul's inspired list of faithful men and women mentioned in Hebrews chapter 11, by contrast, does seem to allude to events recorded in Daniel. (Daniel 6:16-24; Hebrews 11:32, 33) However, the apostle's list is not exhaustive either. There are many, including Isaiah, Jeremiah, and Ezekiel, who are not named in the list, but this hardly proves that they never existed.

Some historians have noted that this would explain why Alexander was so kind to the Jews, who were long-standing friends of the Persians. At the time, Alexander was on a campaign to destroy all friends of Persia.

---

25. (a) How did Josephus attest to the genuineness of Daniel's account? (b) In what way does Josephus' account regarding Alexander the Great and the book of Daniel fit in with known history? (See second footnote.) (c) How does linguistic evidence support the book of Daniel? (See page 26.)

The Matter of Language

THE writing of the book of Daniel was completed in about 536 B.C.E. It was written in the Hebrew and Aramaic languages, with a few Greek and Persian words. Such a mixture of languages is unusual but not unique in Scripture. The Bible book of Ezra too was written in Hebrew and Aramaic. Yet, some critics insist that the writer of Daniel used these languages in a way that proves he was writing at a date later than 536 B.C.E. One critic is widely quoted as saying that the use of Greek words in Daniel *demands* a late date of composition. He asserts that the Hebrew *supports* and the Aramaic at least *permits* such a late date —even one as recent as in the second century B.C.E.

However, not all language scholars agree. Some authorities have said that Daniel's Hebrew is similar to that of Ezekiel and Ezra and unlike that found in such later apocryphal works as Ecclesiasticus. As to Daniel's use of Aramaic, consider two documents found among the Dead Sea Scrolls. They too are in Aramaic and date from the first and second centuries B.C.E.—not long after the supposed forgery of Daniel. But scholars have noted a profound difference between the Aramaic in these documents and that found in Daniel. Thus, some suggest that the book of Daniel must be centuries older than its critics assert.

What about the "problematic" Greek words in Daniel? Some of these have been discovered to be Persian, not Greek at all! The only words still thought to be Greek are the names of three musical instruments. Does the presence of these three words really *demand* that Daniel be assigned a late date? No. Archaeologists have found that Greek culture was influential centuries before Greece became a world power. Furthermore, if the book of Daniel had been composed during the second century B.C.E., when Greek culture and language were all-pervasive, would it contain *only three* Greek words? Hardly. It would likely contain far more. So the linguistic evidence really supports the authenticity of Daniel.

Josephus concerning this passage. They also assail him for noting that some prophecies in the book of Daniel were fulfilled. Yet, as historian Joseph D. Wilson remarked, "[Josephus] probably knew more of the matter than all the critics in the world."

[26] The authenticity of the book of Daniel received further support when the Dead Sea Scrolls were found in the caves of Qumran, Israel. Surprisingly numerous among the finds discovered in 1952 are scrolls and fragments from the book of Daniel. The oldest has been dated to the late second century B.C.E. At that early date, therefore, the book of Daniel was already well-known and widely respected. Notes *The Zondervan Pictorial Encyclopedia of the Bible:* "A Maccabean dating for Daniel has now to be abandoned, if only because there could not possibly be a sufficient interval between the composition of Daniel and its appearance in the form of copies in the library of a Maccabean religious sect."

[27] However, there is far older and more reliable attestation to the book of Daniel. One of Daniel's contemporaries was the prophet Ezekiel. He too served as a prophet during the Babylonian exile. Several times, the book of Ezekiel mentions Daniel by name. (Ezekiel 14:14, 20; 28:3) These references show that even during his own lifetime, in the sixth century B.C.E., Daniel was already well-known as a righteous and a wise man, worthy of being mentioned alongside God-fearing Noah and Job.

THE GREATEST WITNESS

[28] Finally, though, let us consider the greatest of all the

---

26. How have the Dead Sea Scrolls supported the authenticity of the book of Daniel?
27. What is the oldest evidence that Daniel was an actual person who was well-known during the Babylonian exile?
28, 29. (a) What is the most convincing proof of all that the book of Daniel is authentic? (b) Why should we accept Jesus' testimony?

witnesses to the authenticity of Daniel—none other than Jesus Christ. In his discussion of the last days, Jesus refers to "Daniel the prophet" and to one of Daniel's prophecies.—Matthew 24:15; Daniel 11:31; 12:11.

[29] Now if the Maccabean theory of the critics were correct, one of two things would have to be true. Either Jesus was duped by this forgery or he never said what Matthew quotes him as saying. Neither option is viable. If we cannot rely on Matthew's Gospel account, how can we rely on other parts of the Bible? If we remove those sentences, what words will we next pluck from the pages of the Holy Scriptures? The apostle Paul wrote: *"All Scripture is inspired of God and beneficial for teaching, . . . for setting things straight."* (2 Timothy 3:16) So if Daniel was a fraud, then Paul was another one! Could Jesus have been duped? Hardly. He was alive in heaven when the book of Daniel was written. Jesus even said: "Before Abraham came into existence, I have been." (John 8:58) Of all humans who have ever lived, Jesus would be the best one for us to ask for information regarding the authenticity of Daniel. But we do not have to ask. As we have seen, his testimony could scarcely be any clearer.

[30] Jesus further authenticated the book of Daniel at the very time of his baptism. He then became the Messiah, fulfilling a prophecy in Daniel regarding the 69 weeks of years. (Daniel 9:25, 26; see Chapter 11 of this book.) Even if what may be called the late date theory were true, the writer of Daniel still knew the future some 200 years in advance. Of course, God would not inspire a forger to utter true prophecies under a false name. No, the witness of Jesus is wholeheartedly accepted by people faithful to God. If all the experts, all the critics in the world, were to

---

30. How did Jesus further authenticate the book of Daniel?

mount up as one to denounce Daniel, the testimony of Jesus would prove them wrong, for he is "the faithful and true witness."—Revelation 3:14.

³¹ Even this testimony is not enough for many Bible critics. After considering this subject thoroughly, one cannot help but wonder if *any* amount of evidence would be enough to convince them. One professor at Oxford University wrote: "Nothing is gained by a mere answer to objections, so long as the original prejudice, 'there cannot be supernatural prophecy,' remains." So their prejudice blinds them. But that is their choice—and their loss.

³² What about you? If you can see that there is no real reason to doubt the authenticity of the book of Daniel, then you are ready for an exciting voyage of discovery. You will find the narratives in Daniel thrilling, the prophecies fascinating. More important, you will find your faith growing stronger with each chapter. You will never regret paying close attention to Daniel's prophecy!

---

31. Why are many Bible critics still unconvinced as to the authenticity of Daniel?
32. What lies ahead in our study of Daniel?

WHAT DID YOU DISCERN?

- Of what has the book of Daniel been accused?

- Why are the critics' attacks on the book of Daniel not well-founded?

- What evidence supports the authenticity of Daniel's account?

- What is the most convincing proof that the book of Daniel is authentic?

CHAPTER THREE

TESTED—BUT TRUE TO JEHOVAH!

THE curtain rises in the prophetic book of Daniel at a time of momentous change on the international scene. Assyria had just suffered the loss of its capital, Nineveh. Egypt had been restricted to a position of minor importance south of the land of Judah. And Babylon was rapidly rising as the major power in the struggle for world domination.

² In 625 B.C.E., Egyptian Pharaoh Necho made a last-ditch effort to block Babylonian expansion southward. To that end, he led his army to Carchemish, located on the banks of the upper Euphrates River. The battle of Carchemish, as it came to be called, was a decisive, historic event. The Babylonian army, led by Crown Prince Nebuchadnezzar, inflicted a devastating blow on Pharaoh Necho's forces. (Jeremiah 46:2) Riding on the momentum of his victory, Nebuchadnezzar swept over Syria and Palestine and, for all practical purposes, put an end to Egyptian domination in this region. It was only the death of his father, Nabopolassar, that brought a temporary halt to his campaign.

³ The next year, Nebuchadnezzar—now enthroned as king of Babylon—once again turned his attention to his military campaigns in Syria and Palestine. It was during this period that he came to Jerusalem for the first time. The Bible reports: "In his days Nebuchadnezzar the

---

1, 2. What significant events served as a prelude to the account of Daniel?
3. What was the outcome of Nebuchadnezzar's first campaign against Jerusalem?

king of Babylon came up, and so Jehoiakim became his servant for three years. However, he turned back and rebelled against him."—2 Kings 24:1.

NEBUCHADNEZZAR IN JERUSALEM

⁴ The expression "for three years" is of special interest to us, for the opening words of Daniel read: "In the third year of the kingship of Jehoiakim the king of Judah, Nebuchadnezzar the king of Babylon came to Jerusalem and proceeded to lay siege to it." (Daniel 1:1) In the third year of the complete kingship of Jehoiakim, who reigned from 628 to 618 B.C.E., Nebuchadnezzar was not yet "the king of Babylon" but was the crown prince. In 620 B.C.E., Nebuchadnezzar compelled Jehoiakim to pay tribute. But after about three years, Jehoiakim revolted. Thus, it was in 618 B.C.E., or during the third year of the kingship of Jehoiakim as a vassal of Babylon, that King Nebuchadnezzar came to Jerusalem a second time, to punish the rebellious Jehoiakim.

⁵ The outcome of this siege was that "in time Jehovah gave into his hand Jehoiakim the king of Judah and a part of the utensils of the house of the true God." (Daniel 1:2) Jehoiakim probably died, either by assassination or in a revolt, during the early stages of the siege. (Jeremiah 22:18, 19) In 618 B.C.E., his 18-year-old son, Jehoiachin, succeeded him as king. But Jehoiachin's rule lasted only three months and ten days, and he surrendered in 617 B.C.E. —Compare 2 Kings 24:10-15.

⁶ Nebuchadnezzar took as spoils sacred utensils of the
_____
4. How is the expression "in the third year of the kingship of Jehoiakim" at Daniel 1:1 to be understood?
5. What was the outcome of Nebuchadnezzar's second campaign against Jerusalem?
6. What did Nebuchadnezzar do with the sacred utensils of the temple in Jerusalem?

temple in Jerusalem and "brought them to the land of Shinar to the house of his god; and the utensils he brought to the treasure-house of his god," Marduk, or Merodach in Hebrew. (Daniel 1:2; Jeremiah 50:2) A Babylonian inscription was discovered in which Nebuchadnezzar is represented as saying about the temple of Marduk: "I stored up inside silver and gold and precious stones . . . and placed there the *treasure house* of my kingdom." We will read about these sacred utensils once again in the days of King Belshazzar.—Daniel 5:1-4.

THE ELITE OF JERUSALEM'S YOUTH

7 More than the treasures of Jehovah's temple were brought to Babylon. Says the account: "Then the king said to Ashpenaz his chief court official to bring some of the sons of Israel and of the royal offspring and of the nobles, children in whom there was no defect at all, but good in appearance and having insight into all wisdom and being acquainted with knowledge, and having discernment of what is known, in whom also there was ability to stand in the palace of the king."—Daniel 1:3, 4.

8 Who were chosen? We are told: "There happened to be among them some of the sons of Judah, Daniel, Hananiah, Mishael and Azariah." (Daniel 1:6) This sheds some light on the otherwise obscure background of Daniel and his companions. For example, we note that they were "sons of Judah," the kingly tribe. Whether they were from the royal line or not, it is reasonable to think that they were at least from families of some importance and influence. Besides being of sound mind and body, they had insight, wisdom, knowledge, and discernment—all when they were at an age young enough to be called "children," perhaps in their early teens. Daniel

---

7, 8. From Daniel 1:3, 4, and 6, what can we deduce about the background of Daniel and his three companions?

and his companions must have been outstanding—the elite—among the youths in Jerusalem.

⁹ The account does not tell us who the parents of these young people were. Nonetheless, it seems certain that they were godly individuals who had taken their parental responsibilities seriously. Considering the moral and spiritual decadence prevalent in Jerusalem at the time, especially among 'the royal offspring and the nobles,' it is clear that the sterling qualities found in Daniel and his three companions did not come about by accident. Needless to say, it must have been heartbreaking for the parents to see their sons being taken to a distant land. If only they could have known the outcome, how proud they would have been! How important it is for parents to bring their children up "in the discipline and mental-regulating of Jehovah"!—Ephesians 6:4.

A BATTLE FOR THE MIND

¹⁰ Immediately, a battle for the young minds of these exiles began. To make sure that the Hebrew teenagers would be molded to fit in with the Babylonian system, Nebuchadnezzar decreed that his officials "teach them the writing and the tongue of the Chaldeans." (Daniel 1:4) This was no ordinary education. *The International Standard Bible Encyclopedia* explains that it "comprised the study of Sumerian, Akkadian, Aramaic . . . , and other languages, as well as the extensive literature written in them." "The extensive literature" consisted of history, mathematics, astronomy, and so on. However, "associated religious texts, both omina [omens] and astrology . . . , played a large part."

---

9. Why does it seem certain that Daniel and his three companions had God-fearing parents?
10. What were the young Hebrews taught, and what was the purpose of this?

¹¹ So that these Hebrew youths would completely adopt the customs and culture of Babylonian court life, "the king appointed a daily allowance from the delicacies of the king and from his drinking wine, even to nourish them for three years, that at the end of these they might stand before the king." (Daniel 1:5) Furthermore, "to them the principal court official went assigning names. So he assigned to Daniel the name of Belteshazzar; and to Hananiah, Shadrach; and to Mishael, Meshach; and to Azariah, Abednego." (Daniel 1:7) In Bible times it was a common practice for a person to be given a new name to mark a significant event in his life. For instance, Jehovah changed the names of Abram and Sarai to Abraham and Sarah. (Genesis 17:5, 15, 16) For a human to change someone's name is clear evidence of authority or dominance. When Joseph became the food administrator of Egypt, Pharaoh named him Zaphenath-paneah.—Genesis 41:44, 45; compare 2 Kings 23:34; 24:17.

¹² In the case of Daniel and his three Hebrew friends, the name changes were significant. The names their parents had given them were in harmony with the worship of Jehovah. "Daniel" means "My Judge Is God." The meaning of "Hananiah" is "Jehovah Has Shown Favor." "Mishael" possibly means "Who Is Like God?" "Azariah" means "Jehovah Has Helped." No doubt it was their parents' fervent hope that their sons would grow up under the guidance of Jehovah God to become his faithful and loyal servants.

¹³ However, the new names given to the four Hebrews were all closely associated with those of false gods,

---

11. What steps were taken to ensure that the Hebrew youths would be assimilated into Babylonian court life?
12, 13. Why can it be said that changing the names of the young Hebrews was an effort to sabotage their faith?

suggesting that the true God had been subjugated by such deities. What an insidious effort to sabotage the faith of these young people!

¹⁴ Daniel's name was changed to Belteshazzar, meaning "Protect the Life of the King." Evidently, this was a shortened form of an invocation to Bel, or Marduk, the principal god of Babylon. Whether Nebuchadnezzar had a hand in choosing this name for Daniel or not, he was proud to acknowledge that it was "according to the name of [his] god." (Daniel 4:8) Hananiah was renamed Shadrach, which some authorities believe to be a compound name meaning "Command of Aku." Interestingly, Aku was the name of a Sumerian god. Mishael was renamed Meshach (possibly, *Mi·sha·aku*), apparently a clever twist of "Who Is Like God?" to "Who Is What Aku Is?" Azariah's Babylonian name was Abednego, probably meaning "Servant of Nego." And "Nego" is a variant of "Nebo," the name of a deity after which a number of Babylonian rulers were also named.

DETERMINED TO REMAIN TRUE TO JEHOVAH

¹⁵ The Babylonian names, the reeducation program, and the special diet—all of this was an attempt not only to assimilate Daniel and the three young Hebrews into the Babylonian way of life but also to alienate them from their own God, Jehovah, and from their religious training and background. Confronted with all this pressure and temptation, what would these young people do?

¹⁶ The inspired account says: "Daniel determined in his heart that he would not pollute himself with the delicacies of the king and with his drinking wine." (Daniel 1:8a)

---

14. What do the new names given to Daniel and his three companions mean?
15, 16. What dangers now confronted Daniel and his companions, and what was their reaction?

Although Daniel was the only one mentioned by name, it is evident by what followed that his three companions supported his decision. The words "determined in his heart" show that the instruction provided by Daniel's parents and others back home had reached his heart. Similar training undoubtedly guided the other three Hebrews in their decision-making. This amply illustrates the value of teaching our children, even when they may seem to be too young to understand.—Proverbs 22:6; 2 Timothy 3:14, 15.

¹⁷ Why did the young Hebrews object only to the delicacies and the wine but not to the other arrangements? Daniel's reasoning clearly indicates why: "He would not pollute himself." Having to learn "the writing and the tongue of the Chaldeans" and being given a Babylonian name, objectionable though this might be, would not necessarily pollute a person. Consider the example of Moses, nearly 1,000 years earlier. Although he was "instructed in all the wisdom of the Egyptians," he remained loyal to Jehovah. His upbringing by his own parents gave him a solid foundation. Consequently, "by faith Moses, when grown up, refused to be called the son of the daughter of Pharaoh, choosing to be ill-treated with the people of God rather than to have the temporary enjoyment of sin."—Acts 7:22; Hebrews 11:24, 25.

¹⁸ In what way would the Babylonian king's provisions pollute the young men? First, the delicacies may have included foods prohibited by the Mosaic Law. For example, the Babylonians ate unclean animals, forbidden to the Israelites under the Law. (Leviticus 11:1-31; 20:24-26; Deuteronomy 14:3-20) Second, the Babylonians were

17. Why did Daniel and his companions object only to the king's daily provisions and not to the other arrangements?
18. In what ways would the king's provisions pollute the young Hebrews?

not in the habit of bleeding slaughtered animals before eating their flesh. Eating unbled meat would be in direct violation of Jehovah's law on blood. (Genesis 9:1, 3, 4; Leviticus 17:10-12; Deuteronomy 12:23-25) Third, worshipers of false gods customarily offer their food to idols before eating it in a communion meal. Servants of Jehovah would have none of that! (Compare 1 Corinthians 10:20-22.) Finally, indulgence in rich foods and strong drink day after day would hardly be healthful for people of any age, let alone for the young.

¹⁹ It is one thing to know what to do, but it is quite another to have the courage to do it when under pressure or temptation. Daniel and his three friends could have reasoned that since they were far away from their parents and friends, such individuals would not know what they did. They could also have rationalized that it was the king's order and that there appeared to be no alternative. Besides, other young people no doubt readily accepted the arrangements and counted it a privilege rather than a hardship to participate. But such faulty thinking could easily lead to the pitfall of secret sin, which is a snare for many young people. The Hebrew youths knew that "the eyes of Jehovah are in every place" and that "the true God himself will bring every sort of work into the judgment in relation to every hidden thing, as to whether it is good or bad." (Proverbs 15:3; Ecclesiastes 12:14) Let all of us take a lesson from the course of these faithful young people.

COURAGE AND PERSISTENCE WERE REWARDING

²⁰ Having resolved in his heart to resist corrupting influences, Daniel proceeded to act in harmony with his decision. "He kept requesting of the principal court of-

19. How could the Hebrew youths have rationalized, but what helped them to come to the right conclusion?
20, 21. What action did Daniel take, and with what outcome?

ficial that he might not pollute himself." (Daniel 1:8b) "Kept requesting"—that is a noteworthy expression. Most often, persistent effort is needed if we hope to be successful in fighting off temptations or overcoming certain weaknesses.—Galatians 6:9.

21 In Daniel's case, persistence paid off. "Accordingly the true God gave Daniel over to loving-kindness and to mercy before the principal court official." (Daniel 1:9) It was not because Daniel and his companions were personable and intelligent individuals that things eventually worked out well for them. Rather, it was because of Jehovah's blessing. Daniel undoubtedly remembered the Hebrew proverb: "Trust in Jehovah with all your heart and do not lean upon your own understanding. In all your ways take notice of him, and he himself will make your paths straight." (Proverbs 3:5, 6) Following that counsel was rewarding indeed.

22 At first, the principal court official objected: "I am in fear of my lord the king, who has appointed your food and your drink. Why, then, should he see your faces dejected-looking in comparison with the children who are of the same age as yours, and why should you have to make my head guilty to the king?" (Daniel 1:10) These were legitimate objections and fears. King Nebuchadnezzar was not one to take no for an answer, and the official realized that his "head" would be in jeopardy if he were to go against the king's instructions. What would Daniel do?

23 This was where insight and wisdom came into play. Young Daniel probably remembered the proverb: "An answer, when mild, turns away rage, but a word causing pain makes anger to come up." (Proverbs 15:1) Instead of stubbornly insisting that his request be granted and possibly

---

22. What legitimate objection did the court official raise?
23. By the course he took, how did Daniel show insight and wisdom?

provoking others to make a martyr out of him, Daniel let the matter rest. At the right time, he approached "the guardian," who was perhaps more willing to allow a little leeway because he was not directly accountable to the king.—Daniel 1:11.

A TEN-DAY TEST PROPOSED

²⁴ To the guardian, Daniel proposed a test, saying: "Please, put your servants to the test for ten days, and let them give us some vegetables that we may eat and water that we may drink; and let our countenances and the countenance of the children who are eating the delicacies of the king appear before you, and according to what you see do with your servants."—Daniel 1:12, 13.

²⁵ Ten days on 'vegetables and water'—would they become "dejected-looking" as compared with the others? "Vegetables" is translated from a Hebrew word that basically means "seeds." Certain Bible translations render it as "pulse," which is defined as "the edible seeds of various leguminous crops (as peas, beans, or lentils)." Some scholars feel that the context indicates a diet including more than just edible seeds. One reference work states: "What Daniel and his companions were requesting was the plain vegetable fare of the general populace rather than the richer, meaty diet of the royal table." Thus, vegetables could have included nourishing dishes prepared with beans, cucumbers, garlic, leeks, lentils, melons, and onions and bread made from various grains. Surely no one would consider that a starvation diet. Apparently the guardian saw the point. "Finally he listened to them as regards this matter and put them to the test for ten days." (Daniel 1:14) What was the result?

---

24. What test did Daniel propose?
25. What probably were included in the "vegetables" served to Daniel and his three friends?

²⁶ "At the end of ten days their countenances appeared better and fatter in flesh than all the children who were eating the delicacies of the king." (Daniel 1:15) This is not to be taken as evidence that a vegetarian diet is superior to a richer, meaty one. Ten days is a short time for any kind of diet to produce tangible results, but it is not too short for Jehovah to accomplish his purpose. "The blessing of Jehovah—that is what makes rich, and he adds no pain with it," says his Word. (Proverbs 10:22) The four young Hebrews put their faith and trust in Jehovah, and he did not abandon them. Centuries later, Jesus Christ survived without food for 40 days. In this regard, he quoted the words found at Deuteronomy 8:3, where we read: "Not by bread alone does man live but by every expression of Jehovah's mouth does man live." Of this, the experience of Daniel and his friends is a classic example.

INSIGHT AND WISDOM
IN PLACE OF DELICACIES AND WINE

²⁷ The ten days were just a test, but the results were most convincing. "So the guardian kept on taking away their delicacies and their drinking wine and giving them vegetables." (Daniel 1:16) It is not difficult to imagine what the other youths in the training program thought of Daniel and his companions. Turning down a king's feast for vegetables every day must have seemed very foolish to them. But great tests and trials were looming on the horizon, and these would call for all the alertness and sobriety the young Hebrews could muster. Above all, it was their faith and trust in Jehovah that would see them through their tests of faith.—Compare Joshua 1:7.

---

26. What was the outcome of the ten-day test, and why did matters turn out that way?
27, 28. In what ways was the regimen to which Daniel and his three friends submitted themselves a preparation for greater things ahead?

[28] Evidence that Jehovah was with these young people can be seen in what is next said: "As for these children, the four of them, to them the true God gave knowledge and insight in all writing and wisdom; and Daniel himself had understanding in all sorts of visions and dreams." (Daniel 1:17) To deal with the difficult times that were coming, they needed more than physical strength and good health. "When wisdom enters into your heart and knowledge itself becomes pleasant to your very soul, thinking ability itself will keep guard over you, discernment itself will safeguard you, to deliver you from the bad way." (Proverbs 2:10-12) That was precisely what Jehovah bestowed upon the four faithful youths to equip them for what lay ahead.

[29] It is stated that Daniel "had understanding in all sorts of visions and dreams." This is not in the sense that he had become a psychic. Interestingly, though Daniel is regarded as one of the great Hebrew prophets, he was never inspired to utter such declarations as "this is what the Sovereign Lord Jehovah has said" or "this is what Jehovah of armies has said." (Isaiah 28:16; Jeremiah 6:9) Yet, it was only under the guidance of God's holy spirit that Daniel was able to understand and interpret visions and dreams that revealed Jehovah's purpose.

FINALLY, THE CRUCIAL TEST

[30] The three years of reeducation and grooming ended. Next came the crucial test—a personal interview with the king. "At the end of the days that the king had said to bring them in, the principal court official also proceeded to bring them in before Nebuchadnezzar." (Daniel 1:18) It was time for the four youths to render an account of

---

29. Why was Daniel able to 'understand all sorts of visions and dreams'?
30, 31. How did the course chosen by Daniel and his companions prove beneficial for them?

themselves. Would sticking to Jehovah's laws rather than giving in to Babylonian ways prove beneficial for them?

31 "The king began to speak with them, and out of them all no one was found like Daniel, Hananiah, Mishael and Azariah; and they continued to stand before the king." (Daniel 1:19) What a complete vindication of their course of action for the preceding three years! It had been no madness on their part to stick to a regimen dictated by their faith and conscience. By being faithful in what might have seemed to be least, Daniel and his friends were blessed with greater things. The privilege "to stand before the king" was the objective sought by all the young people in the training program. Whether the four Hebrew youths were the only ones selected, the Bible does not say. In any case, their faithful course did indeed bring them "a large reward."—Psalm 19:11.

32 "Have you beheld a man skillful in his work? Before kings is where he will station himself," say the Scriptures. (Proverbs 22:29) Thus, Daniel, Hananiah, Mishael, and Azariah were chosen by Nebuchadnezzar to stand before the king, that is, to be a part of the royal court. In all of this, we can see Jehovah's hand maneuvering matters so that through these young men—especially through Daniel—important aspects of the divine purpose would be made known. Though being selected to be a part of Nebuchadnezzar's royal court was an honor, it was a far greater honor to be used in such a marvelous way by the Universal King, Jehovah.

33 Nebuchadnezzar soon found out that the wisdom and insight Jehovah had granted the four Hebrew youths

---

32. Why can it be said that Daniel, Hananiah, Mishael, and Azariah enjoyed a privilege greater than being in the king's court?
33, 34. (a) Why was the king impressed by the young Hebrews? (b) What lesson can we draw from the experience of the four Hebrews?

was far superior to that possessed by all the counselors and wise men in his court. "As regards every matter of wisdom and understanding that the king inquired about from them, he even got to find them ten times better than all the magic-practicing priests and the conjurers that were in all his royal realm." (Daniel 1:20) How could it be otherwise? The "magic-practicing priests" and "conjurers" relied on the mundane and superstitious learning of Babylon, whereas Daniel and his friends put their trust in wisdom from above. There simply could be no comparison—no contest!

[34] Things really have not changed much down through the ages. In the first century C.E., when Greek philosophy and Roman law were in vogue, the apostle Paul was inspired to write: "The wisdom of this world is foolishness with God; for it is written: 'He catches the wise in their own cunning.' And again: 'Jehovah knows that the reasonings of the wise men are futile.' Hence let no one be boasting in men." (1 Corinthians 3:19-21) Today, we need to hold firmly to what Jehovah has taught us and not be easily swayed by the glamour and glitter of the world. —1 John 2:15-17.

FAITHFUL TO THE END

[35] The strong faith of Hananiah, Mishael, and Azariah is dramatically illustrated in Daniel chapter 3, in connection with Nebuchadnezzar's golden image on the plain of Dura and the test of the fiery furnace. These God-fearing Hebrews unquestionably remained faithful to Jehovah till their death. We know this because the apostle Paul undoubtedly alluded to them when he wrote about those "who through faith . . . stayed the force of fire." (Hebrews 11:33, 34) They are outstanding examples for servants of Jehovah, young and old.

---

35. How much are we told about Daniel's three companions?

³⁶ As for Daniel, the closing verse of chapter 1 says: "Daniel continued on until the first year of Cyrus the king." History reveals that Cyrus overthrew Babylon in one night, in 539 B.C.E. Evidently owing to his reputation and stature, Daniel continued to serve in the court of Cyrus. In fact, Daniel 10:1 tells us that "in the third year of Cyrus the king of Persia," Jehovah revealed a noteworthy matter to Daniel. If he was a teenager when he was brought to Babylon in 617 B.C.E., he would have been nearly 100 years old when he received that final vision. What a long and blessed career of faithful service to Jehovah!

³⁷ The opening chapter of the book of Daniel tells more than a story of four faithful young people successfully meeting tests of faith. It shows us how Jehovah can use whomever he wishes to accomplish his purpose. The account proves that if permitted by Jehovah, what might seem to be a calamity can serve a useful purpose. And it tells us that faithfulness in little things brings a large reward.

---

36. What outstanding career did Daniel have?
37. What lessons can we draw from considering Daniel chapter 1?

WHAT DID YOU DISCERN?

- What can be said about the background of Daniel and his three young friends?

- How was the fine upbringing of the four Hebrew youths put to the test in Babylon?

- How did Jehovah reward the four Hebrews for their courageous stand?

- What lessons can Jehovah's present-day servants learn from Daniel and his three companions?

CHAPTER FOUR

THE RISE AND FALL OF AN IMMENSE IMAGE

A DECADE has passed since King Nebuchadnezzar brought Daniel and other "foremost men of the land" of Judah into captivity in Babylon. (2 Kings 24:15) Young Daniel is serving in the king's court when a life-threatening situation arises. Why should this interest us? Because the way that Jehovah God intervenes in the matter not only saves the lives of Daniel and others but also gives us a view of the march of world powers of Bible prophecy leading into our times.

A MONARCH FACES A DIFFICULT PROBLEM

[2] "In the second year of the kingship of Nebuchadnezzar," wrote the prophet Daniel, "Nebuchadnezzar dreamed dreams; and his spirit began to feel agitated, and his very sleep was made to be something beyond him." (Daniel 2:1) The dreamer was Nebuchadnezzar, the king of the Babylonian Empire. He had effectively become world ruler in 607 B.C.E. when Jehovah God allowed him to destroy Jerusalem and its temple. In the second year of Nebuchadnezzar's reign as world ruler (606/605 B.C.E.), God sent him a terrifying dream.

[3] This dream distressed Nebuchadnezzar so much that he could not sleep. Naturally, he was anxious to know its meaning. But the mighty king had forgotten the dream!

---

1. Why should we be interested in a situation that arose a decade after King Nebuchadnezzar took Daniel and others into captivity?
2. When did Nebuchadnezzar have his first prophetic dream?
3. Who proved unable to interpret the king's dream, and how did Nebuchadnezzar respond?

So he summoned Babylon's magicians, enchanters, and sorcerers, and he demanded that they relate the dream and interpret it. The task was beyond them. Their failure so infuriated Nebuchadnezzar that he issued a command "to destroy all the wise men of Babylon." This decree would bring the prophet Daniel face-to-face with the appointed executioner. Why? Because he and his three Hebrew companions—Hananiah, Mishael, and Azariah—were counted among the wise men of Babylon. —Daniel 2:2-14.

DANIEL COMES TO THE RESCUE

⁴ After learning the reason for Nebuchadnezzar's harsh decree, "Daniel himself went in and asked from the king that he should give him time expressly to show the very interpretation to the king." This was granted. Daniel returned to his house, and he and his three Hebrew friends prayed, asking "for mercies on the part of the God of heaven concerning this secret." In a vision that very night, Jehovah revealed to Daniel the secret of the dream. Gratefully, Daniel said: "Let the name of God become blessed from time indefinite even to time indefinite, for wisdom and mightiness—for they belong to him. And he is changing times and seasons, removing kings and setting up kings, giving wisdom to the wise ones and knowledge to those knowing discernment. He is revealing the deep things and the concealed things, knowing what is in the darkness; and with him the light does dwell." For such insight, Daniel praised Jehovah.—Daniel 2:15-23.

⁵ The following day, Daniel approached Arioch, the

4. (a) How did Daniel learn the content of Nebuchadnezzar's dream and its meaning? (b) What did Daniel say in appreciation to Jehovah God?
5. (a) When before the king, how did Daniel give credit to Jehovah? (b) Why is Daniel's explanation of interest to us today?

chief of the bodyguard, who had been appointed to destroy the wise men of Babylon. Upon learning that Daniel could interpret the dream, Arioch rushed him to the king. Taking no credit for himself, Daniel told Nebuchadnezzar: "There exists a God in the heavens who is a Revealer of secrets, and he has made known to King Nebuchadnezzar what is to occur in the final part of the days." Daniel was ready to reveal not only the future of the Babylonian Empire but an outline of world events from Nebuchadnezzar's day to our time and beyond.—Daniel 2:24-30.

THE DREAM—REMEMBERED

⁶ Nebuchadnezzar listened intently as Daniel explained: "You, O king, happened to be beholding, and, look! a certain immense image. That image, which was large and the brightness of which was extraordinary, was standing in front of you, and its appearance was dreadful. As regards that image, its head was of good gold, its breasts and its arms were of silver, its belly and its thighs were of copper, its legs were of iron, its feet were partly of iron and partly of molded clay. You kept on looking until a stone was cut out not by hands, and it struck the image on its feet of iron and of molded clay and crushed them. At that time the iron, the molded clay, the copper, the silver and the gold were, all together, crushed and became like the chaff from the summer threshing floor, and the wind carried them away so that no trace at all was found of them. And as for the stone that struck the image, it became a large mountain and filled the whole earth." —Daniel 2:31-35.

⁷ How thrilled Nebuchadnezzar must have been to hear Daniel unfold the dream! But wait! Babylon's wise men would be spared only if Daniel also interpreted the dream. Speaking for himself and his three Hebrew friends, Daniel

---

6, 7. What was the dream that Daniel recalled for the king?

declared: "This is the dream, and its interpretation we shall say before the king."—Daniel 2:36.

A KINGDOM OF EMINENT DISTINCTION

[8] "You, O king, the king of kings, you to whom the God of heaven has given the kingdom, the might, and the strength and the dignity, and into whose hand he has given, wherever the sons of mankind are dwelling, the beasts of the field and the winged creatures of the heavens, and whom he has made ruler over all of them, you yourself are the head of gold." (Daniel 2:37, 38) These words applied to Nebuchadnezzar after Jehovah had used him to destroy Jerusalem, in 607 B.C.E. This is so because the kings enthroned in Jerusalem were from the line of David, Jehovah's anointed king. Jerusalem was the capital of Judah, the typical kingdom of God representing Jehovah's sovereignty over the earth. With that city's destruction in 607 B.C.E., this typical kingdom of God ceased to exist. (1 Chronicles 29:23; 2 Chronicles 36:17-21) The successive world powers represented by the metallic parts of the image could now exercise world domination without interference from God's typical kingdom. As the head of gold, the most precious metal known in ancient times, Nebuchadnezzar had had the distinction of overturning that kingdom by destroying Jerusalem.—See "A Warrior King Builds an Empire," on page 63.

[9] Nebuchadnezzar, who reigned for 43 years, headed a dynasty that ruled over the Babylonian Empire. It included his son-in-law Nabonidus and his oldest son, Evil-merodach. That dynasty continued for 43 more years, until the death of Nabonidus' son Belshazzar, in

---

8. (a) Who or what did Daniel interpret the head of gold to be? (b) When did the head of gold come into existence?
9. What was represented by the head of gold?

539 B.C.E. (2 Kings 25:27; Daniel 5:30) So the head of gold in the dream image represented not just Nebuchadnezzar but the entire Babylonian line of rulership.

10 Daniel told Nebuchadnezzar: "After you there will rise another kingdom inferior to you." (Daniel 2:39) A kingdom symbolized by the image's breasts and arms of silver would succeed Nebuchadnezzar's dynasty. Some 200 years earlier, Isaiah had foretold this kingdom, even giving the name of its victorious king—Cyrus. (Isaiah 13:1-17; 21:2-9; 44:24–45:7, 13) This was the Medo-Persian Empire. Even though Medo-Persia developed a great civilization that was not secondary to that of the Babylonian Empire, this latter kingdom is represented by silver, a metal less precious than gold. It was inferior to the Babylonian World Power in that it did not have the distinction of overturning Judah, the typical kingdom of God with its capital at Jerusalem.

11 Some 60 years after interpreting the dream, Daniel witnessed the end of Nebuchadnezzar's dynasty. Daniel was present on the night of October 5/6, 539 B.C.E., when the Medo-Persian army took seemingly impregnable Babylon and executed King Belshazzar. With the death of Belshazzar, the golden head of the dream image—the Babylonian Empire—ceased to exist.

EXILED PEOPLE FREED BY A KINGDOM

12 Medo-Persia replaced the Babylonian Empire as dominant world power in 539 B.C.E. At 62 years of age, Darius

---

10. (a) How did Nebuchadnezzar's dream indicate that the Babylonian World Power would not last? (b) What did the prophet Isaiah foretell about Babylon's conqueror? (c) In what sense was Medo-Persia inferior to Babylon?
11. When did Nebuchadnezzar's dynasty cease to exist?
12. How did the decree issued by Cyrus in 537 B.C.E. benefit the exiled Jews?

the Mede became the first ruler of the conquered city of Babylon. (Daniel 5:30, 31) For a short time, he and Cyrus the Persian reigned jointly over the Medo-Persian Empire. When Darius died, Cyrus became the sole head of the Persian Empire. For the Jews in Babylon, the reign of Cyrus meant release from captivity. In 537 B.C.E., Cyrus issued a decree that allowed Jewish exiles in Babylon to return to their homeland and rebuild Jerusalem and Jehovah's temple. The typical kingdom of God, however, was not reestablished in Judah and Jerusalem.—2 Chronicles 36:22, 23; Ezra 1:1–2:2a.

[13] The silver breasts and arms of the dream image pictured the line of Persian kings beginning with Cyrus the Great. That dynasty lasted for over 200 years. Cyrus is thought to have died while on a military campaign in 530 B.C.E. Of some 12 kings that succeeded him to the throne of the Persian Empire, at least 2 dealt favorably with Jehovah's chosen people. One was Darius I (Persian), and the other was Artaxerxes I.

[14] Darius I was third in the line of Persian kings after Cyrus the Great. The preceding two were Cambyses II and his brother Bardiya (or perhaps a Magian pretender named Gaumata). By the time Darius I, also known as Darius the Great, ascended the throne in 521 B.C.E., the work of rebuilding the temple in Jerusalem was under ban. Upon uncovering the document containing Cyrus' decree in the archives at Ecbatana, Darius did more than remove the ban in 520 B.C.E. He also provided funds from the royal treasury for rebuilding the temple.—Ezra 6:1-12.

[15] The next Persian ruler to assist in Jewish restoration

---

13. What did the silver breasts and arms of Nebuchadnezzar's dream image picture?
14, 15. What assistance did Darius the Great and Artaxerxes I give to the Jews?

efforts was Artaxerxes I, who succeeded his father Ahasuerus (Xerxes I) in 475 B.C.E. Artaxerxes was surnamed Longimanus because his right hand was longer than the left. During the 20th year of his reign, in 455 B.C.E., he commissioned his Jewish cupbearer Nehemiah to be governor of Judah and to rebuild Jerusalem's walls. This action marked the start of the 'seventy weeks of years' outlined in the 9th chapter of Daniel and set the dates for the appearance and the death of the Messiah, or Christ, Jesus of Nazareth.—Daniel 9:24-27; Nehemiah 1:1; 2:1-18.

[16] The last of the six kings to follow Artaxerxes I on the throne of the Persian Empire was Darius III. His reign ended abruptly in 331 B.C.E. when he suffered a terrible defeat by Alexander the Great at Gaugamela, near ancient Nineveh. This defeat ended the Medo-Persian World Power as symbolized by the silver part of the image of Nebuchadnezzar's dream. The power to come was superior in some ways, yet inferior in others. This becomes clear as we listen to Daniel's further interpretation of Nebuchadnezzar's dream.

A KINGDOM—VAST BUT INFERIOR

[17] Daniel told Nebuchadnezzar that the belly and thighs of the immense image constituted "another kingdom, a third one, of copper, that [would] rule over the whole earth." (Daniel 2:32, 39) This third kingdom would follow Babylonia and Medo-Persia. As copper is inferior to silver, this new world power would be inferior to Medo-Persia in that it would not be honored with any privilege like that of liberating Jehovah's people. However, the

---

16. When and with what king did the Medo-Persian World Power end?
17-19. (a) What world power did the belly and thighs of copper represent, and how extensive was its rulership? (b) Who was Alexander III? (c) How did Greek become an international language, and for what was it well suited?

copperlike kingdom would "rule over the whole earth," indicating that it would be more extensive than either Babylonia or Medo-Persia. What do the facts of history bear out about this world power?

[18] Shortly after inheriting the throne of Macedonia in 336 B.C.E. at 20 years of age, ambitious Alexander III embarked upon a campaign of conquest. Because of his military successes, he came to be called Alexander the Great. Gaining one victory after another, he kept moving into the Persian domain. When he defeated Darius III in battle at Gaugamela in 331 B.C.E., the Persian Empire began to collapse and Alexander established Greece as the new world power.

[19] After the victory at Gaugamela, Alexander went on to take the Persian capitals Babylon, Susa, Persepolis, and Ecbatana. Subduing the rest of the Persian Empire, he extended his conquests into western India. Greek colonies were established in the conquered lands. Thus, Greek language and culture spread throughout the realm. The Grecian Empire, in fact, became greater than any that had preceded it. As Daniel had foretold, the copper kingdom 'ruled over the whole earth.' One result of this was that Greek (Koine) became an international language. With its capacity for accurate expression, it proved highly suitable for writing the Christian Greek Scriptures and for spreading the good news of God's Kingdom.

[20] Alexander the Great lived only eight years as world ruler. Young though he was, 32-year-old Alexander fell ill after a banquet and died shortly thereafter, on June 13, 323 B.C.E. In time, his huge empire was divided into four territories, each ruled by one of his generals. Thus out of one great kingdom came four kingdoms that were eventually swallowed up by the Roman Empire. The cop-

---

20. What became of the Grecian Empire after the death of Alexander the Great?

perlike world power continued only until 30 B.C.E. when the last of these four kingdoms—the Ptolemaic dynasty ruling in Egypt—finally fell to Rome.

A KINGDOM THAT CRUSHES AND SHATTERS

21 Daniel continued his explanation of the dream image: "As for the fourth kingdom [after Babylon, Medo-Persia, and Greece], it will prove to be strong like iron. Forasmuch as iron is crushing and grinding everything else, so, like iron that shatters, it will crush and shatter even all these." (Daniel 2:40) In its strength and ability to crush, this world power would be like iron—stronger than the empires represented by gold, silver, or copper. The Roman Empire was such a power.

22 Rome crushed and shattered the Grecian Empire and swallowed up remnants of the Medo-Persian and Babylonian world powers. Showing no respect for God's Kingdom proclaimed by Jesus Christ, it put him to death on a torture stake in 33 C.E. In an effort to shatter true Christianity, Rome persecuted Jesus' disciples. Moreover, the Romans destroyed Jerusalem and its temple in 70 C.E.

23 The iron legs of Nebuchadnezzar's dream image pictured not only the Roman Empire but also its political outgrowth. Consider these words recorded at Revelation 17:10: "There are seven kings: five have fallen, one is, the other has not yet arrived, but when he does arrive he must remain a short while." When the apostle John penned these words, he was being held in exile by the Romans, on the isle of Patmos. The five fallen kings, or world powers, were Egypt, Assyria, Babylon, Medo-Persia, and Greece. The sixth—the Roman Empire—was still in power. But it

---

21. How did Daniel describe "the fourth kingdom"?
22. How was the Roman Empire ironlike?
23, 24. In addition to the Roman Empire, what do the legs of the image picture?

World Powers of Daniel's Prophecy

The immense image
(Daniel 2:31-45)

BABYLONIA
from 607 B.C.E.

MEDO-PERSIA
from 539 B.C.E.

GREECE
from 331 B.C.E.

ROME
from 30 B.C.E.

**ANGLO-AMERICAN WORLD
POWER from 1763 C.E.**

POLITICALLY DIVIDED WORLD
in the time of the end

also was to fall, and the seventh king would arise from one of Rome's captured territories. What world power would that be?

24 Britain was once a northwestern part of the Roman Empire. But by the year 1763, it had become the British Empire—the Britannia that ruled the seven seas. By 1776 its 13 American colonies had declared their independence in order to set up the United States of America. In later years, however, Britain and the United States became partners in both war and peace. Thus, the Anglo-American combination came into existence as the seventh world power of Bible prophecy. Like the Roman Empire, it has proved to be "strong like iron," exercising ironlike authority. The iron legs of the dream image thus include both the Roman Empire and the Anglo-American dual world power.

A FRAGILE AMALGAM

25 Daniel next told Nebuchadnezzar: "Whereas you beheld the feet and the toes to be partly of molded clay of a potter and partly of iron, the kingdom itself will prove to be divided, but somewhat of the hardness of iron will prove to be in it, forasmuch as you beheld the iron mixed with moist clay. And as for the toes of the feet being partly of iron and partly of molded clay, the kingdom will partly prove to be strong and will partly prove to be fragile. Whereas you beheld iron mixed with moist clay, they will come to be mixed with the offspring of mankind; but they will not prove to be sticking together, this one to that one, just as iron is not mixing with molded clay." —Daniel 2:41-43.

26 The succession of world powers represented by the

25. What did Daniel say about the feet and the toes of the image?
26. When does the rulership pictured by the feet and the toes manifest itself?

various parts of the image in Nebuchadnezzar's dream began with the head and extended down to the feet. Logically, the feet and toes of "iron mixed with moist clay" would symbolize the final manifestation of human rule that would exist during "the time of the end." —Daniel 12:4.

²⁷ At the dawn of the 20th century, the British Empire ruled over every fourth person on earth. Other European empires controlled millions more. But World War I resulted in the emergence of groups of nations in place of empires. After World War II, this trend accelerated. As nationalism developed further, the number of nations in the world grew dramatically. The ten toes of the image represent all such coexisting powers and governments, for in the Bible the number ten at times signifies earthly completeness.—Compare Exodus 34:28; Matthew 25:1; Revelation 2:10.

²⁸ Now that we are in "the time of the end," we have reached the feet of the image. Some of the governments pictured by the image's feet and toes of iron mixed with clay are ironlike—authoritarian or tyrannical. Others are claylike. In what way? Daniel associated the clay with "the offspring of mankind." (Daniel 2:43) Despite the fragile nature of clay, of which the offspring of mankind are made, traditional ironlike rulerships have been obliged to listen more and more to the common people, who want their say in the governments ruling over them. (Job 10:9) But there is no sticking together of authoritarian rule and the common people—no more than there could be a uniting of iron with clay. At the time of the image's demise, the world will indeed be politically fragmented!

---

27. (a) What state of affairs do the feet and the toes of iron mixed with clay picture? (b) What is pictured by the ten toes of the image?
28, 29. (a) According to Daniel, what did the clay represent? (b) What can be said about the mixture of iron and clay?

²⁹ Will the divided condition of the feet and toes cause the entire image to collapse? What will happen to the image?

A DRAMATIC CLIMAX!

³⁰ Consider the climax of the dream. Daniel told the king: "You kept on looking until a stone was cut out not by hands, and it struck the image on its feet of iron and of molded clay and crushed them. At that time the iron, the molded clay, the copper, the silver and the gold were, all together, crushed and became like the chaff from the summer threshing floor, and the wind carried them away so that no trace at all was found of them. And as for the stone that struck the image, it became a large mountain and filled the whole earth."—Daniel 2:34, 35.

³¹ By way of explanation, the prophecy continued: "In the days of those kings the God of heaven will set up a kingdom that will never be brought to ruin. And the kingdom itself will not be passed on to any other people. It will crush and put an end to all these kingdoms, and it itself will stand to times indefinite; forasmuch as you beheld that out of the mountain a stone was cut not by hands, and that it crushed the iron, the copper, the molded clay, the silver and the gold. The grand God himself has made known to the king what is to occur after this. And the dream is reliable, and the interpretation of it is trustworthy."—Daniel 2:44, 45.

³² Appreciating that his dream had been called to mind and explained, Nebuchadnezzar acknowledged that only Daniel's God was "a Lord of kings and a Revealer of secrets." The king also gave Daniel and his three Hebrew

---

30. Describe the climax of Nebuchadnezzar's dream.
31, 32. What was foretold with regard to the final part of Nebuchadnezzar's dream?

companions positions of great responsibility. (Daniel 2: 46-49) What, though, is the modern-day significance of Daniel's 'trustworthy interpretation'?

'A MOUNTAIN FILLS THE EARTH'

33 When "the appointed times of the nations" end- ed in October 1914, "the God of heaven" established the heavenly Kingdom by enthroning his anointed Son, Je- sus Christ, as the "King of kings and Lord of lords."* (Luke 21:24; Revelation 12:1-5; 19:16) So it was that by divine power, not by human hands, the Messianic King- dom "stone" was cut out of the "mountain" of Jehovah's universal sovereignty. This heavenly government is in the hands of Jesus Christ, upon whom God has conferred im- mortality. (Romans 6:9; 1 Timothy 6:15, 16) Hence, this "kingdom of our Lord [God] and of his Christ"—an ex- pression of Jehovah's universal sovereignty—will not be passed on to anyone else. It will stand forever.—Revela- tion 11:15.

34 The birth of the Kingdom took place "in the days of those kings." (Daniel 2:44) These were not only the kings pictured by the ten toes of the image but also those symbolized by its iron, copper, silver, and gold parts. Al- though the Babylonian, Persian, Grecian, and Roman empires had passed away as world powers, their remnants still existed in 1914. The Turkish Ottoman Empire then occupied the territory of Babylonia, and national govern- ments were functioning in Persia (Iran) and Greece and Rome, Italy.

---

* See Chapter 6 of this book.

---

33. Out of what "mountain" was the "stone" cut, and when and how did this occur?
34. How was it that God's Kingdom was born "in the days of those kings"?

³⁵ God's heavenly Kingdom will soon strike the symbolic image on its feet. As a result, all the kingdoms pictured by it will be broken to pieces, bringing them to an end. Indeed, at "the war of the great day of God the Almighty," that "stone" will strike with such crushing impact that the image will be ground to powder and the wind of God's storm will sweep it away like the chaff of a threshing floor. (Revelation 16:14, 16) Then, like the stone that grew to mountainous size and filled the earth, God's Kingdom will become the governmental mountain that will affect "the whole earth."—Daniel 2:35.

³⁶ Though the Messianic Kingdom is heavenly, it will extend its power toward our globe for the blessing of all obedient inhabitants of the earth. This stable government "will never be brought to ruin" or be "passed on to any other people." Unlike the kingdoms of dying human rulers, "it itself will stand to times indefinite," forever. (Daniel 2:44) May you have the privilege of being one of its subjects eternally.

---

35. When will the "stone" strike the image, and how thoroughly will the image be disposed of?
36. Why can the Messianic Kingdom be called a stable government?

WHAT DID YOU DISCERN?

- What world powers are represented by the various parts of the immense image of Nebuchadnezzar's dream?

- What world situation do the feet and ten toes of iron mixed with clay represent?

- When and out of what "mountain" was the "stone" cut?

- When will the "stone" strike the image?

A WARRIOR KING BUILDS AN EMPIRE

◆

BABYLON'S crown prince and his army shatter the Egyptian forces of Pharaoh Necho at Carchemish, in Syria. The defeated Egyptians flee south toward Egypt, and the Babylonians pursue them. But a message from Babylon compels the victorious prince to abandon his pursuit. The news is that his father, Nabopolassar, has died. Charging his generals with the responsibility of bringing back the captives and the plunder, Nebuchadnezzar quickly returns home and takes the throne vacated by his father.

Nebuchadnezzar thus ascended the throne of Babylon in the year 624 B.C.E. and became the second ruler of the Neo-Babylonian Empire. During his reign of 43 years, he took possession of the territories once occupied by the

Assyrian World Power and extended his domain, taking in Syria to the north and Palestine to the west down to the border of Egypt.—See map.

BABYLONIAN EMPIRE

In the fourth year of his reign (620 B.C.E.), Nebuchadnezzar made Judah his vassal kingdom. (2 Kings 24:1) Three years later, a Judean rebellion brought Jerusalem under Babylonian siege. Nebuchadnezzar took Jehoiachin, Daniel, and others captive to Babylon. The king also carried along some of the utensils of Jehovah's temple. He made Jehoiachin's uncle, Zedekiah, vassal king of Judah.—2 Kings 24:2-17; Daniel 1:6, 7.

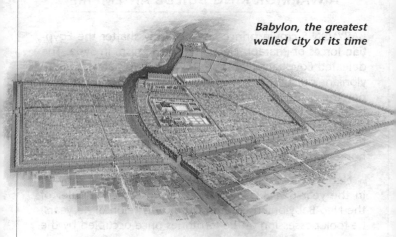

Babylon, the greatest walled city of its time

Sometime later, Zedekiah too rebelled, allying himself with Egypt. Nebuchadnezzar besieged Jerusalem again, and in 607 B.C.E., he breached its wall, burned the temple, and destroyed the city. He slaughtered all of Zedekiah's sons and then blinded Zedekiah and bound him, in order to take him as prisoner to Babylon. Nebuchadnezzar took most of the people captive and transported the remaining temple utensils to Babylon. "Thus Judah went into exile from off its soil."—2 Kings 24:18–25:21.

Nebuchadnezzar also conquered Tyre by laying siege to the city—a siege that lasted 13 years. In the course of the siege, the heads of his soldiers were "made bald" from the chafing of their helmets, and their shoulders were "rubbed bare" from carrying materials used in the construction of the siegeworks. (Ezekiel 29:18) Finally, Tyre capitulated to Babylonian forces.

The Babylonian king evidently was a brilliant military strategist. Some literary references, particularly of Babylonian origin, also describe him as a just king. While the Scriptures do not specifically say that Nebuchadnezzar was just, the prophet Jeremiah said that even though Zedekiah had rebelled, he would be treated fairly 'if he would go out to the princes of the king of Babylon.' (Jeremiah 38:17, 18) And after the destruction of Jerusalem, Nebuchadnezzar treated Jeremiah respectfully. Concerning Jeremiah, the king commanded: "Take him and keep your own eyes set upon him, and do not do to him anything bad at all. But just as he may speak to you, so do with him."—Jeremiah 39: 11, 12; 40:1-4.

As an administrator, Nebuchadnezzar was quick to recognize the qualities and abilities of Daniel and his three companions—Shadrach, Meshach, and Abednego—whose Hebrew names were Hananiah, Mishael, and Azariah. The king therefore used them in responsible positions in his kingdom.—Daniel 1:6, 7, 19-21; 2:49.

Nebuchadnezzar's religious devotion went particularly to Marduk, the chief god of Babylon. The king credited Marduk with all his conquests. In Babylon, he built and beautified the temples of Marduk and numerous other Babylonian deities. The image of gold set up on the plain of Dura may have been dedicated to Marduk. And Nebuchadnezzar appears to have relied heavily on divination in planning his military moves.

The dragon was a symbol of Marduk

Nebuchadnezzar also took pride in restoring Babylon, the greatest walled city of the time. By completing the city's massive double walls that his father had started to build, Nebuchadnezzar made the capital seemingly impregnable. The king repaired an old palace in the heart of the city and built a summer palace one-and-a-half miles to the north. To satisfy his Median queen, who longed for the

WHAT DID YOU DISCERN?

What can be said about Nebuchadnezzar as

- a military strategist?
- an administrator?
- a worshiper of Marduk?
- a builder?

Babylon's famous hanging gardens

hills and forests of her homeland, Nebuchadnezzar reportedly built the hanging gardens—rated as one of the seven wonders of the ancient world.

"Is not this Babylon the Great, that I myself have built for the royal house with the strength of my might and for the dignity of my majesty?" boasted the king one day as he was walking about the royal palace of Babylon. "While the word was yet in the king's mouth," insanity struck him. Unfit to rule for seven years, he ate vegetation, just as Daniel had foretold. At the end of that period, the kingdom was restored to Nebuchadnezzar, who reigned until his death in 582 B.C.E.—Daniel 4:30-36.

CHAPTER FIVE

THEIR FAITH SURVIVED THE CRUCIBLE

SHOULD your devotion be directed to God or to the land in which you live? Many would answer by saying, 'I pay homage to *both*. I worship God according to the dictates of my religion; at the same time, I pledge allegiance to my homeland.'

2 The line between religious devotion and patriotism might seem blurred today, but in ancient Babylon it was virtually nonexistent. Indeed, the civil and the sacred were so entwined that they were at times indistinguishable. "In ancient Babylon," writes Professor Charles F. Pfeiffer, "the king served as both High Priest and civil ruler. He performed sacrifices and determined the religious life of his subjects."

3 Consider King Nebuchadnezzar. His very name means "O Nebo, Protect the Heir!" Nebo was the Babylonian god of wisdom and agriculture. Nebuchadnezzar was a deeply religious man. As noted earlier, he built and beautified the temples of numerous Babylonian gods and was especially devoted to Marduk, to whom he credited his military victories.* It also appears that Nebuchadnezzar relied heavily upon divination to formulate his battle plans.—Ezekiel 21:18-23.

---

* Some believe that Marduk, who was regarded as founder of the Babylonian Empire, represents the deified Nimrod. However, this cannot be stated with certainty.

---

1. How do many feel about devotion to God and to their homeland?
2. How was the king of Babylon both a religious and a political figure?
3. What shows that Nebuchadnezzar was a deeply religious man?

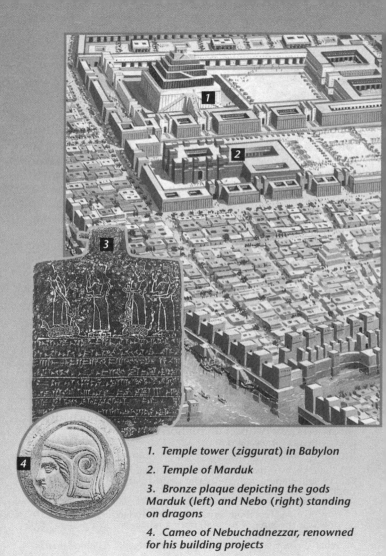

1. *Temple tower (ziggurat) in Babylon*

2. *Temple of Marduk*

3. *Bronze plaque depicting the gods Marduk (left) and Nebo (right) standing on dragons*

4. *Cameo of Nebuchadnezzar, renowned for his building projects*

⁴ Really, a religious spirit pervaded all of Babylon. The city boasted more than 50 temples, at which a vast array of gods and goddesses were worshiped, including the triad of Anu (god of the sky), Enlil (god of the earth, air, and storm), and Ea (god over the waters). Another trinity was made up of Sin (the moon-god), Shamash (the sun-god), and Ishtar (the fertility goddess). Magic, sorcery, and astrology played a prominent role in Babylonian worship.

⁵ Living amid people who venerated many gods posed a formidable challenge for the Jewish exiles. Centuries earlier, Moses had warned the Israelites that there would be dire consequences if they chose to rebel against the Supreme Lawgiver. Moses told them: "Jehovah will march you and your king whom you will set up over you to a nation whom you have not known, neither you nor your forefathers; and there you will have to serve other gods, of wood and of stone."—Deuteronomy 28:15, 36.

⁶ The Jews now found themselves in that very predicament. Keeping integrity to Jehovah would be difficult, especially for Daniel, Hananiah, Mishael, and Azariah. These four young Hebrews had been specially selected to receive training for governmental service. (Daniel 1:3-5) Remember that they had even been assigned Babylonian names—Belteshazzar, Shadrach, Meshach, and Abednego—likely to influence them to conform to their new environment.* The high-profile positions of these men

---

* "Belteshazzar" means "Protect the Life of the King." "Shadrach" may mean "Command of Aku," the Sumerian moon-god. "Meshach" possibly refers to a Sumerian god, and "Abednego" means "Servant of Nego," or Nebo.

---

4. Describe the religious spirit of Babylon.
5. What challenge did the religious environment of Babylon pose for the Jewish exiles?
6. Why did living in Babylon pose a special challenge for Daniel, Hananiah, Mishael, and Azariah?

would make any refusal on their part to worship the gods of the land conspicuous—even treasonous.

A GOLDEN IMAGE PRESENTS A THREAT

[7] Evidently in an effort to strengthen the unity of his empire, Nebuchadnezzar set up a golden image on the plain of Dura. It was 60 cubits (90 feet) in height and 6 cubits (9 feet) in breadth.* Some believe that the image was simply a pillar, or an obelisk. It may have had a very high pedestal on which there was a huge statue in human likeness, perhaps representing Nebuchadnezzar himself or the god Nebo. Whatever the case, this towering monument was a symbol of the Babylonian Empire. As such, it was meant to be seen and revered.—Daniel 3:1.

[8] Accordingly, Nebuchadnezzar arranged an inauguration ceremony. He gathered his satraps, prefects, governors, counselors, treasurers, judges, police magistrates, and all the administrators of the jurisdictional districts. A herald cried out: "To you it is being said, O peoples, national groups and languages, that at the time that you hear the sound of the horn, the pipe, the zither, the triangular harp, the stringed instrument, the bagpipe and all sorts of musical instruments, you fall down and worship the image of gold that Nebuchadnezzar the king has set up. And whoever does not fall down and worship will at the same moment be thrown into the burning fiery furnace."—Daniel 3:2-6.

---

* Considering the immense size of the image, some Bible scholars believe that it was made of wood and then overlaid with gold.

---

7. (a) Describe the image set up by Nebuchadnezzar. (b) What was the purpose of the image?
8. (a) Who were called to the inauguration of the image, and what were all present required to do? (b) What was to be the penalty for refusing to bow down before the image?

⁹ Some believe that Nebuchadnezzar arranged for this ceremony in an attempt to force the Jews to compromise their worship of Jehovah. Likely this was not the case, for evidently only government officials were called to the event. Thus, the only Jews present would be those serving in some governmental capacity. It seems, then, that bowing down before the image was a ceremony intended to strengthen the solidarity of the ruling class. Scholar John F. Walvoord notes: "Such a display of officials was on the one hand a gratifying demonstration of the power of Nebuchadnezzar's empire and on the other hand was significant as recognizing the deities who in their thinking were responsible for their victories."

JEHOVAH'S SERVANTS REFUSE TO COMPROMISE

¹⁰ Despite their devotion to various patron gods, most of those gathered before Nebuchadnezzar's image would have no qualms about worshiping it. "They were all accustomed to worship idols, and the worship of one god did not prevent their doing homage also to another," explained one Bible scholar. He continued: "It accorded with the prevailing views of idolaters that there were many gods . . . and that it was not improper to render homage to the god of any people or country."

¹¹ For the Jews, however, it was a different matter. They had been commanded by their God, Jehovah: "You must not make for yourself a carved image or a form like anything that is in the heavens above or that is on the earth underneath or that is in the waters under the earth. You

---

9. What was the apparent significance of bowing down before the image that Nebuchadnezzar had set up?
10. Why would non-Jews have no problem complying with Nebuchadnezzar's command?
11. Why did Shadrach, Meshach, and Abednego refuse to bow down before the image?

must not bow down to them nor be induced to serve them, because I Jehovah your God am a God exacting exclusive devotion." (Exodus 20:4, 5) Therefore, as the music began and those gathered prostrated themselves before the image, three young Hebrews—Shadrach, Meshach, and Abednego—remained standing.—Daniel 3:7.

[12] The refusal of three Hebrew officials to worship the image infuriated certain Chaldeans. At once, they approached the king and "accused the Jews."* They were not interested in an explanation. Wanting the Hebrews to be punished for disloyalty and treason, the accusers said: "There exist certain Jews whom you appointed over the administration of the jurisdictional district of Babylon, Shadrach, Meshach, and Abednego; these able-bodied men have paid no regard to you, O king, they are not serving your own gods, and the image of gold that you have set up they are not worshiping."—Daniel 3:8-12.

[13] How it must have frustrated Nebuchadnezzar that the three Hebrews disobeyed his order! It was clear that he had not succeeded in turning Shadrach, Meshach, and Abednego into loyal advocates of the Babylonian Empire. Had he not educated them in the wisdom of the Chaldeans? Why, he had even changed their names! But if Nebuchadnezzar thought that a grandiose education would teach them a new way of worship or that changing their names would change their identities, he was sadly mistaken. Shadrach, Meshach, and Abednego remained loyal servants of Jehovah.

---

* The Aramaic expression translated "accused" means to 'eat the pieces' of a person—to chew him up, as it were, by means of slander.

---

12. Certain Chaldeans accused the three Hebrews of what, and why so?
13, 14. How did Nebuchadnezzar respond to the course taken by Shadrach, Meshach, and Abednego?

¹⁴ King Nebuchadnezzar was enraged. At once, he summoned Shadrach, Meshach, and Abednego. He asked: "Is it really so, O Shadrach, Meshach and Abednego, that you are not serving my own gods, and the image of gold that I have set up you are not worshiping?" No doubt Nebuchadnezzar spoke these words in shocked disbelief. After all, he must have reasoned, 'How could three men of sound mind disregard such a plain command—and one that carried such a severe penalty for disobedience?' —Daniel 3:13, 14.

¹⁵ Nebuchadnezzar was willing to give the three Hebrews another chance. "Now if you are ready," he said, "so that when you hear the sound of the horn, the pipe, the zither, the triangular harp, the stringed instrument, and the bagpipe and all sorts of musical instruments, you fall down and worship the image that I have made, all right. But if you do not worship, at that same moment you will be thrown into the burning fiery furnace. And who is that god that can rescue you out of my hands?" —Daniel 3:15.

¹⁶ Apparently, the lesson of the dream image (recorded in Daniel chapter 2) had left no lasting impression on Nebuchadnezzar's mind and heart. Perhaps he had already forgotten his own statement to Daniel: "The God of you men is a God of gods and a Lord of kings." (Daniel 2:47) Now Nebuchadnezzar seemed to be challenging Jehovah, saying that not even He could save the Hebrews from the punishment that awaited them.

¹⁷ Shadrach, Meshach, and Abednego did not need

15, 16. What opportunity did Nebuchadnezzar extend to the three Hebrews?

17. How did Shadrach, Meshach, and Abednego respond to the king's offer?

to reconsider matters. Immediately they responded: "O Nebuchadnezzar, we are under no necessity in this regard to say back a word to you. If it is to be, our God whom we are serving is able to rescue us. Out of the burning fiery furnace and out of your hand, O king, he will rescue us. But if not, let it become known to you, O king, that your gods are not the ones we are serving, and the image of gold that you have set up we will not worship."—Daniel 3:16-18.

INTO THE FIERY FURNACE!

[18] Infuriated, Nebuchadnezzar commanded that his servants heat up the furnace seven times hotter than usual. Then he ordered "certain able-bodied men of vital energy" to bind Shadrach, Meshach, and Abednego and to throw them into the "burning fiery furnace." They followed the king's orders, casting the three Hebrews into the fire, bound and fully clothed—perhaps so that they would be consumed all the more quickly. However, Nebuchadnezzar's henchmen themselves were the ones who were killed by the flames.—Daniel 3:19-22.

[19] But something extraordinary was happening. Although Shadrach, Meshach, and Abednego were in the midst of the fiery furnace, the flames were not consuming them. Imagine Nebuchadnezzar's astonishment! They had been thrown into a blazing fire, securely bound, but they were still alive. Why, they were walking about freely in the fire! But Nebuchadnezzar noticed something else. "Was it not three able-bodied men that we threw bound into the midst of the fire?" he asked his high royal officials. "Yes, O king," they answered.

18, 19. What happened when the three Hebrews were thrown into the fiery furnace?

"Look!" Nebuchadnezzar cried out, "I am beholding four able-bodied men walking about free in the midst of the fire, and there is no hurt to them, and the appearance of the fourth one is resembling a son of the gods."—Daniel 3:23-25.

[20] Nebuchadnezzar approached the door of the fiery furnace. "Shadrach, Meshach and Abednego, you servants of the Most High God," he called out, "step out and come here!" The three Hebrews walked out of the midst of the fire. No doubt all who were eyewitnesses of this miracle—including the satraps, prefects, governors, and high officials—were stunned. Why, it was as if these three young men had never even entered the furnace! The smell of fire had not come onto them, and not a hair of their heads had been singed.—Daniel 3:26, 27.

[21] Now King Nebuchadnezzar was forced to acknowledge that Jehovah is the Most High God. "Blessed be the God of Shadrach, Meshach and Abednego," he declared, "who sent his angel and rescued his servants that trusted in him and that changed the very word of the king and gave over their bodies, because they would not serve and would not worship any god at all except their own God." Then, the king added this stern warning: "From me an order is being put through, that any people, national group or language that says anything wrong against the God of Shadrach, Meshach and Abednego should be dismembered, and its house should be turned into a public privy; forasmuch as there does not exist another god that is able to deliver like this one." At that, the three Hebrews were restored to royal favor and 'prospered in the jurisdictional district of Babylon.'—Daniel 3:28-30.

20, 21. (a) What did Nebuchadnezzar notice about Shadrach, Meshach, and Abednego when they emerged from the furnace? (b) What was Nebuchadnezzar forced to acknowledge?

FAITH AND THE CRUCIBLE TODAY

²² Today, worshipers of Jehovah face circumstances similar to those of Shadrach, Meshach, and Abednego. Granted, God's people may not be exiles in a literal sense. Yet, Jesus said that his followers would be "no part of the world." (John 17:14) They are "foreigners" in that they do not adopt the unscriptural customs, attitudes, and practices of those around them. As the apostle Paul wrote, Christians are to "quit being fashioned after this system of things."—Romans 12:2.

²³ The three Hebrews refused to be fashioned after the Babylonian system. Even thorough instruction in Chaldean wisdom did not sway them. Their position in the matter of worship was nonnegotiable, and their allegiance was to Jehovah. Christians today need to be just as steadfast. They need not be ashamed because they are different from those in the world. Indeed, "the world is passing away and so is its desire." (1 John 2:17) So it would be foolish and futile to conform to this dying system of things.

²⁴ Christians need to be on guard against every form of idolatry, including subtle forms.* (1 John 5:21) Shadrach, Meshach, and Abednego obediently and respectfully stood before the golden image, but they realized that bowing before it was more than a mere gesture of respect. It was an act of worship, and partici-

---

* For example, the Bible links gluttony and covetousness with idolatry.—Philippians 3:18, 19; Colossians 3:5.

---

22. How do Jehovah's present-day servants face circumstances similar to those of Shadrach, Meshach, and Abednego?
23. How did the three Hebrews display steadfastness, and how can Christians today follow their example?
24. How does the stand of true Christians compare with that of the three Hebrews?

pation would incur Jehovah's wrath. (Deuteronomy 5:8-10) John F. Walvoord writes: "It was in effect a saluting of the flag, although, because of the interrelationship of religious with national loyalties, it may also have had religious connotation." Today, true Christians take an equally firm stand against idolatry.

[25] The Bible account of Shadrach, Meshach, and Abednego provides a sterling object lesson for all who are determined to render exclusive devotion to Jehovah. The apostle Paul evidently had these three Hebrews in mind when he spoke of many who exercised faith, including those who "stayed the force of fire." (Hebrews 11:33, 34) Jehovah will reward all who imitate such faith. The three Hebrews were delivered from the fiery furnace, but we can be sure that he will resurrect all loyal ones who lose their lives as integrity keepers and will bless them with everlasting life. Either way, Jehovah "is guarding the souls of his loyal ones; out of the hand of the wicked ones he delivers them."—Psalm 97:10.

---

25. What lesson have you learned from the true-life story of Shadrach, Meshach, and Abednego?

WHAT DID YOU DISCERN?

- Why did Shadrach, Meshach, and Abednego refuse to bow down before the image set up by Nebuchadnezzar?

- How did Nebuchadnezzar respond to the position taken by the three Hebrews?

- How did Jehovah reward the three Hebrews for their faith?

- What have you learned from paying attention to the true-life story of Shadrach, Meshach, and Abednego?

CHAPTER SIX

UNRAVELING THE MYSTERY OF THE GREAT TREE

JEHOVAH allowed King Nebuchadnezzar to become a world ruler. As Babylon's monarch, he had great wealth, a sumptuous table, a grand palace—everything he desired in a material way. But suddenly he suffered humiliation. Becoming mentally deranged, Nebuchadnezzar acted like a beast! Driven away from the royal table and the imperial residence, he lived in the fields and ate grass like a bull. What led up to this calamity? And why should it concern us?—Compare Job 12:17-19; Ecclesiastes 6:1, 2.

THE KING MAGNIFIES THE MOST HIGH

² Shortly after his recovery from that complete mental collapse, Nebuchadnezzar sent throughout his realm a remarkable report of what had occurred. Jehovah inspired the prophet Daniel to preserve an accurate record of these events. It begins with these words: "Nebuchadnezzar the king, to all the peoples, national groups and languages that are dwelling in all the earth: May your peace grow great. The signs and wonders that the Most High God has performed with me, it has seemed good to me to declare. How grand his signs are, and how mighty his wonders are! His kingdom is a kingdom to time indefinite, and his rulership is for generation after generation."—Daniel 4:1-3.

---

1. What happened to King Nebuchadnezzar, raising what questions?
2, 3. What did the king of Babylon wish for his subjects, and how did he view the Most High God?

³ Nebuchadnezzar's subjects were "dwelling in all the earth"—his empire embracing most of the world of Bible record. Regarding Daniel's God, the king said: "His kingdom is a kingdom to time indefinite." How those words magnified Jehovah throughout the Babylonian Empire! Moreover, this was the second time that Nebuchadnezzar had been shown that the Kingdom of God alone is eternal, standing "to times indefinite."—Daniel 2:44.

⁴ What "signs and wonders" did "the Most High God" perform? These began with the king's personal experience related in these words: "I, Nebuchadnezzar, happened to be at ease in my house and flourishing in my palace. There was a dream that I beheld, and it began to make me afraid. And there were mental images upon my bed and visions of my head that began to frighten me." (Daniel 4:4, 5) What did the Babylonian king do about this disturbing dream?

⁵ Nebuchadnezzar summoned Babylon's wise men and told them the dream. But how they failed! They were totally unable to provide an interpretation. The record added: "At last there came in before me Daniel, whose name is Belteshazzar according to the name of my god and in whom there is the spirit of the holy gods; and before him I said what the dream was." (Daniel 4:6-8) Daniel's court name was Belteshazzar, and the false deity that the king called "my god" may have been either Bel or Nebo or Marduk. Being polytheistic, Nebuchadnezzar viewed Daniel as one in whom there was "the spirit of the holy gods." And because of Daniel's position as prefect over all of Babylon's wise men, the

---

4. In connection with Nebuchadnezzar, how did Jehovah's "signs and wonders" begin?
5. How did Nebuchadnezzar view Daniel, and why?

king referred to him as "the chief of the magic-practicing priests." (Daniel 2:48; 4:9; compare Daniel 1: 20.) Of course, faithful Daniel never abandoned the worship of Jehovah to practice magic.—Leviticus 19:26; Deuteronomy 18:10-12.

AN IMMENSE TREE

⁶ What was the content of the Babylonian king's frightening dream? "Now the visions of my head upon my bed I happened to be beholding," said Nebuchadnezzar, "and, look! a tree in the midst of the earth, the height of which was immense. The tree grew up and became strong, and its very height finally reached the heavens, and it was visible to the extremity of the whole earth. Its foliage was fair, and its fruit was abundant, and there was food for all on it. Under it the beast of the field would seek shade, and on its boughs the birds of the heavens would dwell, and from it all flesh would feed itself." (Daniel 4:10-12) Reportedly, Nebuchadnezzar was fond of the great cedars of Lebanon, went to see them, and had some brought to Babylon as lumber. But he had never beheld anything like the tree seen in his dream. It occupied a prominent position "in the midst of the earth," was visible earth wide, and was so fruitful that it provided food for all flesh.

⁷ There was much more to the dream, for Nebuchadnezzar added: "I continued beholding in the visions of my head upon my bed, and, look! a watcher, even a holy one, coming down from the heavens themselves. He was calling out loudly, and this is what he was saying: 'Chop the tree down, and cut off its boughs. Shake off its foliage,

---

6, 7. How would you describe what Nebuchadnezzar saw in his dream?

and scatter its fruitage. Let the beast flee from under it, and the birds from its boughs. However, leave its root-stock itself in the earth, even with a banding of iron and of copper, among the grass of the field; and with the dew of the heavens let it be wet, and with the beast let its portion be among the vegetation of the earth.' "—Daniel 4:13-15.

⁸ The Babylonians had their own religious concept of good and evil spirit creatures. But who was this "watcher," or sentinel, from heaven? Called "a holy one," he was a righteous angel representing God. (Compare Psalm 103:20, 21.) Imagine the questions that must have plagued Nebuchadnezzar! Why chop this tree down? What good is the rootstock restrained from growth by bands of iron and of copper? Indeed, what purpose is served by a mere stump?

⁹ Nebuchadnezzar must have been completely mysti-fied as he heard the watcher's further words: "Let its heart be changed from that of mankind, and let the heart of a beast be given to it, and let seven times pass over it. By the decree of watchers the thing is, and by the say-ing of holy ones the request is, to the intent that people living may know that the Most High is Ruler in the king-dom of mankind and that to the one whom he wants to, he gives it and he sets up over it even the lowliest one of mankind." (Daniel 4:16, 17) The rootstock of a tree does not have a human heart beating inside it. For that matter, how can the heart of a beast be given to a tree's rootstock? What are the "seven times"? And how does all of this relate to rulership in "the kingdom of mankind"? Surely Nebuchadnezzar wanted to know.

---

8. Who was the "watcher"?
9. Basically, what did the watcher say, and what questions are raised?

BAD NEWS FOR THE KING

¹⁰ Upon hearing the dream, Daniel was momentarily astonished, then fearful. Urged by Nebuchadnezzar to explain it, the prophet said: "O my lord, may the dream apply to those hating you, and its interpretation to your adversaries. The tree that you beheld, that grew great and became strong . . . , it is you, O king, because you have grown great and become strong, and your grandeur has grown great and reached to the heavens, and your rulership to the extremity of the earth." (Daniel 4:18-22) In the Scriptures, trees can symbolize individuals, rulers, and kingdoms. (Psalm 1:3; Jeremiah 17:7, 8; Ezekiel, chapter 31) Like the immense tree of his dream, Nebuchadnezzar had "grown great and become strong" as the head of a world power. But "rulership to the extremity of the earth," involving the whole kingdom of mankind, is represented by the great tree. It therefore symbolizes Jehovah's universal sovereignty, particularly in its relationship to the earth.—Daniel 4:17.

¹¹ A debasing change was in store for Nebuchadnezzar. Pointing to this development, Daniel added: "Because the king beheld a watcher, even a holy one, coming down from the heavens, who was also saying: 'Chop the tree down, and ruin it. However, leave its rootstock itself in the earth, but with a banding of iron and of copper, among the grass of the field, and with the dew of the heavens let it become wet, and with the beasts of the field let its portion be until seven times themselves pass over it,' this is the interpretation, O king, and the decree of the Most High is that which must befall my lord

---

10. (a) Scripturally speaking, what can trees symbolize? (b) What is represented by the great tree?
11. How did the king's dream show that he would experience a debasing change?

the king." (Daniel 4:23, 24) Surely courage was needed to give the powerful king that message!

¹² What would befall Nebuchadnezzar? Imagine his reaction as Daniel added: "You they will be driving away from men, and with the beasts of the field your dwelling will come to be, and the vegetation is what they will give even to you to eat just like bulls; and with the dew of the heavens you yourself will be getting wet, and seven times themselves will pass over you, until you know that the Most High is Ruler in the kingdom of mankind, and that to the one whom he wants to he gives it." (Daniel 4:25) Apparently even Nebuchadnezzar's court officials would 'drive him away from men.' But would he be cared for by compassionate herdsmen or shepherds? No, for God had decreed that Nebuchadnezzar would dwell with "the beasts of the field," eating vegetation.

¹³ Just as the tree was cut down, Nebuchadnezzar would be toppled from world rulership—but only for a time. Daniel explained: "Because they said to leave the rootstock of the tree, your kingdom will be sure to you after you know that the heavens are ruling." (Daniel 4: 26) In Nebuchadnezzar's dream the rootstock, or stump, of the felled tree was allowed to remain, although it was banded so that it would not grow. Similarly, the "rootstock" of Babylon's king would remain, though banded from flourishing for "seven times." His position as world ruler would be like the banded tree stump. It would be kept safe till seven times had passed over it. Jehovah would see to it that during that period nobody would succeed Nebuchadnezzar as Babylon's sole ruler, although his son named Evil-merodach may have carried on for him as acting ruler.

---

12. What was going to befall Nebuchadnezzar?
13. What did the tree dream show would happen to Nebuchadnezzar's position as world ruler?

¹⁴ In view of what was foretold concerning Nebuchadnezzar, Daniel courageously urged: "Therefore, O king, may my counsel seem good to you, and remove your own sins by righteousness, and your iniquity by showing mercy to the poor ones. Maybe there will occur a lengthening of your prosperity." (Daniel 4:27) If Nebuchadnezzar would turn away from his sinful course of oppression and pride, perhaps this would change matters for him. After all, some two centuries earlier, Jehovah had determined to destroy the people of Assyria's capital, Nineveh, but he did not do so because its king and his subjects repented. (Jonah 3:4, 10; Luke 11:32) What about proud Nebuchadnezzar? Would he change his ways?

THE DREAM'S INITIAL FULFILLMENT

¹⁵ Nebuchadnezzar remained proud. Walking about on the palace roof 12 months after his tree dream, he boasted: "Is not this Babylon the Great, that I myself have built for the royal house with the strength of my might and for the dignity of my majesty?" (Daniel 4: 28-30) Nimrod had founded Babylon (Babel), but Nebuchadnezzar gave it splendor. (Genesis 10:8-10) In one of his cuneiform inscriptions, he brags: "Nebuchadrezzar, King of Babylon, the restorer of Esagila and Ezida, son of Nabopolassar am I. . . . The fortifications of Esagila and Babylon I strengthened and established the name of my reign forever." (*Archaeology and the Bible,* by George A. Barton, 1949, pages 478-9) Another inscription refers to about 20 temples that he renovated or rebuilt. "Under Nebuchadnezzar's rule," says *The World Book*

---

14. What did Daniel urge Nebuchadnezzar to do?
15. (a) What attitude did Nebuchadnezzar continue to manifest? (b) Inscriptions reveal what about Nebuchadnezzar's activities?

Encyclopedia, "Babylon became one of the most magnificent cities of the ancient world. In his own records, he rarely mentioned his military activities, but wrote of his building projects and his attention to the gods of Babylonia. Nebuchadnezzar probably built the Hanging Gardens of Babylon, one of the Seven Wonders of the Ancient World."

¹⁶ Boast though he did, proud Nebuchadnezzar was about to be humiliated. Says the inspired account: "While the word was yet in the king's mouth, there was a voice that fell from the heavens: 'To you it is being said, O Nebuchadnezzar the king, "The kingdom itself has gone away from you, and from mankind they are driving even you away, and with the beasts of the field your dwelling will be. Vegetation they will give even to you to eat just like bulls, and seven times themselves will pass over you, until you know that the Most High is Ruler in the kingdom of mankind, and that to the one whom he wants to he gives it." ' "—Daniel 4:31, 32.

¹⁷ Nebuchadnezzar promptly lost his reason. Driven away from mankind, he ate vegetation "just like bulls." Out among the beasts of the field, he certainly was not sitting idly in the grass of a virtual paradise, enjoying refreshing breezes daily. In modern-day Iraq, where Babylon's ruins are located, temperatures range from a high of 120 degrees Fahrenheit in the summer months to well below freezing in wintertime. Unattended and exposed to the elements, Nebuchadnezzar's long, matted hair looked like eagles' feathers and his uncut fingernails and toenails became like birds' claws. (Daniel 4:33) What humiliation for this proud world ruler!

---

16. How was Nebuchadnezzar about to be humiliated?
17. What happened to proud Nebuchadnezzar, and in what circumstances did he soon find himself?

[18] In Nebuchadnezzar's dream, the great tree was felled and its stump was banded to prevent growth upward for seven times. Similarly, Nebuchadnezzar "was brought down from the throne of his kingdom" when Jehovah struck him with madness. (Daniel 5:20) In effect, this changed the king's heart from that of a man to that of a bull. Yet, God reserved Nebuchadnezzar's throne for him until the seven times ended. While Evil-merodach possibly acted as the temporary head of government, Daniel served as "the ruler over all the jurisdictional district of Babylon and the chief prefect over all the wise men of Babylon." His three Hebrew companions continued to share in administering that district's affairs. (Daniel 1:11-19; 2:48, 49; 3:30) The four exiles awaited Nebuchadnezzar's restoration to the throne as a sane king who had learned that "the Most High is Ruler in the kingdom of mankind, and that to the one whom he wants to he gives it."

NEBUCHADNEZZAR'S RESTORATION

[19] Jehovah restored Nebuchadnezzar's sanity at the end of seven times. Then acknowledging the Most High God, the king said: "At the end of the days I, Nebuchadnezzar, lifted up to the heavens my eyes, and my own understanding began to return to me; and I blessed the Most High himself, and the One living to time indefinite I praised and glorified, because his rulership is a rulership to time indefinite and his kingdom is for generation after generation. And all the inhabitants of the earth are being considered as merely nothing, and he is doing according to his own will among the army of the heavens and the inhabitants of the earth. And there exists no one that can

---

18. During the seven times, what took place with regard to Babylon's throne?
19. After Jehovah restored Nebuchadnezzar's sanity, what did the Babylonian king come to realize?

check his hand or that can say to him, 'What have you been doing?' " (Daniel 4:34, 35) Yes, Nebuchadnezzar did come to realize that the Most High is indeed the Sovereign Ruler in the kingdom of mankind.

20 When Nebuchadnezzar returned to his throne, it was as though the metal bands around the dream tree's rootstock had been removed. Concerning his restoration, he said: "At the same time my understanding itself began to return to me, and for the dignity of my kingdom my majesty and my brightness themselves began to return to me; and for me even my high royal officers and my grandees began eagerly searching, and I was reestablished upon my own kingdom, and greatness extraordinary was added to me." (Daniel 4:36) If any court officials had despised the deranged king, now they were "eagerly searching" for him in complete subservience.

21 What "signs and wonders" the Most High God had performed! It should not surprise us that the restored Babylonian king said: "Now I, Nebuchadnezzar, am praising and exalting and glorifying the King of the heavens, because all his works are truth and his ways are justice, and because those who are walking in pride he is able to humiliate." (Daniel 4:2, 37) Such an acknowledgment, however, did not make Nebuchadnezzar a Gentile worshiper of Jehovah.

IS THERE SECULAR EVIDENCE?

22 Some have identified Nebuchadnezzar's madness with lycanthropy. Says one medical dictionary:

20, 21. (a) How did the removal of the metal bands around the dream tree's rootstock find a parallel in what happened to Nebuchadnezzar? (b) What acknowledgment did Nebuchadnezzar make, and did this make him a worshiper of Jehovah?
22. With what disorder have some identified Nebuchadnezzar's madness, but what should we realize regarding the cause of his deranged state?

"LYCANTHROPY . . . from [*ly'kos*], *lupus*, wolf; [*an'thropos*], *homo*, man. This name was given to the sickness of people who believe themselves to be changed into an animal, and who imitate the voice or cries, the shapes or manners of that animal. These individuals usually imagine themselves transformed into a wolf, a dog or a cat; sometimes also into a bull, as in the case of Nebuchadnezzar." (*Dictionnaire des sciences médicales, par une société de médicins et de chirurgiens,* Paris, 1818, Volume 29, page 246) The symptoms of lycanthropy are similar to those of Nebuchadnezzar's demented state. Since his mental illness was divinely decreed, however, it cannot specifically be identified with a known disorder.

[23] Scholar John E. Goldingay cites several parallels to Nebuchadnezzar's madness and restoration. For instance, he states: "A fragmentary cuneiform text apparently refers to some mental disorder on Nebuchadnezzar's part, and perhaps to his neglecting and leaving Babylon." Goldingay cites a document called "The Babylonian Job" and says that it "testifies to chastisements by God, illness, humiliation, seeking interpretation of a terrifying dream, being thrown over like a tree, being put outside, eating grass, losing understanding, being like an ox, being rained on by Marduk, nails being marred, hair growing, and being fettered, and then to a restoration for which he praises the god."

SEVEN TIMES THAT AFFECT US

[24] As represented by the great tree, Nebuchadnezzar symbolized world rulership. But remember, the tree

---

23. What secular testimony is there to Nebuchadnezzar's insanity?
24. (a) The great dream tree symbolizes what? (b) What was restrained for seven times, and how did that come about?

stands for rulership and sovereignty far grander than that of Babylon's king. It symbolizes the universal sovereignty of Jehovah, "the King of the heavens," especially with respect to the earth. Before Jerusalem's destruction by the Babylonians, the kingdom centered in that city with David and his heirs sitting on "Jehovah's throne" represented God's sovereignty with reference to the earth. (1 Chronicles 29:23) God himself had such sovereignty chopped down and banded in 607 B.C.E. when he used Nebuchadnezzar to destroy Jerusalem. Exercise of divine sovereignty toward the earth by a kingdom in the line of David was restrained for seven times. How long were these seven times? When did they begin, and what marked their end?

[25] During Nebuchadnezzar's madness, "his very hair grew long just like eagles' feathers and his nails like birds' claws." (Daniel 4:33) This took longer than seven days or seven weeks. Various translations read "seven times," and alternatives are "appointed (definite) times" or "time periods." (Daniel 4:16, 23, 25, 32) A variant of the Old Greek (*Septuagint*) reads "seven years." The "seven times" were treated as "seven years" by the first-century Jewish historian Josephus. (*Antiquities of the Jews*, Book 10, Chapter 10, paragraph 6) And certain Hebrew scholars have viewed these "times" as "years." "Seven years" is the rendering in *An American Translation, Today's English Version,* and the translation by James Moffatt.

[26] Evidently, Nebuchadnezzar's "seven times" involved seven years. In prophecy, a year averages 360 days, or

---

25, 26. (a) In Nebuchadnezzar's case, how long were the "seven times," and why do you so answer? (b) In the major fulfillment, when and how did the "seven times" begin?

12 months of 30 days each. (Compare Revelation 12: 6, 14.) So the king's "seven times," or seven years, were 360 days multiplied by 7, or 2,520 days. But what about the major fulfillment of his dream? The prophetic "seven times" lasted much longer than 2,520 days. This was indicated by Jesus' words: "Jerusalem will be trampled on by the nations, until the appointed times of the nations are fulfilled." (Luke 21:24) That 'trampling' began in 607 B.C.E. when Jerusalem was destroyed and the typical kingdom of God ceased to function in Judah. When would the trampling end? At "the times of restoration of all things," when divine sovereignty would again be manifested toward the earth through symbolic Jerusalem, the Kingdom of God.—Acts 3:21.

[27] If we were to count 2,520 literal days from Jerusalem's destruction in 607 B.C.E., that would bring us only to 600 B.C.E., a year having no Scriptural significance. Even in 537 B.C.E., when the liberated Jews were back in Judah, Jehovah's sovereignty was not manifested on the earth. That was so because Zerubbabel, the heir to David's throne, was made not *king* but only *governor* of the Persian province of Judah.

[28] Since the "seven times" are prophetic, we must apply to the 2,520 days the Scriptural rule: "A day for a year." This rule is set out in a prophecy regarding the Babylonian siege of Jerusalem. (Ezekiel 4:6, 7; compare Numbers 14:34.) The "seven times" of earth's domination by Gentile powers without interference by God's Kingdom therefore spanned 2,520 years. They began

---

27. Why would you say that the "seven times" that began in 607 B.C.E. did not end 2,520 literal days later?
28. (a) What rule must be applied to the 2,520 days of the prophetic "seven times"? (b) How long were the prophetic "seven times," and what dates mark their beginning and their end?

with the desolation of Judah and Jerusalem in the seventh lunar month (Tishri 15) of 607 B.C.E. (2 Kings 25:8, 9, 25, 26) From that point to 1 B.C.E. is 606 years. The remaining 1,914 years stretch from then to 1914 C.E. Thus, the "seven times," or 2,520 years, ended by Tishri 15, or October 4/5, 1914 C.E.

²⁹ In that year "the appointed times of the nations" were fulfilled, and God gave rulership to "the lowliest one of mankind"—Jesus Christ—who had been considered so base by his foes that they even had him impaled. (Daniel 4:17) To enthrone the Messianic King, Jehovah loosened the symbolic iron and copper bands around the "rootstock" of his own sovereignty. The Most High God thus allowed a royal "sprout" to grow from it as a manifestation of divine sovereignty toward the earth by means of the heavenly Kingdom in the hands of David's greatest Heir, Jesus Christ. (Isaiah 11:1, 2; Job 14:7-9; Ezekiel 21:27) How we thank Jehovah for this blessed turn of events and for unraveling the mystery of the great tree!

---

29. Who is "the lowliest one of mankind," and what did Jehovah do to enthrone him?

WHAT DID YOU DISCERN?

- What did the great tree of Nebuchadnezzar's dream symbolize?
- What befell Nebuchadnezzar in the initial fulfillment of his tree dream?
- After his dream's fulfillment, what acknowledgment did Nebuchadnezzar make?
- In the major fulfillment of the prophetic tree dream, how long were the "seven times," and when did they begin and end?

CHAPTER SEVEN

FOUR WORDS THAT CHANGED THE WORLD

FOUR simple words written on a plastered wall. Yet, those four words frightened a powerful ruler nearly out of his wits. They heralded the dethroning of two kings, the death of one of them, and the end of a mighty world power. Those words resulted in the humiliation of a revered religious order. Most important, they exalted the pure worship of Jehovah and reaffirmed his sovereignty at a time when most people showed little regard for either one. Why, those words even shed light on world events today! How could four words do all of that? Let us see.

² Decades had passed since the events described in the 4th chapter of Daniel. Proud King Nebuchadnezzar's 43-year reign in Babylon ended with his death in 582 B.C.E. A series of successors came from his family, but early death or assassination ended the rule of one after another. Finally, a man named Nabonidus gained the throne by means of a revolt. Son of a high priestess of the moon-god Sin, Nabonidus evidently was unrelated by blood to Babylon's royal house. Some authorities suggest that he married a daughter of Nebuchadnezzar to legitimize his own rule, made their son Belshazzar his coregent, and left him in charge of Babylon for years at a time. In that case, Belshazzar would have been

1. How extensive was the impact of four words written long ago on a wall?
2. (a) What happened in Babylon following the death of Nebuchadnezzar? (b) What ruler now held power?

Nebuchadnezzar's grandson. From his grandfather's experiences, had he learned that Jehovah is the Supreme God, able to humiliate any king? Hardly!—Daniel 4:37.

A FEAST GETS OUT OF CONTROL

[3] The 5th chapter of Daniel opens with a banquet. "As regards Belshazzar the king, he made a big feast for a thousand of his grandees, and in front of the thousand he was drinking wine." (Daniel 5:1) As you can imagine, it must have taken a vast hall to seat all these men, along with the king's secondary wives and concubines. One scholar notes: "The Babylonian banquets were magnificent, though they usually ended in drunkenness. Wine, imported from abroad, and luxuries of every kind loaded the table. Perfumes filled the hall; vocalists and instrumental performers entertained the assembled guests." Presiding where all could see him, Belshazzar drank his wine—and drank, and drank.

[4] It seems strange that the Babylonians were in such a festive mood on this night—October 5/6, 539 B.C.E. Their nation was at war, and things were not going well for them. Nabonidus had recently suffered defeat at the hands of the invading Medo-Persian forces and had taken refuge in Borsippa, to the southwest of Babylon. And now the armies of Cyrus were encamped right outside Babylon. Yet, it does not seem that Belshazzar and his grandees were worried. After all, their city was the impregnable Babylon! Her colossal walls loomed over deep moats filled by the great Euphrates River as it flowed through the city. No enemy had taken Babylon by storm

---

3. What was Belshazzar's feast like?
4. (a) Why might it seem strange that the Babylonians were feasting on the night of October 5/6, 539 B.C.E.? (b) What evidently made the Babylonians confident in the face of invading armies?

in over a thousand years. So why worry? Perhaps Belshazzar reasoned that the noise of their revelry would display their confidence to the enemies outside and would dishearten them.

⁵ Before long, excessive drinking took its toll on Belshazzar. As Proverbs 20:1 says, "wine is a ridiculer." In this case, wine indeed led the king to commit folly of a most serious sort. He ordered that the sacred vessels from the temple of Jehovah be brought into the feast. These vessels, taken as spoils during Nebuchadnezzar's conquest of Jerusalem, were to be used only in pure worship. Even the Jewish priests who had been authorized to use them in Jerusalem's temple in times past had been warned to keep themselves clean.—Daniel 5:2; compare Isaiah 52:11.

⁶ However, Belshazzar had a still more insolent act in mind. "The king and his grandees, his concubines and his secondary wives . . . drank wine, and they praised the gods of gold and of silver, copper, iron, wood and stone." (Daniel 5:3, 4) So Belshazzar meant to exalt his false gods above Jehovah! This attitude, it seems, was typical among the Babylonians. They held their Jewish captives in contempt, ridiculing their worship and offering no hope of a return to their beloved homeland. (Psalm 137:1-3; Isaiah 14:16, 17) Perhaps this inebriated monarch felt that humiliating these exiles and insulting their God would impress his women and the officials, giving him an appearance of strength.* But if Belshazzar did feel some thrill of power, it did not last long.

---

* In an ancient inscription, King Cyrus said of Belshazzar: "A weakling has been installed as the [ruler] of his country."

5, 6. What did Belshazzar do under the influence of wine, and why was this a gross insult to Jehovah?

THE HANDWRITING ON THE WALL

⁷ "At that moment," says the inspired account, "the fingers of a man's hand came forth and were writing in front of the lampstand upon the plaster of the wall of the palace of the king, and the king was beholding the back of the hand that was writing." (Daniel 5:5) What an awesome sight! A hand appeared out of nowhere, floating in the air near a well-lit section of the wall. Imagine the hush falling over the party as the guests turned to gape at it. The hand began to write a cryptic message upon the plaster.* So ominous, so unforgettable, was this phenomenon that to this day people use the expression "the handwriting on the wall" to suggest a warning of imminent doom.

⁸ What was the effect upon this proud king who had tried to exalt himself and his gods above Jehovah? "At that time, as regards the king, his very complexion was changed in him, and his own thoughts began to frighten him, and his hip joints were loosening and his very knees were knocking each other." (Daniel 5:6) Belshazzar had aimed to appear grand and majestic before his subjects. Instead, he became a living portrait of abject terror —his face blanched, his hips wobbled, his whole frame trembled so violently that his knees were knocking. True, indeed, were David's words directed to Jehovah in song: "Your eyes are against the haughty ones, that you may bring them low."—2 Samuel 22:1, 28; compare Proverbs 18:12.

_____

* Even this fine detail of Daniel's account has proved accurate. Archaeologists have found that palace walls in ancient Babylon were made of brick coated with plaster.

7, 8. How was Belshazzar's feast interrupted, and what effect did this have upon the king?

⁹ It should be noted that Belshazzar's fear was not the same as godly fear, a profound reverence for Jehovah, which is the beginning of all wisdom. (Proverbs 9:10) No, this was morbid terror, and it did not beget anything like wisdom in the quaking monarch.* Instead of begging forgiveness of the God whom he had just insulted, he called out loudly for "the conjurers, the Chaldeans and the astrologers." He even declared: "Any man that will read this writing and show me its very interpretation, with purple he will be clothed, with a necklace of gold about his neck, and as the third one in the kingdom he will rule." (Daniel 5:7) The third ruler in the kingdom would be mighty indeed, preceded only by the two reigning kings, Nabonidus and Belshazzar himself. Such a place might usually have been reserved for Belshazzar's eldest son. The king was that desperate to have this miraculous message explained!

¹⁰ The wise men filed into the great hall. There was no shortage of them, for Babylon was a city steeped in false religion and abounding with temples. Men who claimed to read omens and decipher cryptic writing were surely in plentiful supply. These wise men must have thrilled at the opportunity before them. Here was their chance to practice their art before a grand audience, win the king's

---

* Babylonian superstitions probably made this miracle all the more terrifying. The book *Babylonian Life and History* notes: "In addition to the number of gods which the Babylonians worshipped, we find them much addicted to the belief in spirits, and this to so great an extent that the prayers and incantations against them form a very large portion of their religious literature."

---

9. (a) Why was Belshazzar's terror not the same as godly fear? (b) What offer did the king make to the wise men of Babylon?
10. How did the wise men fare in their efforts to interpret the handwriting on the wall?

favor, and ascend to a position of great power. But what a failure they were! "They were not competent enough to read the writing itself or to make known to the king the interpretation."*—Daniel 5:8.

11 Whether Babylon's wise men found the writing itself—the very letters—indecipherable is unsure. If they did, these unscrupulous men would have had free rein to invent any fallacious reading whatever, perhaps even one to flatter the king. Another possibility is that the letters were quite readable. Since such languages as Aramaic and Hebrew were written without vowels, however, each word could have had several possible meanings. If so, the wise men would likely have been unable to decide which words were intended. Even if they could have done that, they still would have been unable to grasp the meaning of the words so as to interpret them. In any event, one thing is sure: Babylon's wise men failed—dismally!

12 Thus the wise men were exposed as charlatans, their revered religious order a fraud. What a disappointment they were! When Belshazzar saw that his trust in these religionists had been in vain, he became still more frightened, his complexion grew paler, and even his grandees were "perplexed."#—Daniel 5:9.

---

* Notes the journal *Biblical Archaeology Review*: "Babylonian experts catalogued thousands of ominous signs. . . . When Belshazzar demanded to know what the writing on the wall meant, the wise men of Babylon, no doubt, turned to these omen encyclopedias. But they proved worthless."

Lexicographers note that the word used here for "perplexed" implies a great commotion, as if the gathering was thrown into confusion.

---

11. Why might Babylon's wise men have been unable to read the writing?
12. What did the failure of the wise men prove?

A MAN OF INSIGHT IS SUMMONED

¹³ At this critical moment, the queen herself—evidently the queen mother—entered the banquet hall. She had heard of the commotion at the feast, and she knew of one who could decipher the handwriting on the wall. Decades earlier her father, Nebuchadnezzar, had appointed Daniel over all his wise men. The queen remembered him as a man with "an extraordinary spirit and knowledge and insight." Since Daniel seems to have been unknown to Belshazzar, it is likely that the prophet had lost his high governmental position after Nebuchadnezzar's death. But prominence mattered little to Daniel. He was probably in his 90's by this time, still faithfully serving Jehovah. Despite some eight decades of exile in Babylon, he was yet known by his Hebrew name. Even the queen referred to him as Daniel, not using the Babylonian name once assigned to him. Indeed, she urged the king: "Let Daniel himself be called, that he may show the very interpretation."—Daniel 1:7; 5:10-12.

¹⁴ Daniel was summoned and came in before Belshazzar. It was awkward to beg a favor from this Jew, whose God the king had just insulted. Still, Belshazzar tried to flatter Daniel, offering him the same reward—third place in the kingdom—if he could read and explain the mysterious words. (Daniel 5:13-16) Daniel raised his eyes to the handwriting on the wall, and holy spirit enabled him to discern its meaning. It was a message of doom from Jehovah God! How could Daniel pronounce a harsh judgment of this vain king right to his face—and that in front of his wives and grandees? Imagine Daniel's predic-

---

13. (a) Why did the queen suggest that Daniel be called? (b) What kind of life was Daniel living?
14. What was Daniel's predicament upon seeing the handwriting on the wall?

ament! Was he swayed by the king's flattering words and his offer of riches and prominence? Would the prophet soften Jehovah's pronouncement?

¹⁵ Daniel spoke out courageously, saying: "Let your gifts prove to be to you yourself, and your presents do you give to others. However, I shall read the writing itself to the king, and the interpretation I shall make known to him." (Daniel 5:17) Next, Daniel acknowledged the greatness of Nebuchadnezzar, a king so powerful that he had been able to kill, strike, exalt, or humiliate anyone he chose. However, Daniel reminded Belshazzar that Jehovah, "the Most High God," had made Nebuchadnezzar great. It was Jehovah who had humiliated that mighty king when he became haughty. Yes, Nebuchadnezzar had been forced to learn that "the Most High God is Ruler in the kingdom of mankind, and that the one whom he wants to, he sets up over it."—Daniel 5:18-21.

¹⁶ Belshazzar "knew all this." Yet, he had failed to learn from history. In fact, he had gone far beyond Nebuchadnezzar's sin of wrongful pride and committed an act of outright insolence against Jehovah. Daniel laid bare the king's sin. Furthermore, in front of that pagan assemblage, he boldly told Belshazzar that false gods were "beholding nothing or hearing nothing or knowing nothing." God's courageous prophet added that in contrast with those useless gods, Jehovah is the God "in whose hand your breath is." To this day, people make gods of lifeless things, idolizing money, career, prestige, even pleasure. But none of these things can impart life. Jehovah alone is the one to whom all of us owe our very existence, upon whom we depend for every breath we draw.—Daniel 5:22, 23; Acts 17:24, 25.

15, 16. What vital lesson from history had Belshazzar failed to learn, and how common is similar failure today?

A RIDDLE SOLVED!

¹⁷ The aged prophet now proceeded to do what had proved impossible for all the wise men of Babylon. He read and interpreted the handwriting inscribed on the wall. The words were: "ME'NE, ME'NE, TE'KEL and PAR'-SIN." (Daniel 5:24, 25) What do they mean?

¹⁸ Literally, the words mean "a mina, a mina, a shekel, and half shekels." Each word was a measurement of monetary weight, listed in descending order of value. How puzzling! Even if the Babylonian wise men were able to make out the letters, it is still little wonder that they could not interpret them.

¹⁹ Under the influence of God's holy spirit, Daniel explained: "This is the interpretation of the word: ME'NE, God has numbered the days of your kingdom and has finished it." (Daniel 5:26) The consonants of the first word allowed for both the word "mina" and a form of the Aramaic word for "counted out," or "numbered," depending on the vowels supplied by the reader. Daniel well knew that the exile of the Jews was drawing to a close. Of its foretold 70-year duration, 68 years had already passed. (Jeremiah 29:10) The Great Timekeeper, Jehovah, had numbered the days of Babylon's reign as a world power, and the end was closer than anyone at Belshazzar's banquet thought. In fact, time had run out—not only for Belshazzar but also for his father, Nabonidus. That may be the reason why the word "ME'NE" was written twice—to announce the end of both of these kingships.

²⁰ "TE'KEL," on the other hand, was written only once

17, 18. What were the four words written on the wall, and what is their literal meaning?
19. What was the interpretation of the word "ME'NE"?
20. What was the explanation of the word "TE'KEL," and how did it apply to Belshazzar?

and in the singular form. This may indicate that it was directed primarily to Belshazzar. And this would be appropriate, for he had personally shown gross disrespect for Jehovah. The word itself means "shekel," but the consonants also allow for the word "weighed." Thus, Daniel said to Belshazzar: "TE'KEL, you have been weighed in the balances and have been found deficient." (Daniel 5: 27) To Jehovah, entire nations are as insignificant as the film of dust on a pair of scales. (Isaiah 40:15) They are powerless to thwart his purposes. What, then, could one arrogant king amount to? Belshazzar had tried to exalt himself above the Sovereign of the universe. This mere human had dared to insult Jehovah and ridicule pure worship but had been "found deficient." Yes, Belshazzar fully merited the judgment that was swiftly approaching!

[21] The final word on the wall was "PAR'SIN." Daniel read it in the singular form, "PE'RES," probably because he was addressing one king while the other was absent. This word capped off Jehovah's great riddle with a threefold play on words. Literally, "par'sin" means "half shekels." But the letters also allow for two other meanings—"divisions" and "Persians." Daniel thus foretold: "PE'RES, your kingdom has been divided and given to the Medes and the Persians."—Daniel 5:28.

[22] Thus the riddle was solved. Mighty Babylon was about to fall to the Medo-Persian forces. Though crestfallen in the face of this pronouncement of doom, Belshazzar kept his word. He had his servants clothe

---

21. How was "PAR'SIN" a threefold play on words, and what did this word indicate for Babylon's future as a world power?
22. How did Belshazzar react to the solution of the riddle, and what may have been his hope?

Daniel with purple, bedeck him with a golden necklace, and herald him as the third ruler in the kingdom. (Daniel 5:29) Daniel did not refuse these honors, recognizing that they reflected the honor due Jehovah. Of course, Belshazzar may have hoped to soften Jehovah's judgment by honoring His prophet. If so, it was a case of too little too late.

THE FALL OF BABYLON

23 Even while Belshazzar and his courtiers were drinking to their gods and ridiculing Jehovah, a great drama was unfolding in the darkness outside the palace. Prophecy that had been spoken through Isaiah nearly two centuries earlier was undergoing fulfillment. Concerning Babylon, Jehovah had foretold: "All sighing due to her I have caused to cease." Yes, all of that wicked city's oppression of God's chosen people was to come to an end. By what means? The same prophecy said: "Go up, O Elam! Lay siege, O Media!" Elam became part of Persia after the prophet Isaiah's day. By the time of Belshazzar's feast, which had also been foretold in the same prophecy by Isaiah, Persia and Media had indeed joined forces to "go up" and "lay siege" against Babylon.—Isaiah 21: 1, 2, 5, 6.

24 In fact, the very name of the leader of these forces had been foretold, as had the main points of his battle strategy. Some 200 years in advance, Isaiah had prophesied that Jehovah would anoint one named Cyrus to come against Babylon. In the course of his onslaught, all

---

23. What ancient prophecy was undergoing fulfillment even while Belshazzar's feast was in progress?
24. What details regarding the fall of Babylon had Isaiah's prophecy foretold?

obstacles would be smoothed out before him. Babylon's waters would "dry up," and her mighty doors would be left open. (Isaiah 44:27–45:3) And so it was. The armies of Cyrus diverted the Euphrates River, lowering the water level so that they could move through the riverbed. Doors in Babylon's wall had been left open by careless guards. As secular historians agree, the city was invaded while its inhabitants reveled. Babylon was taken with hardly any opposition. (Jeremiah 51:30) There was, though, at least one notable death. Daniel reported: "In that very night Belshazzar the Chaldean king was killed and Darius the Mede himself received the kingdom, being about sixty-two years old."—Daniel 5:30, 31.

LEARNING FROM THE HANDWRITING ON THE WALL

25 The inspired account in Daniel chapter 5 is rich in meaning for us. As a center of false religious practices, ancient Babylon is a fitting symbol of the world empire of false religion. Pictured in Revelation as a bloodthirsty harlot, this global conglomerate of deceit is called "Babylon the Great." (Revelation 17:5) Heedless of all warnings about her God-dishonoring false doctrines and practices, she has persecuted those preaching the truth of God's Word. Like inhabitants of ancient Jerusalem and Judah, the faithful remnant of anointed Christians were effectively exiled in "Babylon the Great" when clergy-inspired persecution virtually closed down the Kingdom-preaching work in 1918.

26 Suddenly, though, "Babylon the Great" fell! Oh, it was practically a noiseless fall—just as ancient Babylon fell almost noiselessly, in 539 B.C.E. But this figurative fall was devastating nonetheless. It occurred in 1919 C.E. when Jehovah's people were freed from Babylonish captivity and were blessed with divine approval. This ended the power of "Babylon the Great" over God's people and marked the beginning of her public exposure as an unreliable fraud. That fall has proved to be irreversible, and her final destruction is imminent. Jehovah's servants have thus been echoing the warning: "Get out of her, my people, if you do not want to share with her in her sins." (Revelation 18:4) Have you heeded that warning? Do you share it with others?*

---

* See pages 205-71 of the book *Revelation—Its Grand Climax At Hand!*, published by the Watchtower Bible and Tract Society of New York, Inc.

---

25. (a) Why is ancient Babylon a fitting symbol of today's global system of false religion? (b) In what sense were God's modern-day servants held captive in Babylon?
26. (a) How did "Babylon the Great" fall in 1919? (b) What warning should we ourselves heed and share with others?

²⁷ So the handwriting is on the wall today—but not for "Babylon the Great" alone. Remember a vital truth central to Daniel's book: Jehovah is the Universal Sovereign. He, and he alone, has the right to set up a ruler over mankind. (Daniel 4:17, 25; 5:21) Anything standing in opposition to Jehovah's purposes will be removed. It is only a matter of time before Jehovah acts. (Habakkuk 2:3) For Daniel, such a time finally came in the tenth decade of his life. He then saw Jehovah remove a world power—one that had been oppressing God's people since Daniel's boyhood.

²⁸ There is undeniable proof that Jehovah God has established upon a heavenly throne a Ruler for mankind. That the world has ignored this King and has opposed his rulership is sure evidence that Jehovah will soon wipe out all opposers of Kingdom rule. (Psalm 2:1-11; 2 Peter 3:3-7) Are you acting upon the urgency of our times and placing your confidence in God's Kingdom? If so, you have really learned from the handwriting on the wall!

27, 28. (a) Daniel never lost sight of what vital truth? (b) What evidence do we have that Jehovah is soon to act against the wicked world of today?

WHAT DID YOU DISCERN?

- How was Belshazzar's feast interrupted on the night of October 5/6, 539 B.C.E.?

- What was the interpretation of the handwriting on the wall?

- What prophecy about Babylon's fall was being fulfilled while Belshazzar's feast was in progress?

- What meaning does the account of the handwriting on the wall hold for our day?

CHAPTER EIGHT

RESCUED FROM THE JAWS OF LIONS!

BABYLON had fallen! Its century-long splendor as a world power had been snuffed out in just a few hours. A new era was beginning—that of the Medes and the Persians. As successor to Belshazzar's throne, Darius the Mede now faced the challenge of organizing his expanded empire.

² One of the first tasks undertaken by Darius was to appoint 120 satraps. It is believed that those who served in this capacity were sometimes selected from among the king's relatives. In any event, each satrap governed a major district or a smaller subdivision of the empire. (Daniel 6:1) His duties included collecting taxes and remitting the tribute to the royal court. Though subject to periodic scrutiny by a visiting representative of the king, the satrap had considerable authority. His title meant "protector of the Kingdom." In his province the satrap was regarded as a vassal king, with all but sovereign power.

³ Where would Daniel fit into this new arrangement? Would Darius the Mede retire this aged Jewish prophet who was now in his nineties? By no means! Darius no doubt realized that Daniel had accurately foretold the downfall of Babylon and that such a prediction required superhuman discernment. In addition, Daniel had decades of experience in dealing with the varied captive

---

1, 2. (a) How did Darius the Mede organize his expanded empire? (b) Describe the duties and authority of the satraps.
3, 4. Why did Darius favor Daniel, and to what position did the king appoint him?

communities in Babylon. Darius was intent on keeping peaceful relations with his newly conquered subjects. Therefore, he would certainly want someone with Daniel's wisdom and experience close to the throne. In what capacity?

⁴ It would have been startling enough if Darius had appointed the Jewish exile Daniel to be a satrap. But just imagine the commotion when Darius announced his decision to make Daniel one of the three high officials who would oversee the satraps! Not only that but Daniel was "steadily distinguishing himself," proving himself superior to his fellow high officials. Indeed, "an extraordinary spirit" was found in him. Darius was even intent upon giving him the position of prime minister.—Daniel 6:2, 3.

⁵ The other high officials and the satraps must have been seething with anger. Why, they could not stand the thought of having Daniel—who was neither Mede nor Persian nor a member of the royal family—in a position of authority over them! How could Darius elevate a foreigner to such prominence, bypassing his own countrymen, even his own family? Such a maneuver must have seemed unfair. Moreover, the satraps evidently viewed Daniel's integrity as an unwelcome restraint against their own practices of graft and corruption. Yet, the high officials and satraps did not dare to approach Darius about the matter. After all, Darius held Daniel in high esteem.

⁶ So these jealous politicians conspired among themselves. They tried "to find some pretext against Daniel

---

5. How must the other high officials and the satraps have reacted to Daniel's appointment, and why?
6. How did the high officials and satraps try to discredit Daniel, and why did this effort prove futile?

respecting the kingdom." Could anything be amiss about the way he handled his responsibilities? Was he dishonest? The high officials and satraps could find no negligence or corruption whatsoever in the way that Daniel handled his duties. "We shall find in this Daniel no pretext at all," they reasoned, "except we have to find it against him in the law of his God." And so it was that these devious men hatched a plot. They thought it would finish Daniel off once and for all.—Daniel 6:4, 5.

A MURDEROUS PLOT SET IN MOTION

[7] Darius was approached by an entourage of high officials and satraps who "entered as a throng." The Aramaic expression here carries the idea of a thunderous commotion. Apparently, these men made it appear that they had a matter of great urgency to present to Darius. They may have reasoned that he would be less likely to question their proposal if they presented it with conviction and as something that required immediate action. Hence, they came right to the point, saying: "All the high officials of the kingdom, the prefects and the satraps, the high royal officers and the governors, have taken counsel together to establish a royal statute and to enforce an interdict, that whoever makes a petition to any god or man for thirty days except to you, O king, should be thrown to the lions' pit."*—Daniel 6:6, 7.

[8] Historical records confirm that it was common for Mesopotamian kings to be viewed and worshiped as

---

* The existence of a "lions' pit" in Babylon is supported by the testimony of ancient inscriptions showing that Oriental rulers frequently had menageries of wild animals.

---

7. What proposal did the high officials and satraps make to the king, and in what manner did they do so?
8. (a) Why would Darius find the proposed law appealing? (b) What was the true motive of the high officials and satraps?

divine. So Darius undoubtedly was flattered by this proposal. He may also have seen a practical side to it. Remember, to those living in Babylon, Darius was a foreigner and a newcomer. This new law would serve to establish him as king, and it would encourage the multitudes living in Babylon to avow their loyalty and support to the new regime. In proposing the decree, though, the high officials and the satraps were not at all concerned about the king's welfare. Their true motive was to entrap Daniel, for they knew that it was his custom to pray to God three times a day before the open windows of his roof chamber.

⁹ Would this restriction on prayer create a problem for all the religious communities in Babylon? Not necessarily, especially since the prohibition was to last only for a month. Furthermore, few non-Jews would view directing their worship to a human for a time as a compromise. One Bible scholar notes: "King-worship made no strange demands upon the most idolatrous of nations; and therefore the Babylonian when called upon to pay to the conqueror—Darius the Mede—the homage due to a god, readily acceded to the demand. It was the Jew alone who resented such a demand."

¹⁰ In any event, Darius' visitors urged him to "establish the statute and sign the writing, in order for it not to be changed, according to the law of the Medes and the Persians, which is not annulled." (Daniel 6:8) In the ancient East, the will of a king was often regarded as absolute. This perpetuated the notion that he was infallible. Even a law that could cause the death of innocent people had to remain in effect!

---

9. Why would the new law not pose a problem for most non-Jews?
10. How did the Medes and the Persians view a law enacted by their king?

¹¹ Without thinking of Daniel, Darius signed the decree. (Daniel 6:9) In doing so, he unknowingly signed the death warrant of his most valued official. Yes, Daniel was sure to be affected by this edict.

DARIUS FORCED TO
RENDER ADVERSE JUDGMENT

¹² Daniel soon became aware of the law restricting prayer. Immediately, he entered into his house and went to his roof chamber, where the windows were open toward Jerusalem.* There Daniel began praying to God "as he had been regularly doing prior to this." Daniel may have thought that he was alone, but the conspirators were watching him. Suddenly, they "crowded in," no doubt in the same excited manner in which they had approached Darius. Now they were seeing it with their own eyes—Daniel was "petitioning and imploring favor before his God." (Daniel 6:10, 11) The high officials and satraps had all the evidence they needed to accuse Daniel before the king.

¹³ Daniel's enemies slyly asked Darius: "Is there not an interdict that you have signed that any man that asks a petition from any god or man for thirty days except from you, O king, he should be thrown to the lions' pit?" Darius answered: "The matter is well established according to the law of the Medes and the Persians, which is not annulled." Now the conspirators quickly got to the point. "Daniel, who is of the exiles of Judah, has paid no regard

---

* The roof chamber was a private room to which a person could retire when he wished to be left undisturbed.

---

11. How would Daniel be affected by Darius' edict?
12. (a) What did Daniel do as soon as he found out about the new law? (b) Who were watching Daniel, and why?
13. What did Daniel's enemies report to the king?

to you, O king, nor to the interdict that you signed, but three times in a day he is making his petition."—Daniel 6:12, 13.

¹⁴ It is significant that the high officials and satraps referred to Daniel as being "of the exiles of Judah." Evidently, they wanted to emphasize that this Daniel whom Darius had elevated to such prominence was in reality no more than a Jewish slave. They believed that as such, he was certainly not above the law—no matter how the king felt about him!

¹⁵ Perhaps the high officials and satraps expected the king to reward them for their astute detective work. If so, they were in for a surprise. Darius was sorely troubled by the news they brought him. Rather than becoming enraged at Daniel or immediately consigning him to the lions' pit, Darius spent all day striving to deliver him. But his efforts proved futile. Before long, the conspirators returned, and in their shameless spirit, they demanded Daniel's blood.—Daniel 6:14, 15.

¹⁶ Darius felt that he had no choice in the matter. The law could not be annulled, nor could Daniel's "transgression" be pardoned. All that Darius could say to Daniel was "your God whom you are serving with constancy, he himself will rescue you." Darius seemed to respect Daniel's God. It was Jehovah who had given Daniel the ability to foretell the fall of Babylon. God had also given Daniel "an extraordinary spirit," which distinguished

---

14. Evidently, why did the high officials and satraps refer to Daniel as being "of the exiles of Judah"?
15. (a) How did Darius react to the news that the high officials and satraps brought him? (b) How did the high officials and satraps further show their contempt for Daniel?
16. (a) Why did Darius respect Daniel's God? (b) What hope did Darius have regarding Daniel?

him from the other high officials. Perhaps Darius was aware that decades earlier this same God had delivered three young Hebrews from a fiery furnace. Likely, the king hoped that Jehovah would now deliver Daniel, since Darius was unable to reverse the law he had signed. Hence, Daniel was thrown into the lions' pit.* Next, "a stone was brought and placed on the mouth of the pit, and the king sealed it with his signet ring and with the signet ring of his grandees, in order that nothing should be changed in the case of Daniel."—Daniel 6:16, 17.

A DRAMATIC TURN OF EVENTS

[17] A dejected Darius returned to his palace. No musicians were brought in before him, for he was in no mood for entertainment. Instead, Darius lay awake the whole night, fasting. "His very sleep fled from him." At dawn, Darius hastened to the lions' pit. He cried out in a sad voice: "O Daniel, servant of the living God, has your God whom you are serving with constancy been able to rescue you from the lions?" (Daniel 6:18-20) To his amazement—and utter relief—there was an answer!

[18] "O king, live on even to times indefinite." With this respectful greeting, Daniel showed that he did not harbor feelings of animosity toward the king. He realized that the real source of his persecution was, not Darius, but the envious high officials and satraps. (Compare Matthew 5:44; Acts 7:60.) Daniel continued: "My own God sent his angel and shut the mouth of the lions, and they have not

---

* The lions' pit may have been a subterranean chamber with a mouth at the top. Likely it also had doors or gratings that could be raised to allow the animals to enter.

17, 18. (a) What shows that Darius was distressed over Daniel's situation? (b) What happened when the king returned to the lions' pit the following morning?

brought me to ruin, forasmuch as before him innocence itself was found in me; and also before you, O king, no hurtful act have I done."—Daniel 6:21, 22.

¹⁹ How those words must have stung Darius' conscience! He knew all along that Daniel had done nothing to merit being thrown into the lions' pit. Darius was well aware that the high officials and satraps had conspired to have Daniel put to death and that they had manipulated the king to achieve their selfish ends. By their insisting that *"all* the high officials of the kingdom" had recommended the passing of the edict, they implied that Daniel too had been consulted in the matter. Darius would deal with these devious men later. First, however, he gave the command to have Daniel lifted out of the lions' pit. Miraculously, Daniel had not suffered so much as a single scratch!—Daniel 6:23.

²⁰ Now that Daniel was safe, Darius had other business to attend to. "The king commanded, and they brought these able-bodied men who had accused Daniel, and into the lions' pit they threw them, their sons and their wives; and they had not reached the bottom of the pit before the lions had got the mastery over them, and all their bones they crushed."*—Daniel 6:24.

²¹ Putting to death not only the conspirators but also their wives and children may seem unreasonably harsh.

---

* The word "accused" is a translation of an Aramaic expression that may also be rendered "slandered." This highlights the malicious intent of Daniel's enemies.

---

19. How had Darius been deceived and manipulated by the high officials and satraps?
20. What happened to Daniel's malicious enemies?
21. In dealing with family members of wrongdoers, what contrast existed between the Mosaic Law and the laws of some ancient cultures?

In contrast, the Law that God gave through the prophet Moses stated: "Fathers should not be put to death on account of children, and children should not be put to death on account of fathers. Each one should be put to death for his own sin." (Deuteronomy 24:16) Nevertheless, in some ancient cultures, it was not unusual for family members to be executed along with the wrongdoer, in the case of a serious crime. Perhaps this was done so that family members would not be able to seek revenge later on. However, this act against the families of the high officials and the satraps was certainly none of Daniel's doing. Likely, he was distressed over the calamity that these wicked men had brought upon their families.

²² The scheming high officials and satraps were gone. Darius issued a proclamation, which stated: "From before me there has been put through an order that, in every dominion of my kingdom, people are to be quaking and fearing before the God of Daniel. For he is the living God and One enduring to times indefinite, and his kingdom is one that will not be brought to ruin, and his dominion is forever. He is rescuing and delivering and performing signs and wonders in the heavens and on the earth, for he has rescued Daniel from the paw of the lions."—Daniel 6:25-27.

SERVE GOD WITH CONSTANCY

²³ Daniel set a fine example for all modern-day servants of God. His conduct was always above reproach. In his secular work, Daniel "was trustworthy and no negligence or corrupt thing at all was found in him." (Daniel 6:4) In a similar way, a Christian should be industrious

---

22. What new proclamation did Darius issue?
23. What example did Daniel set regarding his secular work, and how can we be like him?

with respect to his employment. This does not mean being a business cutthroat who eagerly pursues material wealth or who steps on others to climb the corporate ladder. (1 Timothy 6:10) The Scriptures require that a Christian fulfill his secular obligations honestly and in a whole-souled way, "as to Jehovah."—Colossians 3:22, 23; Titus 2:7, 8; Hebrews 13:18.

24 In his worship, Daniel was uncompromising. His custom of praying was a matter of public knowledge. Furthermore, the high officials and satraps well knew that Daniel took his worship seriously. Indeed, they were convinced that he would hold to this routine even if a law forbade it. What a fine example for present-day Christians! They too have a reputation for putting God's worship in first place. (Matthew 6:33) This should be readily evident to onlookers, for Jesus commanded his followers: "Let your light shine before men, that they may see your fine works and give glory to your Father who is in the heavens."—Matthew 5:16.

25 Some might say that Daniel could have avoided persecution by praying to Jehovah in secret for the 30-day period. After all, no particular posture or setting is required in order to be heard by God. He can even discern the meditations of the heart. (Psalm 19:14) Nevertheless, Daniel viewed any change in his routine to be tantamount to compromise. Why?

26 Since Daniel's custom of praying was well-known, what message would have been conveyed if he suddenly discontinued it? Observers might well have concluded

---

24. How did Daniel prove himself to be uncompromising in the matter of worship?
25, 26. (a) What might some conclude about Daniel's course of action? (b) Why did Daniel view a change in his routine to be tantamount to compromise?

that Daniel was fearful of man and that the king's decree superseded Jehovah's law. (Psalm 118:6) But Daniel showed by his actions that Jehovah received his exclusive devotion. (Deuteronomy 6:14, 15; Isaiah 42:8) Of course, in doing this Daniel did not disrespectfully flout the king's law. Yet, neither did he cower by compromising. Daniel simply continued to pray in his roof chamber, "as he had been regularly doing" prior to the king's edict.

²⁷ Servants of God today can learn from Daniel's example. They remain "in subjection to the superior authorities," obeying the laws of the land in which they live. (Romans 13:1) When the laws of man conflict with those of God, however, Jehovah's people adopt the position of Jesus' apostles, who boldly stated: "We must obey God as ruler rather than men." (Acts 5:29) In doing so, Christians do not promote insurrection or rebellion. Rather, their aim is simply to live peaceably with all men so that they "may go on leading a calm and quiet life with full godly devotion."—1 Timothy 2:1, 2; Romans 12:18.

²⁸ On two occasions Darius commented that Daniel was serving God "with constancy." (Daniel 6:16, 20) The Aramaic root for the word translated "constancy" means to "move in a circle." It suggests the idea of a continuous cycle, or something that is perpetual. Daniel's integrity was like that. It followed a predictable pattern. There was no question about what Daniel would do when faced with tests, whether large or small. He would continue in the course he had already established decades earlier —that of loyalty and faithfulness to Jehovah.

---

27. How can servants of God today be like Daniel in (a) being in subjection to the superior authorities? (b) obeying God as ruler rather than men? (c) striving to live peaceably with all men?
28. How did Daniel serve Jehovah "with constancy"?

Daniel served Jehovah "with constancy." Do you?

²⁹ God's present-day servants want to follow Daniel's course. Indeed, the apostle Paul admonished all Christians to consider the example of God-fearing men of old. Through faith, they "effected righteousness, obtained promises," and—evidently a reference to Daniel—"stopped the mouths of lions." As servants of Jehovah today, let us display the faith and constancy of Daniel and "run with endurance the race that is set before us."—Hebrews 11:32, 33; 12:1.

---

29. How can servants of Jehovah today benefit from Daniel's faithful course?

CHAPTER NINE

WHO WILL RULE THE WORLD?

DANIEL'S gripping prophecy now takes us back to the first year of Babylonian King Belshazzar. Daniel has long been an exile in Babylon, but never has he wavered in his integrity to Jehovah. Now in his 70's, the faithful prophet beholds "a dream and visions of his head upon his bed." And how those visions frighten him!—Daniel 7:1, 15.

² "See there!" exclaims Daniel. "The four winds of the heavens were stirring up the vast sea. And four huge beasts were coming up out of the sea, each one being different from the others." What remarkable beasts! The first is a winged lion, and the second is like a bear. Then comes a leopard with four wings and four heads! The unusually strong fourth beast has large iron teeth and ten horns. In among its ten horns rises a "small" horn having "eyes like the eyes of a man" and "a mouth speaking grandiose things."—Daniel 7:2-8.

³ Daniel's visions next turn heavenward. The Ancient of Days sits gloriously enthroned as Judge in the heavenly Court. 'There are a thousand thousands that keep ministering to him, and ten thousand times ten thousand that keep standing right before him.' Judging the beasts adversely, he takes rulership away from them and destroys the fourth beast. Lasting rulership over "the peoples, national groups and languages" is vested in "someone like a son of man."—Daniel 7:9-14.

1-3. Describe the dream and visions that Daniel had in the first year of Belshazzar's reign.

⁴ "As for me," says Daniel, "my spirit was distressed within on account of it, and the very visions of my head began to frighten me." So he seeks from an angel "reliable information on all this." The angel indeed provides him "the very interpretation of the matters." (Daniel 7:15-28) What Daniel saw and heard that night is of great interest to us, for it outlined future world events reaching into our times, when "someone like a son of man" is given rulership over all "peoples, national groups and languages." With the help of God's Word and spirit, we too can understand the meaning of these prophetic visions.*

FOUR BEASTS COME OUT OF THE SEA

⁵ "Four huge beasts were coming up out of the sea," said Daniel. (Daniel 7:3) What was symbolized by the windswept sea? Years later, the apostle John saw a seven-headed wild beast come out of the "sea." That sea represented "peoples and crowds and nations and tongues"—the vast body of mankind estranged from God. The sea, then, is a fitting symbol of the masses of mankind alienated from God.—Revelation 13:1, 2; 17:15; Isaiah 57:20.

⁶ "As for these huge beasts," said God's angel, "because they are four, there are four kings that will stand up from the earth." (Daniel 7:17) Clearly, the angel identified the four beasts that Daniel saw as "four kings." Thus, these beasts signify world powers. But which ones?

---

* For clarity and to avoid repetition, we will consolidate explanatory verses found at Daniel 7:15-28 with a verse-by-verse consideration of the visions recorded at Daniel 7:1-14.

---

4. (a) To whom did Daniel turn for reliable information? (b) Why is what Daniel saw and heard that night important to us?
5. What does the windswept sea symbolize?
6. What do the four beasts picture?

⁷ Bible expositors commonly link Daniel's dream-vision of four beasts with Nebuchadnezzar's dream of an immense image. For example, *The Expositor's Bible Commentary* states: "Chapter 7 [of Daniel] parallels chapter 2." *The Wycliffe Bible Commentary* says: "It is generally agreed that the succession of four Gentile dominions . . . is the same here [in Daniel chapter 7] as that contemplated in [Daniel] chapter 2." The four world powers represented by the four metals of Nebuchadnezzar's dream were the Babylonian Empire (gold head), Medo-Persia (silver breasts and arms), Greece (copper belly and thighs), and the Roman Empire (iron legs).* (Daniel 2:32, 33) Let us see how these kingdoms correspond to the four huge beasts that Daniel saw.

FEROCIOUS AS A LION, QUICK AS AN EAGLE

⁸ What beasts Daniel beheld! Describing one, he said: "The first one was like a lion, and it had the wings of an eagle. I kept on beholding until its wings were plucked out, and it was lifted up from the earth and was made to stand up on two feet just like a man, and there was given to it the heart of a man." (Daniel 7:4) This beast pictured the same rulership as that represented by the head of gold of the immense image, the Babylonian World Power (607-539 B.C.E.). Like a predatory "lion," Babylon fiercely devoured nations, including God's people. (Jeremiah 4:5-7; 50:17) As if with the wings of an eagle, this "lion" sped forward in aggressive conquest.—Lamentations 4:19; Habakkuk 1:6-8.

---

* See Chapter 4 of this book.

---

7. (a) What do certain Bible expositors say about Daniel's dream-vision of the four beasts and King Nebuchadnezzar's dream of an immense image? (b) What do each of the four metallic parts of the image represent?
8. (a) How did Daniel describe the first beast? (b) What empire did the first beast represent, and how did it act like a lion?

⁹ In time, the unique winged lion had its wings "plucked out." Near the end of King Belshazzar's rule, Babylon lost its speed of conquest and its lionlike supremacy over the nations. It was no faster than a man on two feet. Getting "the heart of a man," it became weak. Lacking "the heart of the lion," Babylon could no longer behave like king "among the beasts of a forest." (Compare 2 Samuel 17:10; Micah 5:8.) Another huge beast vanquished it.

VORACIOUS AS A BEAR

¹⁰ "See there!" said Daniel, "another beast, a second one, it being like a bear. And on one side it was raised up, and there were three ribs in its mouth between its teeth; and this is what they were saying to it, 'Get up, eat much flesh.'" (Daniel 7:5) The king symbolized by the "bear" was the very same as that represented by the silver breasts and arms of the great image—the line of Medo-Persian rulers (539-331 B.C.E.) starting with Darius the Mede and Cyrus the Great and ending with Darius III.

¹¹ The symbolic bear was 'raised up on one side,' per-

9. What changes did the lionlike beast undergo, and how did these affect it?
10. What line of rulers did the "bear" symbolize?
11. What did the symbolic bear's being raised up on one side and its having three ribs in its mouth signify?

haps to get ready to attack and subdue nations and thus maintain world power. Or this position may have been intended to show that the Persian line of rulers would gain the ascendancy over the sole Median king, Darius. The three ribs between the bear's teeth could denote the three directions in which it pushed its conquests. The Medo-Persian "bear" went to the north to seize

Babylon in 539 B.C.E. Then it went westward through Asia Minor and into Thrace. Finally, the "bear" went to the south to conquer Egypt. Since the number three at times symbolizes intensity, the three ribs may also emphasize the symbolic bear's greed for conquest.

¹² The "bear" assaulted nations in response to the words: "Get up, eat much flesh." By devouring Babylon according to the divine will, Medo-Persia was in a position to perform a valuable service toward Jehovah's people. And it did! (See "A Tolerant Monarch," on page 149.) Through Cyrus the Great, Darius I (Darius the Great), and Artaxerxes I, Medo-Persia freed Babylon's Jewish captives and helped them rebuild Jehovah's temple and repair Jerusalem's walls. In time, Medo-Persia came to rule over 127 jurisdictional districts, and Queen Esther's husband, Ahasuerus (Xerxes I), was "king from India to Ethiopia."

12. What resulted from the symbolic bear's obeying the command: "Get up, eat much flesh"?

(Esther 1:1) However, the rise of another beast was in the offing.

SWIFT AS A WINGED LEOPARD!

¹³ The third beast was "like a leopard, but it had four wings of a flying creature on its back. And the beast had four heads, and there was given to it rulership indeed." (Daniel 7:6) Like its counterpart—the copper belly and thighs of Nebuchadnezzar's dream image—this four-winged, four-headed leopard symbolized the Macedonian, or Grecian, line of rulers starting with Alexander the Great. With the agility and speed of a leopard, Alexander moved through Asia Minor, south into Egypt, and on to the western border of India. (Compare Habakkuk 1:8.) His domain was greater than that of the "bear," for it included Macedonia, Greece, and the Persian Empire.—See "A Young King Conquers the World," on page 153.

¹⁴ The "leopard" became four-headed after Alexander died in 323 B.C.E. Four of his generals eventually became his successors in different sections of his domain. Seleucus held Mesopotamia and Syria. Ptolemy controlled Egypt and Palestine. Lysimachus ruled over Asia Minor and Thrace, and Cassander got Macedonia and Greece.

---

13. (a) What did the third beast symbolize? (b) What can be said about the speed of the third beast and the domain it occupied?
14. How did the "leopard" become four-headed?

(See "A Vast Kingdom Is Divided," on page 162.) Then a new menace arose.

A FEARSOME BEAST PROVES TO BE DIFFERENT

[15] Daniel described the fourth beast as "fearsome and terrible and unusually strong." He continued: "And it had teeth of iron, big ones. It was devouring and crushing, and what was left it was treading down with its feet. And it was something different from all the other beasts that were prior to it, and it had ten horns." (Daniel 7:7) This fearsome beast began as the political and military power of Rome. It gradually took over the four Hellenistic divisions of the Grecian Empire, and by the year 30 B.C.E., Rome had emerged as the next world power of Bible prophecy. Subjugating everything in its path by military force, the Roman Empire eventually grew to cover an area that stretched from the British Isles down across much of Europe, all the way around the Mediterranean, and beyond Babylon to the Persian Gulf.

[16] Desiring to make certain concerning this "extraordinarily fearsome" beast, Daniel listened intently as the angel explained: "As for [its] ten horns, out of that kingdom there are ten kings that will rise up; and still another one will rise up after them, and he himself will be different from the first ones, and three kings he will humiliate." (Daniel 7:19, 20, 24) What were these "ten horns," or "ten kings"?

[17] As Rome became more affluent and increasingly decadent because of the licentious living of its ruling class, it diminished as a military power. In time,

---

15. (a) Describe the fourth beast. (b) What did the fourth beast symbolize, and how did it crush and devour everything in its path?
16. What information did the angel give about the fourth beast?
17. What do the "ten horns" of the fourth beast symbolize?

the decline of Rome's military strength became clearly evident. The mighty empire eventually broke up into many kingdoms. Since the Bible often uses the number ten to denote completeness, the "ten horns" of the fourth beast represent all the kingdoms that resulted from Rome's dissolution.—Compare Deuteronomy 4:13; Luke 15:8; 19:13, 16, 17.

18 The Roman World Power, however, did not end with the removal of its last emperor in Rome in 476 C.E. For many centuries, papal Rome continued to exercise political, and especially religious, domination over Europe. It did so through the feudal system, in which most inhabitants of Europe were subject to a lord, then to a king. And all kings acknowledged the authority of the pope. Thus the Holy Roman Empire with papal Rome as its focal point dominated world affairs throughout that long period of history called the Dark Ages.

19 Who can deny that the fourth beast was "different from all the other kingdoms"? (Daniel 7:7, 19, 23) In this regard, historian H. G. Wells wrote: "This new Roman power . . . was in several respects a different thing from any of the great empires that had hitherto prevailed in the civilised world. . . . [It] incorporated nearly all the Greek people in the world, and its population was less strongly Hamitic and Semitic than that of any preceding empire . . . It was so far a new pattern in history . . . The Roman Empire was a growth, an unplanned novel growth; the Roman people found themselves engaged almost unawares in a vast administrative experiment." Yet, the fourth beast was to have further growth.

---

18. How did Rome continue to exercise domination over Europe for centuries after the removal of its last emperor?
19. According to one historian, how did Rome compare with the preceding empires?

A SMALL HORN GAINS THE ASCENDANCY

20 "I kept on considering the horns," said Daniel, "and, look! another horn, a small one, came up in among them, and there were three of the first horns that were plucked up from before it." (Daniel 7:8) Concerning this outgrowth, the angel told Daniel: "Another one will rise up after them [the ten kings], and he himself will be different from the first ones, and three kings he will humiliate." (Daniel 7:24) Who is this king, when did he rise, and what three kings did he humiliate?

21 Consider the following developments. In 55 B.C.E., Roman General Julius Caesar invaded Britannia but failed to establish a permanent settlement. In 43 C.E.,

20. What did the angel say about the outgrowth of a small horn on the head of the fourth beast?
21. How did Britain come to be the symbolic small horn of the fourth beast?

Emperor Claudius began a more permanent conquest of southern Britain. Then, in 122 C.E., Emperor Hadrian began to build a wall from the Tyne River to the Solway Firth, marking the northern limit of the Roman Empire. Early in the fifth century, the Roman legions left the island. "In the sixteenth century," explained one historian, "England had been a second-rate power. Its wealth was slight compared with that of the Netherlands. Its population was much less than that of France. Its armed forces (including its navy) were inferior to Spain's." Britain evidently was an insignificant kingdom then, making up the symbolic small horn of the fourth beast. But that was to change.

²² In 1588, Philip II of Spain launched the Spanish Armada against Britain. This fleet of 130 ships, carrying more than 24,000 men, sailed up the English Channel, only to suffer defeat by the British navy and to fall victim to contrary winds and fierce Atlantic storms. This event "marked the decisive passing of naval superiority from Spain to England," said one historian. In the 17th century, the Dutch developed the world's largest merchant marine. With growing overseas colonies, however, Britain prevailed over that kingdom. During the 18th century, the British and the French fought each other in North America and India, leading to the Treaty of Paris in 1763. This treaty, said author William B. Willcox, "recognized Britain's new position as the predominant European power in the world beyond Europe." Britain's supremacy was confirmed by the crushing victory over Napoléon of France in 1815 C.E. The "three kings" that Britain thus 'humiliated' were Spain, the Netherlands,

22. (a) What other three horns of the fourth beast did the "small" horn overcome? (b) Britain then emerged as what?

WORLD POWERS OF DANIEL'S PROPHECY

The immense image
(Daniel 2:31-45)

Four beasts out
of the sea
(Daniel 7:3-8, 17, 25)

BABYLONIA
from 607 B.C.E.

MEDO-PERSIA
from 539 B.C.E.

GREECE
from 331 B.C.E

ROME
from 30 B.C.E.

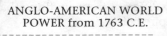

ANGLO-AMERICAN WORLD
POWER from 1763 C.E.

POLITICALLY DIVIDED WORLD
in the time of the end

and France. (Daniel 7:24) As a result, Britain emerged as the world's greatest colonial and commercial power. Yes, the "small" horn grew to become a world power!

²³ The angel told Daniel that the fourth beast, or fourth kingdom, would "devour all the earth." (Daniel 7: 23) That proved true of the Roman province once known as Britannia. It eventually became the British Empire and 'devoured all the earth.' At one time, this empire embraced one fourth of the earth's land surface and a fourth of its population.

²⁴ As the Roman Empire differed from previous world powers, the king depicted by the "small" horn would also "be different from the first ones." (Daniel 7:24) Concerning the British Empire, historian H. G. Wells noted: "Nothing of the sort has ever existed before. First and central to the whole system was the 'crowned republic' of the United British Kingdoms . . . No single office and no single brain had ever comprehended the British Empire as a whole. It was a mixture of growths and accumulations entirely different from anything that has ever been called an empire before."

23. In what way did the symbolic small horn "devour all the earth"?
24. What did a historian say about the British Empire's being different?

²⁵ There was more to the "small" horn than the British Empire. In 1783, Britain recognized the independence of its 13 American colonies. The United States of America eventually became Britain's ally, emerging from World War II as the earth's dominant nation. It still has strong ties with Britain. The resulting Anglo-American dual world power constitutes the 'horn having eyes.' Indeed, this world power is observant, astute! It 'speaks grandiose things,' dictating policy for much of the world and acting as its mouthpiece, or "false prophet."—Daniel 7:8, 11, 20; Revelation 16:13; 19:20.

THE SMALL HORN OPPOSES GOD AND HIS HOLY ONES

²⁶ Daniel continued to describe his vision, saying: "I kept on beholding when that very horn made war upon the holy ones, and it was prevailing against them." (Daniel 7:21) Regarding this "horn," or king, God's angel foretold: "He will speak even words against the Most High, and he will harass continually the holy ones themselves of the Supreme One. And he will intend to change times and law, and they will be given into his hand for a time, and times and half a time." (Daniel 7:25) How and when was this part of the prophecy fulfilled?

²⁷ "The holy ones" persecuted by the "small" horn —the Anglo-American World Power—are Jesus' spirit-anointed followers on earth. (Romans 1:7; 1 Peter 2:9)

25. (a) In its latest development, what constitutes the symbolic small horn? (b) In what sense does the "small" horn have "eyes like the eyes of a man" and "a mouth speaking grandiose things"?
26. What did the angel foretell about the symbolic horn's speech and action toward Jehovah and his servants?
27. (a) Who are "the holy ones" persecuted by the "small" horn? (b) How did the symbolic horn intend "to change times and law"?

For years before World War I, the remnant of these anointed ones publicly warned that 1914 would see the conclusion of "the appointed times of the nations." (Luke 21:24) When war broke out in that year, it was evident that the "small" horn had ignored this warning, for it persisted in harassing the anointed "holy ones." The Anglo-American World Power even opposed their efforts to carry out Jehovah's requirement (or, "law") that the good news of the Kingdom be preached worldwide by his witnesses. (Matthew 24:14) Thus the "small" horn attempted "to change times and law."

²⁸ Jehovah's angel referred to a prophetic period of "a time, and times and half a time." How long is that? Bible expositors generally agree that this expression denotes three and a half times—the sum of one time, two times, and half a time. Since Nebuchadnezzar's "seven times" of madness amounted to seven years, the three and a half times are three and a half years.* (Daniel 4:16, 25) *An American Translation* reads: "They shall be handed over to him for a year, two years, and half a year." James Moffatt's version says: "For three years and half a year." The same period is mentioned at Revelation 11:2-7, which states that God's witnesses would preach dressed in sackcloth for 42 months, or 1,260 days, and then be killed. When did this time period begin and end?

²⁹ For the anointed Christians, World War I meant a time of testing. By the end of 1914, they were expecting persecution. In fact, the very yeartext chosen for 1915 was Jesus' question to his disciples, "Are ye able to drink

---

* See Chapter 6 of this book.

---

28. The "time, and times and half a time" are how long?
29. When and how did the prophetic three and a half years begin?

of my cup?" It was based on Matthew 20:22, *King James Version.* Hence, beginning in December 1914, that small band of witnesses preached "in sackcloth."

³⁰ As war fever took hold, the anointed Christians encountered mounting opposition. Some of them were imprisoned. Individuals, such as Frank Platt in England and Robert Clegg in Canada, were tortured by sadistic authorities. On February 12, 1918, the British Dominion of Canada banned the recently published seventh volume of *Studies in the Scriptures,* entitled *The Finished Mystery,* as well as the tracts entitled *The Bible Students Monthly.* The following month, the U.S. Department of Justice pronounced the distribution of the seventh volume illegal. The result? Why, homes were searched, literature was confiscated, and Jehovah's worshipers were arrested!

³¹ Harassment of God's anointed ones climaxed on June 21, 1918, when the president, J. F. Rutherford, and prominent members of the Watch Tower Bible and Tract Society were sentenced on false charges to long prison terms. Intending "to change times and law," the "small" horn had effectively killed the organized preaching work. (Revelation 11:7) So the foretold period of "a time, and times and half a time" ended in June 1918.

³² But "the holy ones" were not wiped out by the harassment from the "small" horn. As prophesied in the book of Revelation, after a short period of inactivity, the anointed Christians became alive and active again.

---

30. How were anointed Christians harassed by the Anglo-American World Power during World War I?
31. When and how did the "time, and times and half a time" end?
32. Why would you say that "the holy ones" were not wiped out by the "small" horn?

(Revelation 11:11-13) On March 26, 1919, the president of the Watch Tower Bible and Tract Society and his associates were released from prison, and they were later exonerated of the false charges against them. Immediately thereafter, the anointed remnant began to reorganize for further activity. What, though, would be in store for the "small" horn?

THE ANCIENT OF DAYS HOLDS COURT

33 After introducing the four beasts, Daniel shifts his eyes from the fourth beast to a scene in heaven. He beholds the Ancient of Days sit down on his resplendent throne as Judge. The Ancient of Days is none other than Jehovah God. (Psalm 90:2) As the heavenly Court takes its seat, Daniel sees 'books being opened.' (Daniel 7:9, 10) Since Jehovah's existence extends into the infinite past, he knows all human history as if it were written in a book. He has observed all four symbolic beasts and can pass judgment upon them according to firsthand knowledge.

34 Daniel continues: "I kept on beholding at that time because of the sound of the grandiose words that the horn was speaking; I kept on beholding until the beast was killed and its body was destroyed and it was given to the burning fire. But as for the rest of the beasts, their rulerships were taken away, and there was a lengthening in life given to them for a time and a season." (Daniel 7: 11, 12) The angel tells Daniel: "The Court itself proceeded to sit, and his own rulership they finally took away,

---

33. (a) Who is the Ancient of Days? (b) What were the "books that were opened" in the heavenly Court?
34, 35. What will happen to the "small" horn and other beastly powers?

in order to annihilate him and to destroy him totally."
—Daniel 7:26.

35 By decree of the Great Judge, Jehovah God, the horn that blasphemed God and harassed his "holy ones" will have the same experience as the Roman Empire, which persecuted the early Christians. Its rulership will not continue. Neither will that of inferior hornlike "kings" that came out of the Roman Empire. What, though, about the rulerships derived from the previous beastly powers? As foretold, their lives were lengthened "for a time and a season." Their territories have continued to have inhabitants to our day. Iraq, for example, occupies the territory of ancient Babylon. Persia (Iran) and Greece still exist. Remnants of these world powers are part of the United Nations. These kingdoms also will perish with the annihilation of the last world power. All human governments will be obliterated at "the war of the great day of God the Almighty." (Revelation 16:14, 16) But, then, who will rule the world?

LASTING RULERSHIP JUST AHEAD!

36 "I kept on beholding in the visions of the night, and, see there!" exclaimed Daniel. "With the clouds of the heavens someone like a son of man happened to be coming; and to the Ancient of Days he gained access, and they brought him up close even before that One." (Daniel 7:13) When on earth, Jesus Christ called himself "the Son of man," indicating his kinship to mankind. (Matthew 16:13; 25:31) To the Sanhedrin, or Jewish high court, Jesus said: "You will see the Son of man sitting at the right hand of power and coming on the clouds of

36, 37. (a) "Someone like a son of man" refers to whom, and when and for what purpose did he appear in the heavenly Court? (b) What was established in 1914 C.E?

heaven." (Matthew 26:64) So in Daniel's vision, the one coming, invisible to human eyes, and gaining access to Jehovah God was the resurrected, glorified Jesus Christ. When did this occur?

37 With Jesus Christ, God has made a covenant for a Kingdom, just as he had made one with King David. (2 Samuel 7:11-16; Luke 22:28-30) When "the appointed times of the nations" ended in 1914 C.E., Jesus Christ, as David's royal heir, could rightfully receive Kingdom rule. Daniel's prophetic record reads: "To him there were given rulership and dignity and kingdom, that the peoples, national groups and languages should all serve even him. His rulership is an indefinitely lasting rulership that will not pass away, and his kingdom one that will not be brought to ruin." (Daniel 7:14) Thus the Messianic Kingdom was established in heaven in 1914. However, the rulership is given to others also.

38 "The holy ones of the Supreme One will receive the kingdom," said the angel. (Daniel 7:18, 22, 27) Jesus Christ is the chief holy one. (Acts 3:14; 4:27, 30) The other "holy ones" having a share in the rulership are the 144,-000 faithful spirit-anointed Christians, who are Kingdom heirs with Christ. (Romans 1:7; 8:17; 2 Thessalonians 1:5; 1 Peter 2:9) They are resurrected from death as immortal spirits to reign with Christ on heavenly Mount Zion. (Revelation 2:10; 14:1; 20:6) Hence, Christ Jesus and the resurrected anointed Christians will rule the world of mankind.

39 Concerning the rulership of the Son of man and the other resurrected "holy ones," God's angel said: "The kingdom and the rulership and the grandeur of

---

38, 39. Who will receive everlasting rulership over the world?

the kingdoms under all the heavens were given to the people who are the holy ones of the Supreme One. Their kingdom is an indefinitely lasting kingdom, and all the rulerships will serve and obey even them." (Daniel 7:27) What blessings obedient mankind will experience under that Kingdom!

⁴⁰ Daniel was unaware of all the marvelous fulfillments of his God-given visions. He said: "Up to this point is the end of the matter. As for me, Daniel, my own thoughts kept frightening me a great deal, so that my very complexion changed in me; but the matter itself I kept in my own heart." (Daniel 7:28) We, though, live at the time when we can understand the fulfillment of what Daniel saw. Paying attention to this prophecy will strengthen our faith and bolster our conviction that Jehovah's Messianic King will rule the world.

---

40. How can we benefit from paying attention to Daniel's dream and visions?

WHAT DID YOU DISCERN?

- What is symbolized by each of the 'four huge beasts coming up out of the sea'?

- What constitutes the "small" horn?

- How were "the holy ones" harassed by the symbolic small horn during World War I?

- What will happen to the symbolic small horn and the other beastly powers?

- How did you benefit from paying attention to Daniel's dream and visions about the "four huge beasts"?

A TOLERANT MONARCH

◆

A GREEK writer of the fifth century B.C.E. remembered him as a tolerant and ideal monarch. In the Bible he is called God's "anointed one" and "a bird of prey" coming "from the sunrising." (Isaiah 45:1; 46:11) The monarch thus spoken of is Cyrus the Great, of Persia.

Cyrus' march to fame began about 560/559 B.C.E. when he succeeded his father Cambyses I to the throne of Anshan, a city or district in ancient Persia. Anshan was then under suzerainty of the Median King Astyages. Revolting against Median rulership, Cyrus won a swift victory because the army of Astyages defected. Cyrus then gained the loyalty of the Medes. Thereafter, Medes and Persians fought unitedly under his leadership. Thus came into existence the Medo-Persian rule that in time extended its domain from the Aegean Sea to the Indus River.—See map.

With the combined forces of the Medes and the Persians, Cyrus first moved to establish control over a trouble spot

MEDO-PERSIAN EMPIRE

Tomb of Cyrus, at Pasargadae

—the western sector of Media where the Lydian King Croesus had been expanding his domain into Median territory. Advancing to the eastern border of the Lydian Empire in Asia Minor, Cyrus defeated Croesus and captured his capital, Sardis. Cyrus then subdued the Ionian cities and placed all Asia Minor within the realm of the Medo-Persian Empire. He thereby became the major rival of Babylon and its king, Nabonidus.

Cyrus then prepared for a confrontation with mighty Babylon. And from this point forward, he figured in the fulfillment of Bible prophecy. Through the prophet Isaiah, nearly two centuries earlier, Jehovah had named Cyrus as the ruler who would overthrow Babylon and liberate the Jews from bondage. It was by virtue of this advance appointment that the Scriptures refer to Cyrus as Jehovah's "anointed one."—Isaiah 44:26-28.

When Cyrus came up against Babylon in 539 B.C.E., he faced a formidable task. Surrounded by huge walls and a deep and broad moat formed by the river Euphrates, the city seemed impregnable. Where the Euphrates ran through Babylon, a mountainlike wall with huge copper gates ran along the banks of the river. How could Cyrus possibly take Babylon?

Over a century earlier, Jehovah had foretold "a devastation upon her waters" and had said that "they must be dried up." (Jeremiah 50:38) True to the prophecy, Cyrus diverted the waters of the Euphrates River a few miles north of Babylon. Then his army sloshed down the riverbed, climbed the slope leading to the wall, and entered the city easily because the copper gates had been left open. Like "a bird of prey" that swiftly pounces upon its victim, this ruler "from the sunrising"—from the east—captured Babylon in one night!

For the Jews in Babylon, Cyrus' victory meant the arrival of the long-awaited release from captivity and the end of the 70-year desolation of their homeland. How thrilled they must have been when Cyrus issued a proclamation authorizing them to return to Jerusalem and rebuild the temple! Cyrus also restored to them the precious temple utensils that Nebuchadnezzar had carried off to Babylon, gave royal permission for importing timber from Lebanon, and authorized funds from the king's house to cover construction expenses. —Ezra 1:1-11; 6:3-5.

Bas-relief at Pasargadae, depicting Cyrus

Cyrus generally followed a humane and tolerant policy in dealing with the people he conquered. One reason for this behavior could have been his religion. Likely, Cyrus adhered to the teachings of the Persian prophet Zoroaster and worshiped Ahura Mazda—a god thought to be the creator of all that is good. In his book *The Zoroastrian Tradition,* Farhang Mehr writes: "Zoroaster presented God as moral perfection. He told people that *Ahura Mazda* is not revengeful but just and, therefore, should not be feared but loved." Belief in a god that was moral and just may have affected Cyrus' ethics and encouraged magnanimity and fairness.

The king, however, was less tolerant of the climate in Babylon. The torrid summers there were more than he wanted to bear. So while Babylon remained a royal city of the empire, as well as a religious and cultural center, it seldom served as more than his winter capital. In fact, following the conquest of Babylon, Cyrus soon returned to his summer capital, Ecbatana, situated over 6,000 feet above sea level, at the foot of Mount Alwand. There, the cold winters balanced by delightful summers were more to his liking. Cyrus also built an elegant palace in his earlier capital, Pasargadae (near Persepolis), 400 miles southeast of Ecbatana. The residence there served as a retreat for him.

Cyrus thus left his mark as a brave conqueror and a tolerant monarch. His 30-year rule ended with his death in 530 B.C.E. while he was on a military campaign. His son Cambyses II succeeded him to the Persian throne.

WHAT DID YOU DISCERN?

- How did Cyrus the Persian prove to be Jehovah's "anointed one"?
- What valuable service toward Jehovah's people did Cyrus perform?
- How did Cyrus treat the people he conquered?

A YOUNG KING CONQUERS THE WORLD

SOME 2,300 years ago, a blond-haired military general in his 20's stood on the shore of the Mediterranean Sea. His eyes were fixed on an island-city half a mile away. Having been refused entry, the infuriated general was determined to conquer the city. His plan of attack? Construct a causeway to the island and mobilize his forces against the city. The construction of the causeway had already begun.

Alexander

But a message from the great king of the Persian Empire interrupted the young general. Eager to make peace, the Persian ruler made an extraordinary offer: 10,000 talents of gold (over two billion dollars at current values), the hand in marriage of one of the king's daughters, and dominion over the entire western part of the Persian Empire. All of this was offered in return for the king's family, whom the general had captured.

The commander faced with the decision to accept or reject the offer was Alexander III of Macedonia. Should he accept the offer? "It was a fateful moment for the ancient world," says historian Ulrich Wilcken. "The aftereffects of his decision, indeed, stretch through the Middle Ages down to our own day, in the East as in the West." Before considering Alexander's reply, let us see what events led up to this crucial moment.

THE MAKING OF A CONQUEROR

Alexander was born at Pella, Macedonia, in 356 B.C.E. His father was King Philip II, and his mother, Olympias. She taught Alexander that the Macedonian kings descended from Hercules, a son of the Greek god Zeus. According to Olympias, Alexander's ancestor was Achilles, the hero of Homer's poem the *Iliad*. Being thus conditioned by

Aristotle and his pupil Alexander

his parents for conquest and kingly glory, young Alexander had little interest in other pursuits. Asked whether he would run a race in the Olympic Games, Alexander indicated that he would do so if he were to run with kings. His ambition was to perform greater acts than those of his father and to gain glory through accomplishments.

At age 13, Alexander enjoyed the tutorship of the Greek philosopher Aristotle, who helped him develop an interest in philosophy, medicine, and science. The extent to which Aristotle's philosophical teachings shaped Alexander's way of thinking is a matter of debate. "It seems safe to say that there was not a lot on which the two might see eye to eye," observed Bertrand Russell, a 20th-century philosopher. "Aristotle's political views were based on the Greek city state which was all but on the way out." The concept of small city-state government would not have appealed to an ambitious prince wanting to build a great centralized empire. Alexander must also have been skeptical of the Aristotelian precept of treating non-Greeks as slaves, for he envisioned an empire of a flourishing partnership between the victors and the vanquished.

There is little doubt, however, that Aristotle cultivated Alexander's interest in reading and learning. Alexander remained an avid reader throughout his life, having a special passion for Homer's writings. It is claimed that he learned the *Iliad*—all 15,693 lines of poetry—by heart.

Education by Aristotle came to an abrupt end in 340 B.C.E. when the 16-year-old prince went back to Pella to rule Macedonia in the absence of his father. And the crown prince wasted no time distinguishing himself in military exploits. To the delight of Philip, he quickly put down the rebellious Thracian tribe Maedi, took their chief city by storm, and named the place Alexandroúpolis, after himself.

ON WITH THE CONQUEST

The assassination of Philip in 336 B.C.E. led to 20-year-old Alexander's inheriting the throne of Macedonia. Entering Asia at the Hellespont (now the Dardanelles) in the spring

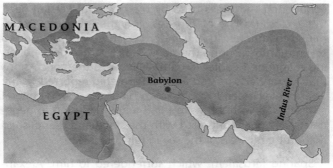

CONQUESTS OF ALEXANDER

of 334 B.C.E., Alexander embarked upon a campaign of conquest with a small but efficient army of 30,000 foot soldiers and 5,000 cavalrymen. Accompanying his army were engineers, surveyors, architects, scientists, and historians.

At the Granicus River in the northwest corner of Asia Minor (now Turkey), Alexander won his first battle against the Persians. That winter he conquered western Asia Minor. The following autumn the second decisive battle with the Persians took place at Issus, in the southeastern corner of Asia Minor. With an army of about half a million men, the great Persian King Darius III came there to meet Alexander. Overconfident Darius also brought along his mother, his wife, and other members of his family so that they could witness what was to have been a spectacular victory. But the Persians were unprepared for the suddenness and vehemence of the Macedonian attack. Alexander's forces utterly defeated the Persian army, and Darius fled, abandoning his family to Alexander's hands.

Rather than pursuing the fleeing Persians, Alexander marched southward along the Mediterranean Coast, conquering the bases used by the powerful Persian fleet. But the island-city of Tyre resisted the invasion. Determined to conquer it, Alexander began a siege that lasted seven months. During the siege came Darius' peace offering mentioned earlier. So attractive were the concessions that Alexander's trusted adviser Parmenio reportedly said: 'Were I Alexander, I would accept.' But the young general retorted: 'So would I, were I Parmenio.' Refusing to negotiate, Alexander continued with the siege and demolished that proud mistress of the sea in July 332 B.C.E.

Sparing Jerusalem, which surrendered to him, Alexander pushed south, conquering Gaza. Weary of Persian rule, Egypt welcomed him as a deliverer. At Memphis he sacrificed to the Apis bull, thus pleasing the Egyptian priests. He also founded the city of Alexandria, which later rivaled Athens as a center of learning and still bears his name.

Next, Alexander turned northeast, moving through Palestine and toward the Tigris River. In the year 331 B.C.E., he engaged in the third major battle with the Persians, at Gaugamela, not far from the crumbling ruins of Nineveh. Here Alexander's 47,000 men overpowered a reorganized Persian army of at least 250,000! Darius fled and was later murdered by his own people.

Medal said to depict Alexander the Great

Flushed with victory, Alexander turned south and took the Persian winter capital Babylon. He also occupied the capitals at Susa and Persepolis, seizing the immense Persian treasury and burning the great palace of Xerxes. Finally, the capital at Ecbatana fell to him. This speedy conqueror then subdued the rest of the Persian domain, going as far to the east as the Indus River, located in modern-day Pakistan.

Upon crossing the Indus, in the region bordering the Persian province of Taxila, Alexander met a formidable rival, the Indian monarch Porus. Against him, Alexander fought his fourth and final major battle, in June 326 B.C.E. Porus' army included 35,000 soldiers and 200 elephants, which terrified the Macedonians' horses. The battle was fierce and bloody, but Alexander's forces prevailed. Porus surrendered and became an ally.

More than eight years had passed since the Macedonian army had crossed into Asia, and the soldiers were weary and homesick. Unnerved by the fierce battle with Porus, they wanted to return home. Although reluctant at first, Alexander complied with their wishes. Greece had indeed become the world power. With Greek colonies established in the conquered lands, the Greek language and culture spread throughout the realm.

THE MAN BEHIND THE SHIELD

The adhesive that held the Macedonian army together through the years of conquest was Alexander's personality. After battles, Alexander customarily visited the wounded, examined their injuries, praised soldiers for their valiant deeds, and honored them by a donation in keeping with their accomplishments. As for those who fell in battle, Alexander arranged a splendid burial for them. The parents and children of the fallen men were exempted from all taxes and forms of service. For diversion after battles, Alexander held games and contests. On one occasion, he even arranged a furlough for recently married men, enabling them to spend the winter with their wives, in Macedonia. Such actions won him the affection and admiration of his men.

Regarding Alexander's marriage to the Bactrian Princess Roxana, the Greek biographer Plutarch writes: "It was, indeed a love affair, yet it seemed at the same time to be conducive to the object he had in hand. For it gratified the conquered people to see him choose a wife from among themselves, and it made them feel the most lively affection for him, to find that in the only passion which he, the most temperate of men, was overcome by, he yet forbore till he could obtain her in a lawful and honourable way."

Alexander also respected the marriages of others. Though the wife of King Darius was his captive, he saw to it that she was treated honorably. Similarly, upon learning that two Macedonian soldiers had abused the wives of some strangers, he ordered that they be executed if found guilty.

Like his mother, Olympias, Alexander was very religious. He would sacrifice before and after battles and consult his diviners regarding the significance of certain omens. He also consulted the oracle of Ammon, in Libya. And at Babylon he carried out the instructions of the Chaldeans regarding sacrifice, particularly to the Babylonian god Bel (Marduk).

Although Alexander was moderate in his eating habits, he eventually gave way to excesses in his drinking. He would speak extendedly over every cup of wine and boast of his achievements. One of the darkest deeds of Alexander was the murder of his friend Clitus, in a fit of drunken rage. But Alexander was so self-condemnatory that for three days he lay in his bed, partaking of neither food nor drink. Finally, his friends were able to persuade him to eat.

As time passed, Alexander's craving for glory brought out other undesirable traits. He began to believe false accusations readily and started to administer punishment with the greatest severity. For instance, having been led to believe that Philotas was implicated in an attempt on his life, Alexander had him and his father, Parmenio, the adviser he had once trusted, executed.

ALEXANDER'S DEFEAT

Shortly after returning to Babylon, Alexander fell victim to malarial fever, from which he never recovered. On June 13, 323 B.C.E., after having lived a mere 32 years and 8 months, Alexander surrendered to the most formidable enemy, death.

It was just as certain Indian wise men had observed: "O King Alexander, each man possesses just so much of the earth as this on which we stand; and you being a man like other men, save that you are full of activity and relentless, are roaming over all this earth far from your home, troubled yourself, and troubling others. But not so long hence you will die, and will possess just so much of the earth as suffices for your burial."

WHAT DID YOU DISCERN?

- What was the background of Alexander the Great?

- Soon after inheriting the throne of Macedonia, upon what campaign did Alexander embark?

- Describe some of Alexander's conquests.

- What can be said of Alexander's personality?

A VAST KINGDOM IS DIVIDED

CONCERNING the kingdom of Alexander the Great, the Bible foretold a breakup and a division "but not to his posterity." (Daniel 11:3, 4) Accordingly, within 14 years after Alexander's sudden death in 323 B.C.E., his legitimate son Alexander IV and his illegitimate son Heracles were assassinated.

By the year 301 B.C.E., four of Alexander's generals established themselves in power over the vast empire their commander had built. General Cassander took control of Macedonia and Greece. General Lysimachus received Asia Minor and Thrace. To Seleucus I Nicator went Mesopotamia and Syria. And Ptolemy Lagus, or Ptolemy I, ruled Egypt and Palestine. From Alexander's one great kingdom thus arose four Hellenistic, or Grecian, kingdoms.

Of the four Hellenistic kingdoms, Cassander's rule proved to be of the shortest duration. A few years after Cassander came to power, his male lineage died out, and in 285 B.C.E., Lysimachus took possession of the European part of the Greek Empire. Four years later, Lysimachus fell in battle before Seleucus I Nicator, giving him control of the

Ptolemy I

Seleucus I

major portion of the Asiatic territories. Seleucus became the first of the line of Seleucid kings in Syria. He founded Antioch in Syria and made that his new capital. Seleucus was assassinated in 281 B.C.E., but the dynasty that he established continued in power until 64 B.C.E. when Roman General Pompey made Syria a province of Rome.

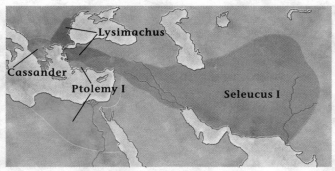

BREAKUP OF ALEXANDER'S EMPIRE

Of the four divisions of Alexander's empire, the Ptolemaic kingdom lasted the longest. Ptolemy I assumed the title of king in 305 B.C.E. and became the first of the Macedonian kings, or Pharaohs, of Egypt. Making Alexandria the capital, he immediately began an urban-development program. One of his greatest building projects was the famous Alexandrian Library. To oversee this grand project, Ptolemy brought from Greece a noted Athenian scholar, Demetrius Phalereus. Reportedly, by the first century C.E., the library housed one million scrolls. The Ptolemaic dynasty continued to rule in Egypt until it fell to Rome in 30 B.C.E. Rome then replaced Greece as the dominant world power.

WHAT DID YOU DISCERN?

- How was Alexander's vast empire divided?
- Until when did the line of Seleucid kings continue to rule in Syria?
- When did the Ptolemaic kingdom of Egypt come to an end?

CHAPTER TEN

WHO CAN STAND AGAINST THE PRINCE OF PRINCES?

FIFTY-SEVEN years have passed since the destruction of Jehovah's temple in Jerusalem. Belshazzar and his father, Nabonidus, jointly rule the Babylonian Empire, the third world power of Bible prophecy.* God's prophet Daniel is exiled in Babylon. And during "the third year of the kingship of Belshazzar the king," Jehovah sends Daniel a vision revealing certain details of the restoration of true worship.—Daniel 8:1.

² The prophetic vision that Daniel saw had a profound effect on him and is of great interest to us living in "the time of the end." The angel Gabriel tells Daniel: "Here I am causing you to know what will occur in the final part of the denunciation, because it is for the appointed time of the end." (Daniel 8:16, 17, 19, 27) With keen interest, then, let us consider what Daniel saw and what it means for us today.

A RAM WITH TWO HORNS

³ "I began to see in the vision," writes Daniel, "and it came about, while I was seeing, that I was in Shushan the castle, which is in Elam the jurisdictional district; and

---

* Seven world powers of special Biblical significance are Egypt, Assyria, Babylonia, Medo-Persia, Greece, Rome, and the Anglo-American dual world power. All of these are noteworthy because they have had dealings with Jehovah's people.

1, 2. Why is the vision that Daniel had in the third year of Belshazzar's reign of importance to us?
3, 4. What animal did Daniel see standing before the watercourse, and what does it symbolize?

Medo-Persian Empire

I proceeded to see in the vision, and I myself happened to be by the watercourse of Ulai." (Daniel 8:2) Whether Daniel actually was in Shushan (Susa)—the capital of Elam, located some 220 miles east of Babylon—or was there only in a visionary way is not stated.

⁴ Daniel continues: "When I raised my eyes, then I saw, and, look! a ram standing before the watercourse, and it had two horns." (Daniel 8:3a) The identity of the ram does not remain a mystery for Daniel. The angel Gabriel later states: "The ram that you saw possessing the two horns stands for the kings of Media and Persia." (Daniel 8:20) The Medes came from the mountainous plateau to the east of Assyria, and the Persians originally led an often nomadic life in the region north of the Persian Gulf. As the Medo-Persian Empire grew, however, its inhabitants developed an outstanding taste for luxury.

⁵ "The two horns were tall," reports Daniel, "but the one was taller than the other, and the taller was the one that came up afterward." (Daniel 8:3b) The taller horn that came up later pictures the Persians, whereas the other horn represents the Medes. At first, the Medes were dominant. But in 550 B.C.E., Cyrus the ruler of Persia gained an

5. How did the horn that "came up afterward" become taller?

easy victory over Median King Astyages. Cyrus combined the customs and laws of the two peoples, united their kingdoms, and expanded their conquests. From then on, the empire had a dual nature.

THE RAM PUTS ON GREAT AIRS

⁶ Continuing his description of the ram, Daniel states: "I saw the ram making thrusts to the west and to the north and to the south, and no wild beasts kept standing before it, and there was no one doing any delivering out of its hand. And it did according to its will, and it put on great airs."—Daniel 8:4.

⁷ In the preceding vision given to Daniel, Babylon had been pictured by the wild beast that came up out of the sea and that was like a lion having the wings of an eagle. (Daniel 7:4, 17) That symbolic beast proved to be unable to stand before "the ram" of this new vision. Babylon fell to Cyrus the Great in 539 B.C.E. For almost 50 years thereafter, "no wild beasts," or political governments, were able to stand up against the Medo-Persian Empire—the fourth world power of Bible prophecy.

⁸ Coming from 'the rising of the sun'—the east—the Medo-Persian World Power did as it pleased, making "thrusts to the west and to the north and to the south." (Isaiah 46:11) King Cambyses II, who succeeded Cyrus the Great, conquered Egypt. His successor was Persian King Darius I, who moved westward across the straits of Bosporus in 513 B.C.E. and invaded the European territory of Thrace, the capital of which was Byzantium (now Istanbul). In the year 508 B.C.E., he subdued Thrace, and he conquered Macedonia in 496 B.C.E. Thus, by the time

---

6, 7. How was it that "no wild beasts kept standing before" the ram?
8, 9. (a) How did "the ram" make "thrusts to the west and to the north and to the south"? (b) What does the book of Esther say regarding the successor of Persian King Darius I?

of Darius, the Medo-Persian "ram" had seized territory in three principal directions: north into Babylonia and Assyria, west through Asia Minor, and south into Egypt.

9 Testifying to the greatness of the Medo-Persian Empire, the Bible speaks of Darius' successor, Xerxes I, as "the Ahasuerus who was ruling as king from India to Ethiopia, over a hundred and twenty-seven jurisdictional districts." (Esther 1:1) But this great empire was to give way to another, and in this regard, Daniel's vision reveals some intriguing details that should strengthen our faith in God's prophetic word.

THE HE-GOAT STRIKES DOWN THE RAM

10 Imagine Daniel's astonishment at what he now sees. The account says: "I, for my part, kept on considering, and, look! there was a male of the goats coming from the sunset upon the surface of the whole earth, and it was not touching the earth. And as regards the he-goat, there was a conspicuous horn between its eyes. And it kept coming all the way to the ram possessing the two horns, which I had seen standing before the watercourse; and it came running toward it in its powerful rage. And I saw it coming into close touch with the ram, and it began showing bitterness toward it, and it proceeded to strike down the ram and to break its two horns, and there proved to be no power in the ram to stand before it. So it threw it to the earth and trampled it down, and the ram proved to have no deliverer out of its hand." (Daniel 8:5-7) What does all of this mean?

11 Neither Daniel nor we are left to guess about the meaning of this vision. "The hairy he-goat stands for the king of Greece; and as for the great horn that was

10. In Daniel's vision, what animal struck down "the ram"?
11. (a) How did the angel Gabriel explain "the hairy he-goat" and its "great horn"? (b) Who was pictured by the conspicuous horn?

Grecian Empire

between its eyes, it stands for the first king," the angel Gabriel informs Daniel. (Daniel 8:21) In 336 B.C.E., the last king of the Persian Empire, Darius III (Codommanus), was crowned. In that same year, Alexander became king in Macedonia. History shows that Alexander the Great proved to be the foretold first "king of Greece." Starting "from the sunset," or the west, in the year 334 B.C.E., Alexander moved quickly. As if "not touching the earth," he conquered territories and struck down "the ram." Ending the Medo-Persian dominion of nearly two centuries, Greece thus became the fifth world power of Biblical significance. What a remarkable fulfillment of divine prophecy!

¹² But Alexander's power was to be short-lived. The vision further reveals: "And the male of the goats, for its part, put on great airs to an extreme; but as soon as it became mighty, the great horn was broken, and there proceeded to come up conspicuously four instead of it, toward the four winds of the heavens." (Daniel 8:8) Explaining the prophecy, Gabriel says: "That one having been broken, so that there were four that finally stood up instead of it, there are four kingdoms from his nation

---

12. How was "the great horn" of the symbolic goat "broken," and what were the four horns that came up in its place?

that will stand up, but not with his power." (Daniel 8:22) As predicted, at the very height of his victorious career, Alexander was "broken," or died, at the age of only 32. And his great empire eventually came to be divided among four of his generals.

A MYSTERIOUS SMALL HORN

13 The next part of the vision spans more than 2,200 years, its fulfillment stretching into modern times. Daniel writes: "Out of one of them [the four horns] there came forth another horn, a small one, and it kept getting very much greater toward the south and toward the sunrising and toward the Decoration. And it kept getting greater all the way to the army of the heavens, so that it caused some of the army and some of the stars to fall to the earth, and it went trampling them down. And all the way to the Prince of the army it put on great airs, and from him the constant feature was taken away, and the established place of his sanctuary was thrown down. And an army itself was gradually given over, together with the constant feature, because of transgression; and it kept throwing truth to the earth, and it acted and had success."—Daniel 8:9-12.

14 Before we can understand the meaning of the words just quoted, we must pay attention to God's angel. After pointing to the coming to power of the four kingdoms from Alexander's empire, the angel Gabriel says: "In the final part of their kingdom, as the transgressors act to a completion, there will stand up a king fierce in countenance and understanding ambiguous sayings. And his power must become mighty, but not by his own power. And in a wonderful way he will cause ruin, and he will

13. What grew out of one of the four horns, and how did it act?
14. What did the angel Gabriel say about the activities of the symbolic small horn, and what would happen to that horn?

certainly prove successful and do effectively. And he will actually bring mighty ones to ruin, also the people made up of the holy ones. And according to his insight he will also certainly cause deception to succeed in his hand. And in his heart he will put on great airs, and during a freedom from care he will bring many to ruin. And against the Prince of princes he will stand up, but it will be without hand that he will be broken."—Daniel 8:23-25.

¹⁵ "You, for your part, keep secret the vision," the angel tells Daniel, "because it is yet for many days." (Daniel 8: 26) The fulfillment of this part of the vision was not to occur for "many days," and Daniel was to "keep secret the vision." Its meaning apparently remained a mystery to Daniel. By now, however, those "many days" must surely have passed by. So we ask: 'What does world history reveal regarding the fulfillment of this prophetic vision?'

THE SMALL HORN BECOMES MIGHTY IN POWER

¹⁶ According to history, the small horn was an offshoot of one of the four symbolic horns—the one farthest to the west. This was the Hellenistic kingdom of General Cassander over Macedonia and Greece. Later, this kingdom was absorbed by the kingdom of General Lysimachus, the king of Thrace and Asia Minor. In the second century before our Common Era, these western sectors of the Hellenistic domain were conquered by Rome. And by the year 30 B.C.E., Rome took over all the Hellenistic kingdoms, making itself the sixth world power of Bible prophecy. But the Roman Empire was not the small horn of Daniel's vision, for that empire did not continue till "the appointed time of the end."—Daniel 8:19.

---

15. What did the angel tell Daniel to do with regard to the vision?
16. (a) Out of which symbolic horn did the small horn come forth? (b) How did Rome become the sixth world power of Bible prophecy, but why was it not the symbolic small horn?

Roman Empire

¹⁷ What, then, does history identify as that aggressive "king fierce in countenance"? Britain actually was a north-western offshoot of the Roman Empire. Down till the early part of the fifth century C.E., there were Roman provinces in what is now Britain. In the course of time, the Roman Empire declined, but the influence of the Greco-Roman civilization continued in Britain and in other parts of Europe that had been under Roman dominion. "At the fall of the Roman Empire," wrote Nobel Prize winning Mexican poet and author Octavio Paz, "the Church took its place." He added: "The Church fathers, as well as the later scholars, grafted Greek philosophy onto Christian doctrine." And the 20th-century philosopher and mathematician Bertrand Russell observed: "The civilization of the West, which has sprung from Greek sources, is based on a philosophic and scientific tradition that began in Miletus [a Greek city in Asia Minor] two and a half thousand years ago." Thus, it could be said that the British Empire had its cultural roots in the Hellenistic kingdom of Macedonia and Greece.

17. (a) What relationship did Britain have with the Roman Empire? (b) How is the British Empire related to the Hellenistic kingdom of Macedonia and Greece?

[18] By 1763 the British Empire had defeated her powerful rivals, Spain and France. From then on she demonstrated herself to be the mistress of the seas and the seventh world power of Bible prophecy. Even after the 13 American colonies broke away from Britain in 1776 to establish the United States of America, the British Empire grew to embrace a quarter of the earth's surface and a quarter of its population. The seventh world power gained still greater strength when the United States of America collaborated with Britain to form the Anglo-American dual world power. Economically and militarily, this power had indeed become "a king fierce in countenance." The small horn that became a fierce political power in the "time of the end," then, is the Anglo-American World Power.

[19] Daniel saw that the small horn "kept getting very much greater" toward "the Decoration." (Daniel 8:9) The Promised Land, which Jehovah gave to his chosen people, was so beautiful that it was called "the decoration of all the lands," that is, of the entire earth. (Ezekiel 20:6, 15) True, Britain did capture Jerusalem on December 9, 1917, and in the year 1920, the League of Nations assigned the mandate over Palestine to Great Britain, to continue until May 14, 1948. But the vision is prophetic, containing many symbols. And "the Decoration" mentioned in the vision symbolizes, not Jerusalem, but the earthly condition of the people whom God views as holy during the time of the seventh world power. Let us see how the Anglo-American World Power tries to threaten the holy ones.

"PLACE OF HIS SANCTUARY" THROWN DOWN

[20] The small horn "kept getting greater all the way to the

---

18. What is the small horn that became "a king fierce in countenance" in the "time of the end"? Explain.
19. What is "the Decoration" mentioned in the vision?
20. Who are "the army of the heavens" and "the stars" that the small horn tries to bring down?

army of the heavens, so that it caused some of the army and some of the stars to fall to the earth." According to the angelic explanation, "the army of the heavens" and "the stars" that the small horn attempts to bring down are "the people made up of the holy ones." (Daniel 8:10, 24) These "holy ones" are spirit-anointed Christians. Because of being brought into a relationship with God by means of the new covenant, made operative by the shed blood of Jesus Christ, they are sanctified, cleansed, and set apart for God's exclusive service. (Hebrews 10:10; 13:20) Having assigned them as heirs with his Son in the heavenly inheritance, Jehovah views them as holy. (Ephesians 1:3, 11, 18-20) In Daniel's vision, then, "the army of the heavens" refers to the remnant on earth of the 144,000 "holy ones," who will reign in heaven with the Lamb.—Revelation 14:1-5.

[21] Today the remaining ones of the 144,000 are earthly representatives of the "heavenly Jerusalem"—the citylike Kingdom of God—and its temple arrangement. (Hebrews 12:22, 28; 13:14) In this sense they occupy a "holy place" that the seventh world power tries to trample on and make desolate. (Daniel 8:13) Speaking of that holy place also as "the established place of [Jehovah's] sanctuary," Daniel says: "From him [Jehovah] the constant feature was taken away, and the established place of his sanctuary was thrown down. And an army itself was gradually given over, together with the constant feature, because of

---

21. Who occupy a "holy place" that the seventh world power attempts to desolate?

Some prominent figures of the Anglo-American World Power:
1. George Washington, first U.S. president (1789-97)
2. Queen Victoria of Britain (1837-1901)
3. Woodrow Wilson, U.S. president (1913-21)
4. David Lloyd George, prime minister of Britain (1916-22)
5. Winston Churchill, prime minister of Britain (1940-45, 1951-55)
6. Franklin D. Roosevelt, U.S. president (1933-45)

transgression; and it kept throwing truth to the earth, and it acted and had success." (Daniel 8:11, 12) How was this fulfilled?

²² What was the experience of Jehovah's Witnesses during World War II? They suffered intense persecution! It started in Nazi and Fascist countries. But soon 'truth was being thrown to the earth' throughout the vast domain of the 'small horn whose power had become mighty.' "The army" of Kingdom proclaimers and their work of preaching "the good news" were banned in almost all of the British Commonwealth. (Mark 13:10) When these nations conscripted their manpower, they refused to grant ministerial exemption to Jehovah's Witnesses, showing no respect for their theocratic appointment as ministers of God. Mob violence and various indignities were experienced by Jehovah's faithful servants in the United States. The seventh world power, in effect, tried to take away a sacrifice of praise—"the fruit of lips"—regularly offered to Jehovah by his people as "the constant feature" of their worship. (Hebrews 13:15) That world power thus committed the "transgression" of invading the rightful domain of the Most High God—"the established place of his sanctuary."

²³ By persecuting "the holy ones" during World War II, the small horn put on great airs "all the way to the Prince of the army." Or, as the angel Gabriel states, it stood up "against the Prince of princes." (Daniel 8:11, 25) The title "the Prince of princes" applies exclusively to Jehovah God. The Hebrew word *sar,* translated "prince," is related to a verb meaning "exercise dominion." In addition to referring to the son of a king or a person of royal rank, the word applies to a head, or a chief one. The book of Dan-

---

22. During World War II, how did the seventh world power commit a notable "transgression"?
23. (a) During World War II, how did the Anglo-American World Power stand up "against the Prince of princes"? (b) Who is "the Prince of princes"?

iel mentions other angelic princes—for example, Michael. God is the Chief Prince of all such princes. (Daniel 10:13, 21; compare Psalm 83:18.) Can we imagine that anyone could stand up against Jehovah—the Prince of princes?

"HOLY PLACE" BROUGHT INTO RIGHT CONDITION

²⁴ No one can stand up against the Prince of princes —not even a king as "fierce in countenance" as the Anglo-American World Power! This king's attempts to desolate God's sanctuary do not succeed. After a period of "two thousand three hundred evenings and mornings," says the angelic messenger, "the holy place will certainly be brought into its right condition," or "shall emerge victorious."—Daniel 8:13, 14; *The New English Bible.*

²⁵ The 2,300 days constitute a prophetic period. Hence, a prophetic year of 360 days is involved. (Revelation 11:2, 3; 12:6, 14) This 2,300 days, then, would amount to 6 years, 4 months, and 20 days. When was this period? Well, in the 1930's, God's people began to experience increasing persecution in various countries. And during World War II, Jehovah's Witnesses were fiercely persecuted in the lands of the Anglo-American dual world power. Why? Because of their insistence on 'obeying God as ruler rather than men.' (Acts 5:29) Therefore, the 2,300 days must be associated with that war.* But what can be said about the beginning and the end of this prophetic period?

²⁶ For "the holy place" to be "brought," or restored,

---

* Daniel 7:25 also speaks of a period of time when 'the holy ones of the Supreme One are harassed continually.' As explained in the preceding chapter, this was associated with the first world war.

---

24. What assurance does Daniel 8:14 give us?
25. How long is the prophetic period of 2,300 days, and with what event must it be associated?
26. (a) From when, at the earliest, should the counting of the 2,300 days begin? (b) When did the period of 2,300 days end?

to what it should be, the 2,300 days must have begun when it previously was in the "right condition" from God's standpoint. At the earliest, this was on June 1, 1938, when *The Watchtower* published part 1 of the article "Organization." Part 2 appeared in the issue of June 15, 1938. Counting 2,300 days (6 years, 4 months, and 20 days on the Hebrew calendar) from June 1 or 15, 1938, brings us to October 8 or 22, 1944. On the first day of a special assembly held at Pittsburgh, Pennsylvania, U.S.A., on September 30 and October 1, 1944, the Watch Tower Society's president spoke on the subject "The Theocratic Alignment Today." At the annual corporate meeting on October 2, the Society's charter was amended in an effort to bring it as close to a theocratic arrangement as the law would allow. With the publication of clarified Biblical requirements, theocratic organization was soon more fully installed in the congregations of Jehovah's Witnesses.

[27] While the 2,300 days ran their course during World War II, which began in 1939, the offering of "the constant feature" at God's sanctuary was severely restricted because of persecution. In 1938 the Watch Tower Society had 39 branches supervising the work of the Witnesses worldwide, but by 1943 there were only 21. Increases in the number of Kingdom proclaimers were also small during that period.

[28] As we have noted, during the closing months of World War II, Jehovah's Witnesses reaffirmed their determination to magnify God's rulership by serving him as a theocratic organization. It was with this objective that the rearrangement of their work and governing structure was

---

27. What evidence was there that "the constant feature" was restricted during the persecution-filled years of World War II?
28, 29. (a) As World War II drew to a close, what development took place in Jehovah's organization? (b) What can be said of the enemy's vicious attempts to desolate and destroy "the holy place"?

initiated in 1944. In fact, *The Watchtower* of October 15, 1944, contained an article entitled "Organized for Final Work." It and other service-oriented articles of the same period indicated that the 2,300 days had ended and that "the holy place" was again in its "right condition."

29 The enemy's vicious attempts to desolate and destroy "the holy place" had failed completely. Indeed, the remaining "holy ones" on earth, along with their companions of the "great crowd," had come off victorious. (Revelation 7:9) And the sanctuary, in its rightful theocratic state, now continues to render sacred service to Jehovah.

30 The Anglo-American World Power still holds its position. "But it will be without hand that he will be broken," said the angel Gabriel. (Daniel 8:25) Very soon, this seventh world power of Bible prophecy—this "king fierce in countenance"—will be broken, not by human hands, but by superhuman power at Armageddon. (Daniel 2:44; Revelation 16:14, 16) How thrilling it is to know that the sovereignty of Jehovah God, the Prince of princes, will then be vindicated!

---

30. What will soon happen to the "king fierce in countenance"?

WHAT DID YOU DISCERN?

- What is pictured by
  "the ram" with "two horns"?
  "the hairy he-goat" with its "great horn"?
  the four horns coming up in place of "the great horn"?
  the small horn that came forth from one of the four horns?

- During World War II, how did the Anglo-American World Power try to desolate "the holy place," and did it succeed?

CHAPTER ELEVEN

THE TIME OF MESSIAH'S COMING REVEALED

JEHOVAH is the Great Timekeeper. Under his control are all the times and seasons connected with his work. (Acts 1:7) All events that he has assigned to these times and seasons are sure to occur. They will not fail.

2 As a diligent student of the Scriptures, the prophet Daniel had faith in Jehovah's ability to schedule events and bring them about. Of particular interest to Daniel were prophecies regarding the devastation of Jerusalem. Jeremiah had recorded God's revelation about how long the holy city would remain desolate, and Daniel gave this prophecy careful consideration. He wrote: "In the first year of Darius the son of Ahasuerus of the seed of the Medes, who had been made king over the kingdom of the Chaldeans; in the first year of his reigning I myself, Daniel, discerned by the books the number of the years concerning which the word of Jehovah had occurred to Jeremiah the prophet, for fulfilling the devastations of Jerusalem, namely, seventy years."—Daniel 9:1, 2; Jeremiah 25:11.

3 Darius the Mede was then ruling over "the kingdom of the Chaldeans." The earlier prediction that Daniel had made when interpreting the handwriting on the wall had undergone swift fulfillment. The Babylonian Empire was no more. It had been "given to the Medes and the Persians" in 539 B.C.E.—Daniel 5:24-28, 30, 31.

---

1. Since Jehovah is the Great Timekeeper, of what can we be sure?
2, 3. To what prophecy did Daniel give his attention, and what empire was ruling Babylon at that time?

DANIEL HUMBLY PETITIONS JEHOVAH

⁴ Daniel realized that Jerusalem's 70-year desolation was about to end. What would he do next? He himself tells us: "I proceeded to set my face to Jehovah the true God, in order to seek him with prayer and with entreaties, with fasting and sackcloth and ashes. And I began to pray to Jehovah my God and to make confession." (Daniel 9: 3, 4) A proper heart condition was needed to experience God's merciful deliverance. (Leviticus 26:31-46; 1 Kings 8: 46-53) There was a need for faith, a humble spirit, and full repentance over the sins that had led to exile and slavery. In behalf of his sinful people, Daniel therefore proceeded to approach God. How? By fasting, mourning, and clothing himself in sackcloth, a symbol of repentance and sincerity of heart.

⁵ Jeremiah's prophecy had given Daniel hope, for it indicated that the Jews would soon be restored to their homeland of Judah. (Jeremiah 25:12; 29:10) Doubtless, Daniel felt confident that relief would come for the subjugated Jews because a man named Cyrus was already ruling as king of Persia. Had not Isaiah prophesied that Cyrus would be instrumental in releasing the Jews to rebuild Jerusalem and the temple? (Isaiah 44:28–45:3) But Daniel had no idea just how that would come about. So he continued to supplicate Jehovah.

⁶ Daniel drew attention to God's mercy and lovingkindness. Humbly, he acknowledged that the Jews had sinned by rebelling, turning aside from Jehovah's commandments, and ignoring his prophets. God had rightly

4. (a) What was needed in order to experience God's deliverance? (b) How did Daniel proceed to approach Jehovah?
5. Why could Daniel feel confident that the Jews would be restored to their homeland?
6. What acknowledgment did Daniel make in prayer?

"dispersed them because of their unfaithfulness." Daniel prayed: "O Jehovah, to us belongs the shame of face, to our kings, to our princes and to our forefathers, because we have sinned against you. To Jehovah our God belong the mercies and the acts of forgiveness, for we have rebelled against him. And we have not obeyed the voice of Jehovah our God by walking in his laws that he set before us by the hand of his servants the prophets. And all those of Israel have overstepped your law, and there has been a turning aside by not obeying your voice, so that you poured out upon us the curse and the sworn oath that is written in the law of Moses the servant of the true God, for we have sinned against Him."—Daniel 9:5-11; Exodus 19:5-8; 24:3, 7, 8.

⁷ God had warned the Israelites of the consequences of disobeying him and disregarding the covenant he had made with them. (Leviticus 26:31-33; Deuteronomy 28:15; 31:17) Daniel acknowledges the rightness of God's actions, saying: "He proceeded to carry out his words that he had spoken against us and against our judges who judged us, by bringing upon us great calamity, such as was not done under the whole heavens as what has been done in Jerusalem. Just as it is written in the law of Moses, all this calamity—it has come upon us, and we have not softened the face of Jehovah our God by turning back from our error and by showing insight into your trueness. And Jehovah kept alert to the calamity and finally brought it upon us, for Jehovah our God is righteous in all his works that he has done; and we have not obeyed his voice."—Daniel 9:12-14.

⁸ Daniel does not seek to justify the actions of his

---

7. Why can it be said that Jehovah acted rightly in allowing the Jews to go into captivity?
8. On what does Daniel base his appeal to Jehovah?

people. Their exile was justly deserved, as he readily confesses: "We have sinned, we have acted wickedly." (Daniel 9:15) Neither is his concern simply for relief from suffering. No, he bases his appeal on Jehovah's own glory and honor. By pardoning the Jews and restoring them to their homeland, God would fulfill his promise through Jeremiah and would sanctify His holy name. Daniel pleads: "O Jehovah, according to all your acts of righteousness, please, may your anger and your rage turn back from your city Jerusalem, your holy mountain; for, because of our sins and because of the errors of our forefathers, Jerusalem and your people are an object of reproach to all those round about us."—Daniel 9:16.

⁹ In fervent prayer, Daniel continues: "Now listen, O our God, to the prayer of your servant and to his entreaties, and cause your face to shine upon your sanctuary that is desolated, for the sake of Jehovah. Incline your ear, O my God, and hear. Do open your eyes and see our desolated conditions and the city that has been called by your name; for not according to our righteous acts are we letting our entreaties fall before you, but according to your many mercies. O Jehovah, do hear. O Jehovah, do forgive. O Jehovah, do pay attention and act. Do not delay, for your own sake, O my God, for your own name has been called upon your city and upon your people." (Daniel 9:17-19) If God were unforgiving and left his people in exile, allowing his holy city, Jerusalem, to lay desolate indefinitely, would nations regard him as the Universal Sovereign? Might they not conclude that Jehovah was powerless against the might of the Babylonian gods? Yes, Jehovah's name would be reproached, and this distresses

---

9. (a) With what entreaties does Daniel conclude his prayer? (b) What distresses Daniel, but how does he show regard for God's name?

Daniel. Of the 19 times that the divine name, Jehovah, is found in the book of Daniel, 18 occur in connection with this prayer!

GABRIEL COMES SPEEDILY

[10] While Daniel is yet praying, the angel Gabriel appears. He says: "O Daniel, now I have come forth to make you have insight with understanding. At the start of your entreaties a word went forth, and I myself have come to make report, because you are someone very desirable. So give consideration to the matter, and have understanding in the thing seen." But why does Daniel speak of him as "the man Gabriel"? (Daniel 9:20-23) Well, when Daniel sought understanding of his earlier vision of the he-goat and the ram, "someone in appearance like an able-bodied man" appeared before him. It was the angel Gabriel, sent to give Daniel insight. (Daniel 8:15-17) Similarly, after Daniel's prayer, this angel came near to him in humanlike form and spoke to him as one man does to another.

[11] Gabriel arrives "at the time of the evening gift offering." Jehovah's altar had been destroyed along with the temple in Jerusalem, and the Jews were captives of the pagan Babylonians. So sacrifices were not being offered to God by the Jews in Babylon. At the prescribed times for offerings under the Mosaic Law, however, it was appropriate for devout Jews in Babylon to praise and supplicate Jehovah. As a man deeply devoted to God, Daniel was called "someone very desirable." Jehovah, the "Hearer of prayer," took pleasure in him, and Gabriel was dispatched speedily to answer Daniel's prayer of faith.—Psalm 65:2.

[12] Even when praying to Jehovah had imperiled his life,

---

10. (a) Who was dispatched to Daniel, and why? (b) Why did Daniel speak of Gabriel as a "man"?
11, 12. (a) Although there was no temple or altar of Jehovah in Babylon, how did devout Jews show regard for offerings required by the Law? (b) Why was Daniel called "someone very desirable"?

Daniel continued to pray to God three times a day. (Daniel 6:10, 11) No wonder Jehovah found him so desirable! In addition to prayer, Daniel's meditation on God's Word enabled him to determine Jehovah's will. Daniel persisted in prayer and knew how to approach Jehovah properly so as to have his prayers answered. He highlighted God's righteousness. (Daniel 9:7, 14, 16) And although his enemies could find no fault in him, Daniel knew that he was a sinner in God's eyes and readily confessed his sin.—Daniel 6:4; Romans 3:23.

"SEVENTY WEEKS" TO FINISH OFF SIN

¹³ What an answer prayerful Daniel receives! Jehovah not only assures him that the Jews will be restored to their homeland but also gives him insight into something of far greater significance—the appearance of the foretold Messiah. (Genesis 22:17, 18; Isaiah 9:6, 7) Gabriel tells Daniel: "There are seventy weeks that have been determined upon your people and upon your holy city, in order to terminate the transgression, and to finish off sin, and to make atonement for error, and to bring in righteousness for times indefinite, and to imprint a seal upon vision and prophet, and to anoint the Holy of Holies. And you should know and have the insight that from the going forth of the word to restore and to rebuild Jerusalem until Messiah the Leader, there will be seven weeks, also sixty-two weeks. She will return and be actually rebuilt, with a public square and moat, but in the straits of the times."—Daniel 9:24, 25.

¹⁴ This was good news indeed! Not only would Jerusalem be rebuilt and worship be restored at a new temple but also "Messiah the Leader" would appear at a specific

---

13, 14. (a) What important information did Gabriel disclose to Daniel? (b) How long are the "seventy weeks," and how do we know?

time. This would occur within "seventy weeks." Since Gabriel does not mention days, these are not weeks of seven days each, which would amount to 490 days—a mere year and a third. The foretold rebuilding of Jerusalem "with a public square and moat" took much longer than that. The weeks are weeks of years. That each week is seven years long is suggested by a number of modern translations. For example, "seventy weeks of years" is a rendering indicated by a footnote on Daniel 9:24 in *Tanakh—The Holy Scriptures,* published by The Jewish Publication Society. *An American Translation* reads: "Seventy weeks of years are destined for your people and for your holy city." Similar renderings appear in the translations by Moffatt and Rotherham.

[15] According to the angel's words, the "seventy weeks" would be divided into three periods: (1) "seven weeks," (2) "sixty-two weeks," and (3) one week. That would be 49 years, 434 years, and 7 years—totaling 490 years. Interestingly, *The Revised English Bible* reads: "Seventy times seven years are marked out for your people and your holy city." Following their exile and suffering in Babylon for 70 years, the Jews would experience special favor from God for 490 years, or 70 years multiplied by 7. The starting point would be "the going forth of the word to restore and to rebuild Jerusalem." When would this be?

THE "SEVENTY WEEKS" BEGIN

[16] Three noteworthy incidents deserve consideration with regard to the beginning of the "seventy weeks." The first occurred in 537 B.C.E. when Cyrus issued his decree

---

15. Into what three periods are the "seventy weeks" divided, and when would they start?
16. As shown by his decree, for what purpose did Cyrus restore the Jews to their homeland?

restoring the Jews to their homeland. It reads: "This is what Cyrus the king of Persia has said, 'All the kingdoms of the earth Jehovah the God of the heavens has given me, and he himself has commissioned me to build him a house in Jerusalem, which is in Judah. Whoever there is among you of all his people, may his God prove to be with him. So let him go up to Jerusalem, which is in Judah, and rebuild the house of Jehovah the God of Israel —he is the true God—which was in Jerusalem. As for anyone that is left from all the places where he is residing as an alien, let the men of his place assist him with silver and with gold and with goods and with domestic animals along with the voluntary offering for the house of the true God, which was in Jerusalem.'" (Ezra 1:2-4) Clearly, the express purpose of this decree was to have the temple —"the house of Jehovah"—rebuilt on its former site.

¹⁷ The second incident occurred in the seventh year of the reign of Persian King Artaxerxes (Artaxerxes Longimanus, son of Xerxes I). At that time, Ezra the copyist made a four-month journey from Babylon to Jerusalem. He carried a special letter from the king, but it did not authorize the rebuilding of Jerusalem. Instead, Ezra's

---

17. The letter given to Ezra gave what reason for his journey to Jerusalem?

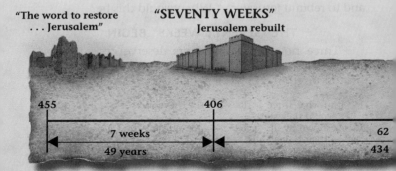

"The word to restore . . . Jerusalem"   "SEVENTY WEEKS"
                                            Jerusalem rebuilt

455   406   62

        7 weeks   434
        49 years

commission was limited to 'beautifying the house of Jehovah.' That is why the letter referred to gold and silver, sacred vessels, and contributions of wheat, wine, oil, and salt for support of worship at the temple, as well as freedom from taxation for those serving there.—Ezra 7:6-27.

¹⁸ The third incident occurred 13 years later, in the 20th year of Persian King Artaxerxes. Nehemiah was then serving as his cupbearer in "Shushan the castle." Jerusalem had been rebuilt to some extent by the remnant that had returned from Babylon. But all was not well. Nehemiah learned that 'the wall of Jerusalem was broken down and its very gates had been burned with fire.' This disturbed him greatly, and gloom settled upon his heart. Questioned about his sadness, Nehemiah replied: "Let the king himself live to time indefinite! Why should not my face become gloomy when the city, the house of the burial places of my forefathers, is devastated, and its very gates have been eaten up with fire?"—Nehemiah 1:1-3; 2:1-3.

¹⁹ The account involving Nehemiah continues: "In

18. What news disturbed Nehemiah, and how did King Artaxerxes learn of it?
19. (a) When questioned by King Artaxerxes, what did Nehemiah do first? (b) What did Nehemiah request, and how did he acknowledge God's role in the matter?

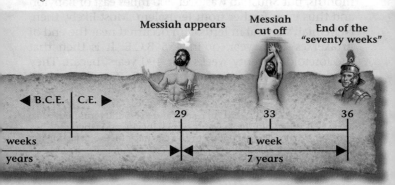

Messiah appears

Messiah cut off

End of the "seventy weeks"

◀ B.C.E. | C.E. ▶

	29	33	36
weeks		1 week	
years		7 years	

turn the king said to me: 'What is this that you are seeking to secure?' At once I prayed to the God of the heavens. After that I said to the king: 'If to the king it does seem good, and if your servant seems good before you, that you would send me to Judah, to the city of the burial places of my forefathers, that I may rebuild it.'" This proposal pleased Artaxerxes, who also acted on Nehemiah's further request: "If to the king it does seem good, let letters be given me to the governors beyond the River [Euphrates], that they may let me pass until I come to Judah; also a letter to Asaph the keeper of the park that belongs to the king, that he may give me trees to build with timber the gates of the Castle that belongs to the house, and for the wall of the city and for the house into which I am to enter." Nehemiah acknowledged Jehovah's role in all of this, saying: "So the king gave [the letters] to me, according to the good hand of my God upon me."—Nehemiah 2:4-8.

[20] Although permission was given in the month of Nisan, during the early part of the 20th year of Artaxerxes' reign, the actual "going forth of the word to restore and to rebuild Jerusalem" took effect months later. This occurred when Nehemiah arrived in Jerusalem and began his work of restoration. Ezra's journey had taken four months, but Shushan was over 200 miles east of Babylon and thus even farther from Jerusalem. Most likely, then, Nehemiah's arrival in Jerusalem occurred near the end of Artaxerxes' 20th year, or in 455 B.C.E. It is then that the foretold "seventy weeks," or 490 years, began. They would end in the latter part of 36 C.E.—See "When Did Artaxerxes' Reign Begin?" on page 197.

---

20. (a) When did the word "to restore and to rebuild Jerusalem" take effect? (b) When did the "seventy weeks" begin, and when did they end? (c) What evidence points to the accuracy of the dates for the beginning and the end of the "seventy weeks"?

"MESSIAH THE LEADER" APPEARS

²¹ How many years elapsed before Jerusalem was actually rebuilt? Well, the restoration of the city was to be accomplished "in the straits of the times" because of difficulties among the Jews themselves and opposition from the Samaritans and others. The work was evidently completed to the extent necessary by about 406 B.C.E. —within the "seven weeks," or 49 years. (Daniel 9:25) A period of 62 weeks, or 434 years, would follow. After that time period, the long-promised Messiah would appear. Counting 483 years (49 plus 434) from 455 B.C.E. brings us to 29 C.E. What happened at that time? The Gospel writer Luke tells us: "In the fifteenth year of the reign of Tiberius Caesar, when Pontius Pilate was governor of Judea, and Herod was district ruler of Galilee, . . . God's declaration came to John the son of Zechariah in the wilderness. So he came into all the country around the Jordan, preaching baptism in symbol of repentance for forgiveness of sins." At that time "the people were in expectation" of the Messiah.—Luke 3:1-3, 15.

²² John was not the promised Messiah. But concerning what he witnessed at the baptism of Jesus of Nazareth, in the fall of 29 C.E., John said: "I viewed the spirit coming down as a dove out of heaven, and it remained upon him. Even I did not know him, but the very One who sent me to baptize in water said to me, 'Whoever it is upon whom you see the spirit coming down and remaining, this is the one that baptizes in holy spirit.' And I have seen it, and I have borne witness that this one is the Son of God." (John 1:32-34) At his baptism, Jesus became the

---

21. (a) What was to be accomplished during the first "seven weeks," and despite what circumstances? (b) In what year was the Messiah due to appear, and what does Luke's Gospel say happened at that time?
22. When and by what means did Jesus become the foretold Messiah?

Anointed One—the Messiah, or Christ. Shortly thereafter, John's disciple Andrew met the anointed Jesus and then told Simon Peter: "We have found the Messiah." (John 1: 41) Thus, "Messiah the Leader" appeared exactly on time —at the end of 69 weeks!

THE EVENTS OF THE FINAL WEEK

[23] What was to be accomplished during the 70th week? Gabriel said that the period of "seventy weeks" had been determined "in order to terminate the transgression, and to finish off sin, and to make atonement for error, and to bring in righteousness for times indefinite, and to imprint a seal upon vision and prophet, and to anoint the Holy of Holies." For this to be accomplished, "Messiah the Leader" had to die. When? Gabriel said: "After the sixty-two weeks Messiah will be cut off, with nothing for himself. . . . And he must keep the covenant in force for the many for one week; and at the half of the week he will cause sacrifice and gift offering to cease." (Daniel 9:26a, 27a) The critical time was "at the half of the week," that is, the middle of the last week of years.

[24] Jesus Christ's public ministry began in the latter part of 29 C.E. and lasted for three and a half years. As prophesied, early in 33 C.E., Christ was "cut off" when he died on a torture stake, giving his human life as a ransom for mankind. (Isaiah 53:8; Matthew 20:28) The need for the animal sacrifices and the gift offerings prescribed by the Law ceased when the resurrected Jesus presented the value of his sacrificed human life to God in heaven. Although the Jewish priests continued to make offerings until the destruction of Jerusalem's temple in 70 C.E.,

---

23. Why did "Messiah the Leader" have to die, and when was this to happen?
24, 25. (a) As prophesied, when did Christ die, and to what did his death and resurrection bring an end? (b) What did Jesus' death make possible?

194 *Pay Attention to Daniel's Prophecy!*

such sacrifices were no longer acceptable to God. They had been replaced by a better sacrifice, one that never had to be repeated. The apostle Paul wrote: "[Christ] offered one sacrifice for sins perpetually . . . For it is by one sacrificial offering that he has made those who are being sanctified perfect perpetually."—Hebrews 10:12, 14.

²⁵ Though sin and death continued to afflict mankind, Jesus' being cut off in death and his resurrection to heavenly life fulfilled prophecy. It 'terminated transgression, finished off sin, made atonement for error, and brought in righteousness.' God had removed the Law covenant, which had exposed and condemned the Jews as sinners. (Romans 5:12, 19, 20; Galatians 3:13, 19; Ephesians 2:15; Colossians 2:13, 14) Now the sins of repentant wrongdoers could be canceled, and the penalties thereof could be lifted. By means of the Messiah's propitiatory sacrifice, reconciliation with God was possible for those exercising faith. They could look forward to receiving God's gift of "everlasting life by Christ Jesus."—Romans 3:21-26; 6:22, 23; 1 John 2:1, 2.

²⁶ So it was that Jehovah removed the Law covenant by means of Christ's death in 33 C.E. How, then, could it be said that the Messiah "must keep the covenant in force for the many for one week"? Because he kept the *Abrahamic* covenant in force. Until the 70th week ended, God extended the blessings of that covenant to Abraham's Hebrew offspring. But at the end of the "seventy weeks" of years, in 36 C.E., the apostle Peter preached to the devout Italian man Cornelius, his household, and other Gentiles. And from that day on, the good news began to be declared among people of the nations.—Acts 3:25, 26; 10:1-48; Galatians 3:8, 9, 14.

---

26. (a) Although the Law covenant had been removed, what covenant was 'kept in force for one week'? (b) What took place at the end of the 70th week?

²⁷ The prophecy also foretold the anointing of "the Holy of Holies." This does not refer to anointing the Most Holy, or innermost compartment, of the temple in Jerusalem. The expression "Holy of Holies" here refers to the heavenly sanctuary of God. There, Jesus presented the value of his human sacrifice to his Father. That sacrifice anointed, or set apart, that heavenly, spiritual reality represented by the Most Holy of the earthly tabernacle and of the later temple.—Hebrews 9:11, 12.

THE PROPHECY AFFIRMED BY GOD

²⁸ The Messianic prophecy uttered by the angel Gabriel also spoke of 'imprinting a seal upon vision and prophet.' This meant that everything foretold regarding the Messiah—all that he accomplished by means of his sacrifice, resurrection, and appearance in heaven, as well as the other things occurring during the 70th week—would be stamped with the seal of divine backing, would prove true, and could be trusted. The vision would be sealed, restricted to the Messiah. Its fulfillment would be in him and in God's work through him. Only in connection with the foretold Messiah could we find the correct interpretation of the vision. Nothing else would unseal its meaning.

²⁹ Gabriel had previously prophesied that Jerusalem would be rebuilt. Now he foretells the destruction of that rebuilt city and its temple, saying: "The city and the holy place the people of a leader that is coming will bring to their ruin. And the end of it will be by the flood. And until the end there will be war; what is decided upon is desolations. . . . And upon the wing of disgusting things there will be the one causing desolation; and until an extermination, the very thing decided upon will go pouring

27. What "Holy of Holies" was anointed, and how?
28. What was meant by 'imprinting a seal upon vision and prophet'?
29. What was to happen to rebuilt Jerusalem, and for what reason?

out also upon the one lying desolate." (Daniel 9:26b, 27b) Although this desolation would take place after the "seventy weeks," it would be a direct result of happenings during the final "week," when the Jews rejected Christ and had him put to death.—Matthew 23:37, 38.

[30] Historical records show that in 66 C.E., Roman legions under Syrian Governor Cestius Gallus surrounded Jerusalem. Despite Jewish resistance, the Roman forces bearing their idolatrous ensigns, or standards, penetrated the city and started to undermine the temple wall on the north. Their standing there made them a "disgusting thing" that could cause complete desolation. (Matthew 24:15, 16) In 70 C.E., the Romans under General Titus came like a "flood" and desolated the city and its temple. Nothing stopped them, for this had been decreed—"decided upon"—by God. The Great Timekeeper, Jehovah, had again fulfilled his word!

---

30. As shown by the historical record, how was the decree of the Great Timekeeper fulfilled?

WHAT DID YOU DISCERN?

- When the 70 years of Jerusalem's desolation were coming to an end, what entreaties did Daniel make to Jehovah?

- How long were the "seventy weeks," and when did they begin and end?

- When did "Messiah the Leader" appear, and at what critical time was he "cut off"?

- What covenant was kept "in force for the many for one week"?

- What took place following the "seventy weeks"?

When Did Artaxerxes' Reign Begin?

HISTORIANS disagree regarding the year in which the reign of Persian King Artaxerxes began. Some have placed his accession year in 465 B.C.E. because his father, Xerxes, started to rule in 486 B.C.E. and died in the 21st year of his reign. But there is evidence that Artaxerxes ascended to the throne in 475 B.C.E. and began his first regnal year in 474 B.C.E.

Inscriptions and sculptures unearthed at the ancient Persian capital Persepolis indicate a coregency between Xerxes and his father, Darius I. If this covered 10 years and Xerxes ruled alone for 11 years after Darius died in 486 B.C.E., the first year of Artaxerxes' reign would have been 474 B.C.E.

A second line of evidence involves Athenian General Themistocles, who defeated Xerxes' forces in 480 B.C.E. He later fell out of favor with the Greek people and was accused of treason. Themistocles fled and sought protection at the Persian court, where he was well received. According to the Greek historian Thucydides, this happened when Artaxerxes had but "lately come to the throne." The Greek historian Diodorus Siculus puts the death of Themistocles at 471 B.C.E. Since Themistocles requested a year to learn Persian before having an audience with King Artaxerxes, he must have arrived in Asia Minor no later than 473 B.C.E. That date is supported by Jerome's *Chronicle of Eusebius*. As Artaxerxes had "lately come to the throne" when Themistocles arrived in Asia in 473 B.C.E., German scholar Ernst Hengstenberg stated in his *Christology of the Old Testament* that Artaxerxes' reign commenced in 474 B.C.E., as do other sources. He added: "The twentieth year of Artaxerxes is the year 455 before Christ."

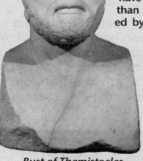

Bust of Themistocles

CHAPTER TWELVE

STRENGTHENED BY A MESSENGER FROM GOD

DANIEL'S keen interest in the outworking of Jehovah's purpose was richly rewarded. He was given the stirring prophecy of the 70 weeks regarding the time of Messiah's appearance. Daniel was also blessed with seeing the faithful remnant of his people return to their homeland. That occurred in 537 B.C.E, toward the end of "the first year of Cyrus the king of Persia."—Ezra 1:1-4.

² Daniel was not among those who traveled back to the land of Judah. Traveling may have been difficult at his advanced age. In any case, God still had further service in mind for him in Babylon. Two years passed. Then, the account tells us: "In the third year of Cyrus the king of Persia there was a matter revealed to Daniel, whose name was called Belteshazzar; and the matter was true, and there was a great military service. And he understood the matter, and he had understanding in the thing seen." —Daniel 10:1.

³ "The third year of Cyrus" would correspond to 536/535 B.C.E. More than 80 years had passed since Daniel was brought to Babylon along with the royal offspring and Judah's youths of noble birth. (Daniel 1:3) If he was in his early teens when he first arrived in Babylon, he would be nearly 100 years of age by now. What a marvelous record of faithful service he had!

---

1. How was Daniel blessed for having a keen interest in the outworking of Jehovah's purpose?
2, 3. Why may Daniel not have returned to the land of Judah with the Jewish remnant?

⁴ In spite of his advanced age, however, Daniel's role in Jehovah's service was not over. Through him, God would yet proclaim a prophetic message having far-reaching significance. It was to be a prophecy that would reach down to our times and beyond. To prepare Daniel for this further task, Jehovah saw fit to act in his behalf, to strengthen him for the service ahead.

A CAUSE FOR ANXIETY

⁵ Though Daniel did not return to the land of Judah with the Jewish remnant, he was keenly interested in what was taking place back in his beloved homeland. From reports that reached him, Daniel learned that all was not going well there. The altar had been reestablished and the foundation of the temple had been laid in Jerusalem. (Ezra, chapter 3) But the neighboring nations were in opposition to the reconstruction project, and they were scheming mischief against the returned Jews. (Ezra 4:1-5) Indeed, Daniel could easily have become anxious about many things.

⁶ Daniel was familiar with Jeremiah's prophecy. (Daniel 9:2) He knew that the rebuilding of the temple in Jerusalem and the restoration of true worship there were closely related to Jehovah's purpose regarding His people and that all of this would precede the appearance of the promised Messiah. In fact, Daniel was highly privileged to have received from Jehovah the prophecy of the "seventy weeks." From it he understood that Messiah would come 69 "weeks" after the going forth of the word to restore and to rebuild Jerusalem. (Daniel 9:24-27) In view of the devastated state of Jerusalem and the delay in

---

4. In spite of Daniel's advanced age, what significant role would he still play in Jehovah's service?
5. What reports were likely causes for concern to Daniel?
6. Why were conditions in Jerusalem troubling to Daniel?

building the temple, however, it is easy to see why Daniel could have become discouraged, dejected, and low in spirits.

7 "In those days I myself, Daniel, happened to be mourning for three full weeks," says the account. "Dainty bread I did not eat, and no flesh or wine entered into my mouth, and in no way did I grease myself until the completing of the three full weeks." (Daniel 10:2, 3) "Three full weeks," or 21 days, of mourning and fasting was an unusually long period. It apparently ended on the "twenty-fourth day of the first month." (Daniel 10:4) Hence, the period of Daniel's fast included the Passover, observed on the 14th day of the first month, Nisan, and the following seven-day festival of unleavened bread.

8 Daniel had had a similar experience on an earlier occasion. At that time, he was perplexed about the fulfillment of Jehovah's prophecy regarding the 70-year desolation of Jerusalem. What did Daniel then do? "I proceeded to set my face to Jehovah the true God," said Daniel, "in order to seek him with prayer and with entreaties, with fasting and sackcloth and ashes." Jehovah answered Daniel's prayer by sending the angel Gabriel to him with a message that greatly encouraged him. (Daniel 9:3, 21, 22) Would Jehovah now act in a similar way and provide Daniel with the encouragement he sorely needed?

AN AWE-INSPIRING VISION

9 Daniel is not disappointed. He goes on to tell us what happens next, saying: "While I myself happened to be

7. What did Daniel do for three weeks?
8. On what earlier occasion had Daniel earnestly sought Jehovah's direction, and what had been the outcome?
9, 10. (a) Where was Daniel when a vision came to him? (b) Describe what Daniel saw in the vision.

on the bank of the great river, that is, Hiddekel, I also proceeded to raise my eyes and see, and here was a certain man clothed in linen, with his hips girded with gold of Uphaz." (Daniel 10:4, 5) Hiddekel was one of the four rivers that had their source in the garden of Eden. (Genesis 2:10-14) In Old Persian, Hiddekel was known as the *Tigra,* from which came the Greek name Tigris. The region between it and the Euphrates came to be called Mesopotamia, meaning "Land Between Rivers." This confirms that when Daniel received this vision, he was still in the land of Babylonia, though perhaps not in the city of Babylon.

¹⁰ What a vision Daniel received! Obviously, he saw no ordinary man when he raised his eyes. Daniel provided this vivid description: "His body was like chrysolite, and his face like the appearance of lightning, and his eyes like fiery torches, and his arms and the place of his feet were like the sight of burnished copper, and the sound of his words was like the sound of a crowd."—Daniel 10:6.

¹¹ In spite of the brilliance of the vision, 'the men that happened to be with me did not see the appearance,' said Daniel. For some unexplained reason, "there was a great trembling that fell upon them, so that they went running away in hiding themselves." Hence, Daniel was left all by himself on the bank of the river. The sight of "this great appearance" was so overwhelming that he confessed: "There was left remaining in me no power, and my own dignity became changed upon me to ruination, and I retained no power."—Daniel 10:7, 8.

¹² Let us take a closer look at this striking messenger

---

11. What effect did the vision have on Daniel and on the men with him?

12, 13. What is indicated about the messenger by (a) his clothing? (b) his appearance?

who so frightened Daniel. He was "clothed in linen, with his hips girded with gold of Uphaz." In ancient Israel, the high priest's girdle, ephod, and breastpiece, as well as the robes of the other priests, were made with fine twisted linen and were decorated with gold. (Exodus 28:4-8; 39:27-29) Thus, the messenger's clothing indicates holiness and dignity of office.

[13] Daniel was also awed by the appearance of the messenger—the luminous glow of his gemlike body, the blinding radiance of his shining face, the penetrating power of his fiery eyes, and the glitter of his powerful arms and feet. Even his commanding voice was fear-inspiring. All of this clearly indicates that he was superhuman. This "man clothed in linen" was none other than an angel of high rank, one who served in the holy presence of Jehovah, from which he came forth with a message.*

A "VERY DESIRABLE MAN" STRENGTHENED

[14] The message that Jehovah's angel had for Daniel was weighty and complex. Before Daniel could receive it, he needed help to recover from his physical and mental distress. Apparently aware of this, the angel lovingly gave Daniel personal assistance and encouragement. Let us follow Daniel's own narration of what happened.

[15] "While I was hearing the sound of his words, I

---

* Though this angel is unnamed, it appears that he is the same one whose voice was heard directing Gabriel to help Daniel with a vision that he had just seen. (Compare Daniel 8:2, 15, 16 with 12:7, 8.) Further, Daniel 10:13 shows that Michael, "one of the foremost princes," came to assist this angel. Thus, this unnamed angel must enjoy the privilege of working closely with Gabriel and Michael.

---

14. What help did Daniel need in order to receive the angelic message?
15. What did the angel do to help Daniel?

Angelic Guardians or Demonic Rulers?

WE CAN learn much from what the book of Daniel says about the angels. It tells us about the role they play in carrying out Jehovah's word and the effort they put forth to fulfill their assignments.

God's angel said that on his way to speak to Daniel, he was hindered by "the prince of the royal realm of Persia." After contending with him for 21 days, the angelic messenger was able to proceed only with the help of "Michael, one of the foremost princes." The angel also said that he would again have to fight that enemy and possibly "the prince of Greece." (Daniel 10:13, 20) No easy task, even for an angel! Who, though, were these princes of Persia and Greece?

First of all, we note that Michael was called "one of the foremost princes" and "the prince of you people." Later, Michael was referred to as "the great prince who is standing in behalf of the sons of [Daniel's] people." (Daniel 10:21; 12:1) This points to Michael as the angel assigned by Jehovah to lead the Israelites through the wilderness.—Exodus 23:20-23; 32:34; 33:2.

Lending support to this conclusion is the disciple Jude's statement that "Michael the archangel had a difference with

myself also happened to be fast asleep upon my face, with my face to the earth." Likely, fear and apprehension had caused Daniel to fall into a stupor. What did the angel do to help him? "Look!" said Daniel, "there was a hand that touched me, and it gradually stirred me up to get upon my knees and the palms of my hands." In addition, the angel encouraged the prophet with these words: "O Daniel, you very desirable man, have understanding in the words that I am speaking to you, and stand up

the Devil and was disputing about Moses' body." (Jude 9) Michael's position, power, and authority made him truly "the archangel," meaning "the chief angel," or "the principal angel." Most fittingly, this lofty position can be applied to none other than Jesus Christ, the Son of God, before and after his life on earth.—1 Thessalonians 4:16; Revelation 12:7-9.

Does this mean that Jehovah also appointed angels over such nations as Persia and Greece to guide them in their affairs? Well, Jesus Christ, the Son of God, openly stated: "The ruler of the world . . . has no hold on me." Jesus also said: "My kingdom is no part of this world . . . my kingdom is not from this source." (John 14:30; 18:36) The apostle John declared that "the whole world is lying in the power of the wicked one." (1 John 5:19) It is clear that the nations of the world never were and are not now under the guidance or rulership of God or Christ. While Jehovah permits "the superior authorities" to exist and maintain control of earthly governmental affairs, he does not appoint his angels over them. (Romans 13:1-7) Any "princes" or "rulers" over them could be placed there only by "the ruler of the world," Satan the Devil. They would have to be demonic rulers rather than angelic guardians. There are, then, invisible demonic forces, or "princes," behind the visible rulers, and national conflicts involve more than mere humans.

where you were standing, for now I have been sent to you." The helping hand and the consoling words revived Daniel. Although he was "shivering," Daniel did "stand up."—Daniel 10:9-11.

¹⁶ The angel pointed out that he had come specifically to strengthen Daniel. "Do not be afraid, O Daniel,"

16. (a) How can it be seen that Jehovah responds quickly to his servants' prayers? (b) Why was the angel delayed in coming to Daniel's aid? (Include box.) (c) What message did the angel have for Daniel?

said the angel, "for from the first day that you gave your heart to understanding and humbling yourself before your God your words have been heard, and I myself have come because of your words." The angel then explained why there had been a delay. He said: "But the prince of the royal realm of Persia was standing in opposition to me for twenty-one days, and, look! Michael, one of the foremost princes, came to help me; and I, for my part, remained there beside the kings of Persia." With the assistance of Michael, the angel was able to accomplish his mission, coming to Daniel with this most urgent message: "I have come to cause you to discern what will befall your people in the final part of the days, because it is a vision yet for the days to come."—Daniel 10:12-14.

[17] Instead of Daniel's being aroused by the prospect of receiving such an intriguing message, it appears that the things he heard had an adverse effect on him. The account states: "Now when he spoke with me words like these, I had set my face to the earth and had become speechless." But the angelic messenger was ready to render loving help—a second time. Said Daniel: "Look! one similar to the likeness of the sons of mankind was touching my lips, and I began to open my mouth and speak."*
—Daniel 10:15, 16a.

[18] Daniel was strengthened when the angel touched his lips. (Compare Isaiah 6:7.) With his power of speech restored, Daniel was able to explain to the angelic

-----

* Although the same angel who was speaking with Daniel may have touched his lips and revived him, the wording here leaves room for the possibility that another angel, perhaps Gabriel, did this. In any case, Daniel was strengthened by an angelic messenger.

17, 18. How was Daniel helped a second time, and what did that enable him to do?

messenger the hardship that he was enduring. Daniel said: "O my lord, because of the appearance my convulsions were turned within me, and I did not retain any power. So how was the servant of this my lord able to speak with this my lord? And as for me, up to now there kept standing in me no power, and no breath at all was left remaining in me."—Daniel 10:16b, 17.

[19] Daniel was not voicing any complaint or making an excuse. He was merely stating his predicament, and the angel accepted his statement. Thus, for a third time, Daniel was helped by the angelic messenger. "The one like the appearance of an earthling man proceeded to touch me again and strengthen me," said the prophet. The messenger followed that energizing touch with these consoling words: "Do not be afraid, O very desirable man. May you have peace. Be strong, yes, be strong." That loving touch and those upbuilding words seemed to be just what Daniel needed. The result? Daniel declared: "As soon as he spoke with me I exerted my strength and finally said: 'Let my lord speak, because you have strengthened me.'" Daniel was now ready for another challenging assignment.—Daniel 10:18, 19.

[20] Having strengthened Daniel and helped him to recover his mental and physical capabilities, the angel restated the purpose of his mission. He said: "Do you really know why I have come to you? And now I shall go back to fight with the prince of Persia. When I am going forth, look! also the prince of Greece is coming. However, I shall tell you the things noted down in the writing of truth, and there is no one holding strongly with me

---

19. How was Daniel helped a third time, and with what result?
20. Why had effort been required in order for the angelic messenger to carry out his assignment?

in these things but Michael, the prince of you people."
—Daniel 10:20, 21.

²¹ How loving and considerate of Jehovah! He always deals with his servants according to their potential and limitations. On the one hand, he gives them assignments according to what he knows they can accomplish, even though they may sometimes feel otherwise. On the other hand, he is willing to listen to them and then provide what is needed to help them carry out their assignments. May we always imitate our heavenly Father, Jehovah, by lovingly encouraging and strengthening our fellow worshipers.—Hebrews 10:24.

²² The angel's comforting message was of great encouragement to Daniel. In spite of his advanced age, Daniel was now strengthened and prepared to receive and to record further remarkable prophecy for our benefit.

21, 22. (a) From Daniel's experience, what can we learn about Jehovah's way of dealing with his servants? (b) For what was Daniel now strengthened?

WHAT DID YOU DISCERN?

- Why was Jehovah's angel delayed in coming to Daniel's aid in 536/535 B.C.E.?

- What did the clothing and appearance of God's angelic messenger indicate about him?

- What help did Daniel need, and how did the angel provide it three times?

- What message did the angel have for Daniel?

CHAPTER THIRTEEN

TWO KINGS IN CONFLICT

TWO rival kings are locked in an all-out struggle for supremacy. As the years pass, first one, then the other, gains ascendancy. At times, one king rules supreme while the other becomes inactive, and there are periods of no conflict. But then another battle suddenly erupts, and the conflict continues. Among the participants in this drama have been Syrian King Seleucus I Nicator, Egyptian King Ptolemy Lagus, Syrian Princess and Egyptian Queen Cleopatra I, Roman Emperors Augustus and Tiberius, and Palmyrene Queen Zenobia. As the conflict nears its end, Nazi Germany, the Communist bloc of nations, the Anglo-American World Power, the League of Nations, and the United Nations have also been involved. The finale is an episode unforeseen by any of these political entities. Jehovah's angel declared this exciting prophecy to the prophet Daniel some 2,500 years ago.—Daniel, chapter 11.

² How thrilled Daniel must have been to hear the angel reveal to him in detail the rivalry between two forthcoming kings! The drama is of interest to us as well, for the power struggle between the two kings stretches into our day. Seeing how history has shown the first part of the prophecy to be true will strengthen our faith and confidence in the certainty of fulfillment of the last part of the prophetic account. Paying attention to this prophecy will give us a clear view of where we are in the stream of time. It will also fortify our resolve to remain neutral in the conflict as we patiently wait for God to act in our behalf.

1, 2. Why should we be interested in the prophecy recorded in Daniel chapter 11?

(Psalm 146:3, 5) With keen attention, then, let us listen as Jehovah's angel speaks to Daniel.

AGAINST THE KINGDOM OF GREECE

³ "As for me," said the angel, "in the first year of Darius the Mede [539/538 B.C.E.] I stood up as a strengthener and as a fortress to him." (Daniel 11:1) Darius was no longer living, but the angel referred to his reign as the starting point of the prophetic message. It was this king who had ordered that Daniel be taken out of the lions' pit. Darius had also decreed that all his subjects should fear Daniel's God. (Daniel 6:21-27) However, the one for whom the angel stood up as a supporter was, not Darius the Mede, but the angel's associate Michael—the prince of Daniel's people. (Compare Daniel 10:12-14.) God's angel provided this support while Michael contended with the demon prince of Medo-Persia.

⁴ God's angel continued: "Look! There will yet be three kings standing up for Persia, and the fourth one will amass greater riches than all others. And as soon as he has become strong in his riches, he will rouse up everything against the kingdom of Greece." (Daniel 11:2) Just who were these Persian rulers?

⁵ The first three kings were Cyrus the Great, Cambyses II, and Darius I (Hystaspes). Since Bardiya (or perhaps a pretender named Gaumata) ruled for only seven months, the prophecy did not take his brief reign into consideration. In 490 B.C.E., the third king, Darius I, attempted to invade Greece for the second time. However, the Persians were routed at Marathon and retreated to Asia Minor. Though Darius made careful preparations for

---

3. Whom did the angel support "in the first year of Darius the Mede"?
4, 5. Who were the foretold four kings of Persia?

a further campaign against Greece, he could not carry it out before his death four years later. That was left up to his son and successor, the "fourth" king, Xerxes I. He was the King Ahasuerus who married Esther.—Esther 1:1; 2:15-17.

⁶ Xerxes I did indeed "rouse up everything against the kingdom of Greece," that is, the independent Grecian states as a group. "Urged on by ambitious courtiers," says the book *The Medes and Persians—Conquerors and Diplomats,* "Xerxes launched an assault by land and sea." Greek historian Herodotus, of the fifth century B.C.E., writes that "no other expedition compared to this seems of any account." His record states that the sea force "amounted in all to 517,610 men. The number of the foot soldiers was 1,700,000; that of the horsemen 80,000; to which must be added the Arabs who rode on camels, and the Libyans who fought in chariots, whom I reckon at 20,000. The whole number, therefore, of the land and sea forces added together amounts to 2,317,610 men."

⁷ Planning on nothing less than a complete conquest, Xerxes I moved his huge force against Greece in 480 B.C.E. Overcoming a Greek delaying action at Thermopylae, the Persians ravaged Athens. At Salamis, though, they met with terrible defeat. Another Greek victory took place at Plataea, in 479 B.C.E. None of the seven kings who succeeded Xerxes on the throne of the Persian Empire during the next 143 years carried war into Greece. But then there arose a mighty king in Greece.

A GREAT KINGDOM DIVIDED INTO FOUR

⁸ "A mighty king will certainly stand up and rule with

6, 7. (a) How did the fourth king "rouse up everything against the kingdom of Greece"? (b) What was the result of Xerxes' campaign against Greece?
8. What "mighty king" stood up, and how did he come to "rule with extensive dominion"?

extensive dominion and do according to his will," said the angel. (Daniel 11:3) Twenty-year-old Alexander 'stood up' as king of Macedonia in 336 B.C.E. He did become "a mighty king"—Alexander the Great. Driven by a plan of his father, Philip II, he took the Persian provinces in the Middle East. Crossing the Euphrates and Tigris rivers, his 47,000 men scattered the 250,000 troops of Darius III at Gaugamela. Subsequently, Darius fled and was murdered, ending the Persian dynasty. Greece now became the world power, and Alexander 'ruled with extensive dominion and did according to his will.'

⁹ Alexander's rulership over the world was to be brief, for God's angel added: "When he will have stood up, his kingdom will be broken and be divided toward the four winds of the heavens, but not to his posterity and not according to his dominion with which he had ruled; because his kingdom will be uprooted, even for others than these." (Daniel 11:4) Alexander was not quite 33 years old when sudden illness took his life in Babylon in 323 B.C.E.

¹⁰ Alexander's vast empire did not pass to "his posterity." His brother Philip III Arrhidaeus reigned for less than seven years and was murdered at the instance of Olympias, Alexander's mother, in 317 B.C.E. Alexander's son Alexander IV ruled until 311 B.C.E. when he met death at the hands of Cassander, one of his father's generals. Alexander's illegitimate son Heracles sought to rule in his father's name but was murdered in 309 B.C.E. Thus ended the line of Alexander, "his dominion" departing from his family.

¹¹ Following the death of Alexander, his kingdom was "divided toward the four winds." His many generals quar-

---

9, 10. How did the prophecy prove true that Alexander's kingdom would not go to his posterity?
11. How was Alexander's kingdom "divided toward the four winds of the heavens"?

reled among themselves as they grabbed for territory. One-eyed General Antigonus I tried to bring all of Alexander's empire under his control. But he was killed in a battle at Ipsus in Phrygia. By the year 301 B.C.E., four of Alexander's generals were in power over the vast territory that their commander had conquered. Cassander ruled Macedonia and Greece. Lysimachus gained control over Asia Minor and Thrace. Seleucus I Nicator secured Mesopotamia and Syria. And Ptolemy Lagus took Egypt and Palestine. True to the prophetic word, Alexander's great empire was divided into four Hellenistic kingdoms.

Seleucus I Nicator

TWO RIVAL KINGS EMERGE

¹² A few years after coming to power, Cassander died, and in 285 B.C.E., Lysimachus took possession of the European part of the Greek Empire. In 281 B.C.E., Lysimachus fell in battle before Seleucus I Nicator, giving Seleucus control over the major portion of the Asiatic territories. Antigonus II Gonatas, grandson of one of Alexander's generals, ascended to the throne of Macedonia in 276 B.C.E. In time, Macedonia became dependent upon Rome and ended up as a Roman province in 146 B.C.E.

¹³ Only two of the four Hellenistic kingdoms now remained prominent—one under Seleucus I Nicator and the other under Ptolemy Lagus. Seleucus established the Seleucid dynasty in Syria. Among the cities he founded were Antioch—the new Syrian capital—and the seaport of Seleucia. The apostle Paul later taught in Antioch, where the followers of Jesus first came to be called Christians. (Acts

12, 13. (a) How were four Hellenistic kingdoms reduced to two? (b) What dynasty did Seleucus establish in Syria?

MACEDONIA

ASIA MINOR

GREECE

Ptolemy II

ISRAEL

LIBYA

EGYPT

The designations "the king
of the north" and "the king
of the south" refer to kings north
and south of the land of
Daniel's people

ETHIOPIA

11:25, 26; 13:1-4) Seleucus was assassinated in 281 B.C.E.,
but his dynasty ruled until 64 B.C.E. when Roman General Gnaeus Pompey made Syria a Roman province.

¹⁴ The Hellenistic kingdom that lasted the longest of
the four was that of Ptolemy Lagus, or Ptolemy I, who
assumed the title of king in 305 B.C.E. The Ptolemaic dynasty that he established continued to rule Egypt until it
fell to Rome in 30 B.C.E.

14. When was the Ptolemaic dynasty established in Egypt?

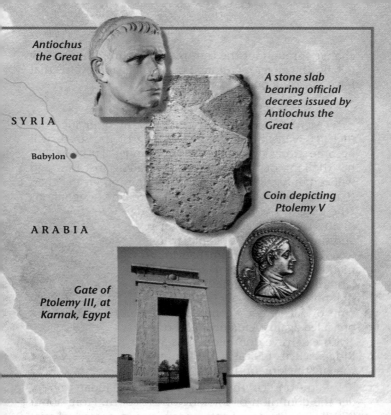

Antiochus the Great

A stone slab bearing official decrees issued by Antiochus the Great

SYRIA

Babylon

ARABIA

Coin depicting Ptolemy V

Gate of Ptolemy III, at Karnak, Egypt

15 Thus out of four Hellenistic kingdoms, there emerged two strong kings—Seleucus I Nicator over Syria and Ptolemy I over Egypt. With these two kings began the long struggle between "the king of the north" and "the king of the south," described in Daniel chapter 11. Jehovah's angel left the names of the kings unmentioned, for the identity and nationality of these two kings would

---

15. What two strong kings emerged out of the four Hellenistic kingdoms, and what struggle did they begin?

change throughout the centuries. Omitting unnecessary details, the angel mentioned only rulers and events that have a bearing on the conflict.

THE CONFLICT BEGINS

¹⁶ Listen! Describing the start of this dramatic conflict, Jehovah's angel says: "The king of the south will become strong, even one of his [Alexander's] princes; and he [the king of the north] will prevail against him and will certainly rule with extensive dominion greater than that one's ruling power." (Daniel 11:5) The designations "the king of the north" and "the king of the south" refer to kings north and south of Daniel's people, who were by then freed from Babylonian captivity and restored to the land of Judah. The initial "king of the south" was Ptolemy I of Egypt. One of Alexander's generals who prevailed against Ptolemy I and ruled "with extensive dominion" was Syrian King Seleucus I Nicator. He assumed the role of "the king of the north."

Ptolemy I

¹⁷ At the onset of the conflict, the land of Judah was under the dominion of the king of the south. From about 320 B.C.E., Ptolemy I influenced Jews to come to Egypt as colonists. A Jewish colony flourished in Alexandria, where Ptolemy I founded a famous library. The Jews in Judah remained under the control of Ptolemaic Egypt, the king of the south, until 198 B.C.E.

---

16. (a) The two kings were to the north and to the south of whom? (b) What kings first assumed the roles of "the king of the north" and "the king of the south"?
17. Under whose dominion was the land of Judah at the onset of the conflict between the king of the north and the king of the south?

¹⁸ Concerning the two kings, the angel prophesied: "At the end of some years they will ally themselves with each other, and the very daughter of the king of the south will come to the king of the north in order to make an equitable arrangement. But she will not retain the power of her arm; and he will not stand, neither his arm; and she will be given up, she herself, and those bringing her in, and he who caused her birth, and the one making her strong in those times." (Daniel 11:6) How did this come to be?

¹⁹ The prophecy did not take note of Seleucus I Nicator's son and successor, Antiochus I, because he did not wage a decisive war against the king of the south. But his successor, Antiochus II, fought a long war against Ptolemy II, the son of Ptolemy I. Antiochus II and Ptolemy II respectively constituted the king of the north and the king of the south. Antiochus II was married to Laodice, and they had a son named Seleucus II, whereas Ptolemy II had a daughter named Berenice. In 250 B.C.E., these two kings entered into "an equitable arrangement." To pay the price of this alliance, Antiochus II divorced his wife Laodice and married Berenice, "the very daughter of the king of the south." By Berenice, he had a son who became heir to the Syrian throne instead of the sons of Laodice.

²⁰ Berenice's "arm," or supporting power, was her father, Ptolemy II. When he died in 246 B.C.E., she did not "retain the power of her arm" with her husband. Antiochus II rejected her, remarried Laodice, and named their son to be his successor. As Laodice planned, Berenice and her son were murdered. Evidently, the attendants who had brought Berenice from Egypt to Syria

18, 19. In the course of time, how did the two rival kings enter into "an equitable arrangement"?
20. (a) How did Berenice's "arm" not stand? (b) How were Berenice, "those bringing her in," and "the one making her strong" given up? (c) Who became the Syrian king after Antiochus II lost "his arm," or power?

—"those bringing her in"—suffered the same end. Laodice even poisoned Antiochus II, and thus "his arm," or power, also did "not stand." Hence, Berenice's father—"he who caused her birth"—and her Syrian husband—who had temporarily made her "strong"—both died. This left Seleucus II, the son of Laodice, as Syrian king. How would the next Ptolemaic king react to all of this?

A KING AVENGES HIS SISTER'S MURDER

²¹ "One from the sprout of her roots will certainly stand up in his position," said the angel, "and he will come to the military force and come against the fortress of the king of the north and will certainly act against them and prevail." (Daniel 11:7) "One from the sprout" of Berenice's parents, or "roots," was her brother. At his father's death, he 'stood up' as the king of the south, the Egyptian Pharaoh Ptolemy III. At once he set out to avenge his sister's murder. Marching against Syrian King Seleucus II, who Laodice had used to murder Berenice and her son, he came against "the fortress of the king of the north." Ptolemy III took the fortified part of Antioch and dealt a deathblow to Laodice. Moving eastward through the domain of the king of the north, he plundered Babylonia and marched on to India.

²² What happened next? God's angel tells us: "And also with their gods, with their molten images, with their desirable articles of silver and of gold, and with the captives he will come to Egypt. And he himself will for some years stand off from the king of the north." (Daniel 11:8) Over 200 years earlier, Persian King Cambyses II had conquered Egypt and carried home Egyptian gods, "their mol-

---

21. (a) Who was "one from the sprout" of Berenice's "roots," and how did he "stand up"? (b) How did Ptolemy III "come against the fortress of the king of the north" and prevail against him?
22. What did Ptolemy III bring back to Egypt, and why did he "for some years stand off from the king of the north"?

ten images." Plundering Persia's former royal capital Susa, Ptolemy III recovered these gods and took them 'captive' to Egypt. He also brought back as spoils of war a great many "desirable articles of silver and of gold." Obliged to quell revolt at home, Ptolemy III 'stood off from the king of the north,' inflicting no further injuries upon him.

THE SYRIAN KING RETALIATES

²³ How did the king of the north react? Daniel was told: "He will actually come into the kingdom of the king of the south and go back to his own soil." (Daniel 11:9) The king of the north—Syrian King Seleucus II—struck back. He entered "the kingdom," or realm, of the Egyptian king of the south but met defeat. With only a small remnant of his army, Seleucus II 'went back to his own soil,' retreating to the Syrian capital Antioch in about 242 B.C.E. At his death, his son Seleucus III succeeded him.

²⁴ What was foretold concerning the offspring of Syrian King Seleucus II? The angel told Daniel: "Now as for his sons, they will excite themselves and actually gather together a crowd of large military forces. And in coming he will certainly come and flood over and pass through. But he will go back, and he will excite himself all the way to his fortress." (Daniel 11:10) Assassination ended the reign of Seleucus III in less than three years. His brother, Antiochus III, succeeded him on the Syrian throne. This son of Seleucus II assembled great forces for an assault on the king of the south, who was by then Ptolemy IV. The new Syrian king of the north successfully fought against Egypt and won back the seaport of Seleucia, the province of Coele-Syria, the cities of Tyre and Ptolemaïs,

---

23. Why did the king of the north "go back to his own soil" after coming into the kingdom of the king of the south?
24. (a) What happened to Seleucus III? (b) How did Syrian King Antiochus III "come and flood over and pass through" the domain of the king of the south?

and nearby towns. He routed an army of King Ptolemy IV and took many cities of Judah. In the spring of 217 B.C.E., Antiochus III left Ptolemaïs and went north, "all the way to his fortress" in Syria. But a change was in sight.

THE TIDE TURNS

²⁵ Like Daniel, we expectantly listen as Jehovah's angel next foretells: "The king of the south will embitter himself and will have to go forth and fight with him, that is, with the king of the north; and he will certainly have a large crowd stand up, and the crowd will actually be given into the hand of that one." (Daniel 11:11) With 75,000 troops, the king of the south, Ptolemy IV, moved northward against the enemy. The Syrian king of the north, Antiochus III, had raised "a large crowd" of 68,000 to stand up against him. But "the crowd" was "given into the hand" of the king of the south in battle at the coastal city of Raphia, not far from Egypt's border.

²⁶ The prophecy continues: "And the crowd will certainly be carried away. His heart will become exalted, and he will actually cause tens of thousands to fall; but he will not use his strong position." (Daniel 11:12) Ptolemy IV, the king of the south, "carried away" 10,000 Syrian infantry and 300 cavalry into death and took 4,000 as prisoners. The kings then made a treaty whereby Antiochus III kept his Syrian seaport of Seleucia but lost Phoenicia and Coele-Syria. Over this victory, the heart of the Egyptian king of the south 'became exalted,' especially against Jehovah. Judah remained under the control

---

25. Where did Ptolemy IV meet Antiochus III in battle, and what was "given into the hand" of the Egyptian king of the south?
26. (a) What "crowd" was carried away by the king of the south at the battle at Raphia, and what were the terms of the peace treaty made there? (b) How did Ptolemy IV "not use his strong position"? (c) Who became the next king of the south?

of Ptolemy IV. However, he did not "use his strong position" to follow up his victory against the Syrian king of the north. Instead, Ptolemy IV turned to a life of debauchery, and his five-year-old son, Ptolemy V, became the next king of the south some years before the death of Antiochus III.

THE EXPLOITER RETURNS

27 Because of all his exploits, Antiochus III came to be called Antiochus the Great. Of him, the angel said: "The king of the north must return and set up a crowd larger than the first; and at the end of the times, some years, he will come, doing so with a great military force and with a great deal of goods." (Daniel 11:13) These "times" were 16 or more years after the Egyptians defeated the Syrians at Raphia. When young Ptolemy V became king of the south, Antiochus III set out with "a crowd larger than the first" to recover the territories he had lost to the Egyptian king of the south. To that end, he joined forces with Macedonian King Philip V.

28 The king of the south also had troubles within his kingdom. "In those times there will be many who will stand up against the king of the south," said the angel. (Daniel 11:14a) Many did "stand up against the king of the south." Besides facing the forces of Antiochus III and his Macedonian ally, the young king of the south faced problems at home in Egypt. Because his guardian Agathocles, who ruled in his name, dealt arrogantly with the Egyptians, many revolted. The angel added: "And the sons of the robbers belonging to your people will, for their part, be carried along to try making a vision come true;

27. How did the king of the north return "at the end of the times" to recover territory from Egypt?
28. What troubles did the young king of the south have?

and they will have to stumble." (Daniel 11:14b) Even some of Daniel's people became 'sons of robbers,' or revolutionaries. But any "vision" such Jewish men had of ending Gentile domination of their homeland was false, and they would fail, or "stumble."

29 Jehovah's angel further foretold: "The king of the north will come and throw up a siege rampart and actually capture a city with fortifications. And as for the arms of the south, they will not stand, neither the people of his picked ones; and there will be no power to keep standing. And the one coming against him will do according to his will, and there will be no one standing before him. And he will stand in the land of the Decoration, and there will be extermination in his hand."—Daniel 11:15, 16.

30 Military forces under Ptolemy V, or "arms of the south," succumbed to assault from the north. At Paneas (Caesarea Philippi), Antiochus III drove Egypt's General Scopas and 10,000 select men, or "picked ones," into Sidon, "a city with fortifications." There Antiochus III 'threw up a siege rampart,' taking that Phoenician seaport in 198 B.C.E. He acted "according to his will" because the forces of the Egyptian king of the south were unable to stand before him. Antiochus III then marched against Jerusalem, the capital of "the land of the Decoration," Judah. In 198 B.C.E., Jerusalem and Judah passed from domination by the Egyptian king of the south to that of the Syrian king of the north. And Antiochus III, the king of the north, began to "stand in the land of the Decoration." There was "extermination in his hand" for all opposing Jews and Egyptians. For how long would this king of the north be able to do as he pleased?

29, 30. (a) How did "the arms of the south" succumb to the assault from the north? (b) How did the king of the north come to "stand in the land of the Decoration"?

ROME CONSTRAINS THE EXPLOITER

[31] Jehovah's angel gives us this answer: "He [the king of the north] will set his face to come with the forcefulness of his entire kingdom, and there will be equitable terms with him; and he will act effectively. And as regards the daughter of womankind, it will be granted to him to bring her to ruin. And she will not stand, and she will not continue to be his."—Daniel 11:17.

[32] The king of the north, Antiochus III, "set his face" to dominate Egypt "with the forcefulness of his entire kingdom." But he ended up making "equitable terms" of peace with Ptolemy V, the king of the south. Rome's demands had caused Antiochus III to change his plan. When he and King Philip V of Macedonia leagued against the Egyptian king of tender years to take over his territories, the guardians of Ptolemy V turned to Rome for protection. Taking advantage of the opportunity to expand its sphere of influence, Rome flexed its muscles.

[33] Under compulsion by Rome, Antiochus III brought terms of peace to the king of the south. Rather than surrendering conquered territories, as Rome had demanded, Antiochus III planned to make a nominal transfer of them by having his daughter Cleopatra I—"the daughter of womankind"—marry Ptolemy V. Provinces that included Judah, "the land of the Decoration," would be given as her dowry. At the marriage in 193 B.C.E., however, the Syrian king did not let these provinces go to Ptolemy V. This was a political marriage, formed to make Egypt subject to Syria. But the scheme failed because Cleopatra I did

31, 32. Why did the king of the north end up making "equitable terms" of peace with the king of the south?

33. (a) What were the terms of peace between Antiochus III and Ptolemy V? (b) What was the purpose of the marriage between Cleopatra I and Ptolemy V, and why did the scheme fail?

"not continue to be his," for she later sided with her husband. When war broke out between Antiochus III and the Romans, Egypt took the side of Rome.

[34] Referring to the reverses of the king of the north, the angel added: "And he [Antiochus III] will turn his face back to the coastlands and will actually capture many. And a commander [Rome] will have to make the reproach from him cease for himself [Rome], so that his reproach [that from Antiochus III] will not be. He [Rome] will make it turn back upon that one. And he [Antiochus III] will turn his face back to the fortresses of his own land, and he will certainly stumble and fall, and he will not be found." —Daniel 11:18, 19.

[35] The "coastlands" were those of Macedonia, Greece, and Asia Minor. A war broke out in Greece in 192 B.C.E., and Antiochus III was induced to come to Greece. Displeased because of the Syrian king's efforts to capture additional territories there, Rome formally declared war on him. At Thermopylae he suffered a defeat at Roman hands. About a year after losing the battle of Magnesia in 190 B.C.E., he had to give up everything in Greece, Asia Minor, and in areas west of the Taurus Mountains. Rome exacted a heavy fine and established its domination over the Syrian king of the north. Driven from Greece and Asia Minor and having lost nearly all his fleet, Antiochus III 'turned his face back to the fortresses of his own land,' Syria. The Romans had 'turned back upon him his reproach against them.' Antiochus III died while trying to rob a temple at Elymaïs, Persia, in 187 B.C.E. He thus 'fell' in death and was succeeded by his son Seleucus IV, the next king of the north.

34, 35. (a) To what "coastlands" did the king of the north turn his face? (b) How did Rome bring an end to "the reproach" from the king of the north? (c) How did Antiochus III die, and who came to be the next king of the north?

THE CONFLICT CONTINUES

[36] As the king of the south, Ptolemy V tried to gain the provinces that should have come to him as Cleopatra's dowry, but poison ended his efforts. He was succeeded by Ptolemy VI. What about Seleucus IV? In need of money to pay the heavy fine owed to Rome, he sent his treasurer Heliodorus to seize riches said to be stored in Jerusalem's temple. Desiring the throne, Heliodorus murdered Seleucus IV. However, King Eumenes of Pergamum and his brother Attalus had the slain king's brother Antiochus IV enthroned.

[37] The new king of the north, Antiochus IV, sought to show himself mightier than God by trying to eradicate Jehovah's arrangement of worship. Defying Jehovah, he dedicated Jerusalem's temple to Zeus, or Jupiter. In December 167 B.C.E., a pagan altar was erected on top of the great altar in the temple courtyard where a daily burnt offering had been made to Jehovah. Ten days later, a sacrifice to Zeus was offered on the pagan altar. This desecration led to a Jewish uprising under the Maccabees. Antiochus IV battled them for three years. In 164 B.C.E., on the anniversary of the desecration, Judas Maccabaeus rededicated the temple to Jehovah and the festival of dedication—Hanukkah—was instituted.—John 10:22.

[38] The Maccabees probably made a treaty with Rome in 161 B.C.E. and established a kingdom in 104 B.C.E. But the friction between them and the Syrian king of the north continued. Finally, Rome was called upon to intervene.

---

36. (a) How did the king of the south try to continue the struggle, but what became of him? (b) How did Seleucus IV fall, and who succeeded him?
37. (a) How did Antiochus IV try to show himself mightier than Jehovah God? (b) To what did the desecration of the temple in Jerusalem by Antiochus IV lead?
38. How did Maccabean rule come to an end?

KINGS IN DANIEL 11:5-19

	The King of the North	The King of the South
Daniel 11:5	Seleucus I Nicator	Ptolemy I
Daniel 11:6	Antiochus II (wife Laodice)	Ptolemy II (daughter Berenice)
Daniel 11:7-9	Seleucus II	Ptolemy III
Daniel 11:10-12	Antiochus III	Ptolemy IV
Daniel 11:13-19	Antiochus III (daughter Cleopatra I) Successors: Seleucus IV and Antiochus IV	Ptolemy V Successor: Ptolemy VI

Coin portraying Ptolemy II and his wife

Seleucus I Nicator

Antiochus III

Ptolemy VI

Ptolemy III and his successors built this temple of Horus at Idfu, Upper Egypt

The Roman General Gnaeus Pompey took Jerusalem in 63 B.C.E. after a three-month siege. In 39 B.C.E., the Roman Senate appointed Herod—an Edomite—to be king of Judea. Ending the Maccabean rule, he took Jerusalem in 37 B.C.E.

³⁹ How thrilling it is to see the first part of the prophecy of the two kings in conflict fulfilled in detail! Indeed, how exciting to peer into the history of some 500 years after the prophetic message was delivered to Daniel and identify the rulers occupying the positions of the king of the north and the king of the south! However, the political identities of these two kings change as the battle between them continues through the time when Jesus Christ walked the earth and down into our day. By matching historical developments with intriguing details revealed in this prophecy, we will be able to identify these two contending kings.

39. How have you benefited from considering Daniel 11:1-19?

WHAT DID YOU DISCERN?

- What two lines of strong kings emerged out of Hellenistic kingdoms, and what struggle did the kings begin?

- As foretold at Daniel 11:6, how did the two kings enter into "an equitable arrangement"?

- How did the conflict continue between
  Seleucus II and Ptolemy III (Daniel 11:7-9)?
  Antiochus III and Ptolemy IV (Daniel 11:10-12)?
  Antiochus III and Ptolemy V (Daniel 11:13-16)?

- What was the purpose of the marriage between Cleopatra I and Ptolemy V, and why did the scheme fail (Daniel 11:17-19)?

- How has paying attention to Daniel 11:1-19 benefited you?

CHAPTER FOURTEEN

THE TWO KINGS
CHANGE IDENTITIES

SYRIAN monarch Antiochus IV invades Egypt and crowns himself its king. At the request of Egyptian King Ptolemy VI, Rome sends Ambassador Caius Popilius Laenas to Egypt. He has with him an impressive fleet and orders from the Roman Senate that Antiochus IV renounce his kingship of Egypt and withdraw from the country. At Eleusis, a suburb of Alexandria, the Syrian king and the Roman ambassador come face-to-face. Antiochus IV requests time for consultation with his advisers, but Laenas draws a circle around the king and tells him to answer before stepping across the line. Humiliated, Antiochus IV complies with Roman demands and returns to Syria in 168 B.C.E. Thus ends the confrontation between the Syrian king of the north and the Egyptian king of the south.

[2] Playing a dominant role in the affairs of the Middle East, Rome goes on dictating to Syria. Hence, even though other kings of the Seleucid dynasty rule Syria after Antiochus IV dies in 163 B.C.E., they do not occupy the position of "the king of the north." (Daniel 11:15) Syria finally becomes a Roman province in 64 B.C.E.

[3] Egypt's Ptolemaic dynasty continues to hold the position of "king of the south" for a little over 130 years after the death of Antiochus IV. (Daniel 11:14) During the battle of Actium, in 31 B.C.E., Roman ruler Octavian

---

1, 2. (a) What led Antiochus IV to bow to Rome's demands? (b) When did Syria become a Roman province?
3. When and how did Rome gain supremacy over Egypt?

defeats the combined forces of the last Ptolemaic queen —Cleopatra VII—and her Roman lover, Mark Antony. After Cleopatra's suicide the following year, Egypt too becomes a Roman province and no longer plays the role of the king of the south. By the year 30 B.C.E., Rome has supremacy over both Syria and Egypt. Should we now expect other rulerships to assume the roles of the king of the north and the king of the south?

A NEW KING SENDS OUT "AN EXACTOR"

⁴ In the spring of 33 C.E., Jesus Christ told his disciples: "When you catch sight of the disgusting thing that causes desolation, as spoken of through Daniel the prophet, standing in a holy place, . . . then let those in Judea begin fleeing to the mountains." (Matthew 24:15, 16) Quoting from Daniel 11:31, Jesus warned his followers about a future 'disgusting thing causing desolation.' This prophecy involving the king of the north was given some 195 years after the death of Antiochus IV, the last Syrian king in that role. Surely, another ruling entity would have to assume the identity of the king of the north. Who would that be?

⁵ Jehovah God's angel foretold: "There must stand up in his position [that of Antiochus IV] one who is causing an exactor to pass through the splendid kingdom, and in a few days he will be broken, but not in anger nor in warfare." (Daniel 11:20) The one 'standing up' in this way proved to be the first Roman emperor, Octavian, who was known as Caesar Augustus.—See "One Honored, the Other Despised," on page 248.

---

4. Why should we expect another ruling entity to assume the identity of the king of the north?
5. Who stood up as the king of the north, taking the position once occupied by Antiochus IV?

⁶ "The splendid kingdom" of Augustus included "the land of the Decoration"—the Roman province of Judea. (Daniel 11: 16) In 2 B.C.E., Augustus sent out "an exactor" by ordering a registration, or census, probably so that he could learn the number of the population for purposes of taxation and military conscription. Because of this decree, Joseph and Mary traveled to Bethlehem for registration, resulting in Jesus' birth at that foretold location. (Micah 5:2; Matthew

Augustus

2:1-12) In August 14 C.E.—"in a few days," or not long after decreeing the registration—Augustus died at the age of 76, neither "in anger" at an assassin's hands nor "in warfare," but as a result of illness. The king of the north had indeed changed identity! This king had by now become the Roman Empire in the person of its emperors.

'THE DESPISED ONE STANDS UP'

⁷ Continuing with the prophecy, the angel said: "There must stand up in his [Augustus'] position one who is to be despised, and they will certainly not set upon him the dignity of the kingdom; and he will actually come in

---

6. (a) When was "an exactor" caused to pass through "the splendid kingdom," and what was the importance of this? (b) Why can it be said that Augustus died "not in anger nor in warfare"? (c) What change took place in the identity of the king of the north?
7, 8. (a) Who stood up in Augustus' position as the king of the north? (b) Why was "the dignity of the kingdom" unwillingly bestowed upon the successor of Augustus Caesar?

Tiberius

during a freedom from care and take hold of the kingdom by means of smoothness. And as regards the arms of the flood, they will be flooded over on account of him, and they will be broken; as will also the Leader of the covenant."—Daniel 11: 21, 22.

⁸ The "one who is to be despised" was Tiberius Caesar, the son of Livia, Augustus' third wife. (See "One Honored, the Other Despised," on page 248.) Augustus hated this stepson because of his bad traits and did not want him to become the next Caesar. "The dignity of the kingdom" was unwillingly bestowed upon him only after all other likely successors were dead. Augustus adopted Tiberius in 4 C.E. and made him heir to the throne. After the death of Augustus, 54-year-old Tiberius—the despised one—'stood up,' assuming power as the Roman emperor and the king of the north.

⁹ "Tiberius," says *The New Encyclopædia Britannica*, "played politics with the Senate and did not allow it to name him emperor for almost a month [after Augustus died]." He told the Senate that no one but Augustus was capable of carrying the burden of ruling the Roman Empire and asked the senators to restore the republic by entrusting such authority to a group of men rather than

---

9. How did Tiberius "take hold of the kingdom by means of smoothness"?

Because of Augustus' decree, Joseph and Mary traveled to Bethlehem

to one man. "Not daring to take him at his word," wrote historian Will Durant, "the Senate exchanged bows with him until at last he accepted power." Durant added: "The play was well acted on both sides. Tiberius wanted the principate, or he would have found some way to evade it; the Senate feared and hated him, but shrank from re-establishing a republic based, like the old, upon theoretically sovereign assemblies." Thus Tiberius 'took hold of the kingdom by means of smoothness.'

[10] "As regards the arms of the flood"—the military forces of the surrounding kingdoms—the angel said: 'They will be flooded over and will be broken.' When Tiberius became the king of the north, his nephew Germanicus Caesar was commander of the Roman troops on the Rhine River. In 15 C.E., Germanicus led his forces against the German hero Arminius, with some success. However, the limited victories were won at great cost, and Tiberius thereafter aborted operations in Germany. Instead, by promoting civil war, he tried to prevent German tribes from uniting. Tiberius generally favored a defensive foreign policy and focused on strengthening the frontiers. This stance was fairly successful. In this way "the arms of the flood" were controlled and were "broken."

[11] "Broken" too was "the Leader of the covenant" that Jehovah God had made with Abraham for blessing all the families of the earth. Jesus Christ was the Seed of Abraham promised in that covenant. (Genesis 22:18; Galatians 3:16) On Nisan 14, 33 C.E., Jesus stood before Pontius Pilate in the Roman governor's palace in Jerusalem. The Jewish priests had charged Jesus with treason against the

---

10. How were 'the arms of the flood broken'?
11. How was 'the Leader of the covenant broken'?

As foretold, Jesus was "broken" in death

emperor. But Jesus told Pilate: "My kingdom is no part of this world. . . . My kingdom is not from this source." So that the Roman governor might not free the faultless Jesus, the Jews shouted: "If you release this man, you are not a friend of Caesar. Every man making himself a king speaks against Caesar." After calling for Jesus' execution, they said: "We have no king but Caesar." According to the law of "injured majesty," which Tiberius had broadened to include virtually any insult to Caesar, Pilate handed Jesus over to be "broken," or impaled on a torture stake. —John 18:36; 19:12-16; Mark 15:14-20.

A TYRANT 'SCHEMES OUT HIS SCHEMES'

12 Still prophesying about Tiberius, the angel said: "Because of their allying themselves with him he will carry on deception and actually come up and become mighty by means of a little nation." (Daniel 11:23) Members of the Roman Senate had constitutionally 'allied themselves' with Tiberius, and he formally depended upon them. But he was deceptive, actually becoming "mighty by means of a little nation." That little nation was the Roman Praetorian Guard, encamped close to Rome's walls. Its proximity intimidated the Senate and helped Tiberius keep in check any uprisings against his authority among the populace. By means of some 10,000 guards, therefore, Tiberius remained mighty.

13 The angel added prophetically: "During freedom from care, even into the fatness of the jurisdictional district he will enter in and actually do what his fathers and the fathers of his fathers have not done. Plunder and spoil and goods he will scatter among them; and against forti-

---

12. (a) Who allied themselves with Tiberius? (b) How did Tiberius "become mighty by means of a little nation"?
13. In what way did Tiberius exceed his forefathers?

fied places he will scheme out his schemes, but only until a time." (Daniel 11:24) Tiberius was extremely suspicious, and his reign abounded with ordered killings. Largely because of the influence of Sejanus, commander of the Praetorian Guard, the latter part of his reign was marked by terror. Finally, Sejanus himself fell under suspicion and was executed. In tyrannizing over people, Tiberius exceeded his forefathers.

[14] Tiberius, however, scattered "plunder and spoil and goods" throughout the Roman provinces. By the time of his death, all the subject peoples were enjoying prosperity. Taxes were light, and he could be generous to those in areas undergoing hard times. If soldiers or officials oppressed anyone or promoted irregularity in handling matters, they could expect imperial vengeance. A firm grip on power maintained public security, and an improved communications system helped commerce. Tiberius made sure that affairs were administered fairly and steadily inside and outside Rome. The laws were improved, and social and moral codes were enhanced by the furthering of reforms instituted by Augustus Caesar. Yet, Tiberius 'schemed out his schemes,' so that Roman historian Tacitus described him as a hypocritical man, skilled at putting on false appearances. By the time he died in March 37 C.E., Tiberius was considered to be a tyrant.

[15] The successors to Tiberius who filled the role of the king of the north included Gaius Caesar (Caligula), Claudius I, Nero, Vespasian, Titus, Domitian, Nerva, Trajan, and Hadrian. "For the most part," says *The New Encyclopædia Britannica,* "the successors to Augustus continued

---

14. (a) How did Tiberius scatter "plunder and spoil and goods" throughout the Roman provinces? (b) In what way was Tiberius regarded by the time he died?
15. How did Rome fare in the late first and early second centuries C.E.?

his administrative policies and building program, though with less innovation and more ostentation." The same reference work further points out: "In the late 1st and early 2nd centuries Rome was at the peak of its grandeur and population." Although Rome had some trouble on the imperial frontiers during this time, its first foretold confrontation with the king of the south did not occur until the third century C.E.

AROUSED AGAINST THE KING OF THE SOUTH

[16] God's angel continued with the prophecy, saying: "He [the king of the north] will arouse his power and his heart against the king of the south with a great military force; and the king of the south, for his part, will excite himself for the war with an exceedingly great and mighty military force. And he [the king of the north] will not stand, because they will scheme out against him schemes. And the very ones eating his delicacies will bring his breakdown. And as for his military force, it will be flooded away, and many will certainly fall down slain."—Daniel 11:25, 26.

[17] About 300 years after Octavian had made Egypt a Roman province, Roman Emperor Aurelian assumed the role of the king of the north. Meanwhile, Queen Septimia Zenobia of the Roman colony of Palmyra occupied the position of the king of the south.* (See "Zenobia—The Warrior Queen of Palmyra," on page 252.) The Palmy-

---

* Since the designations "the king of the north" and "the king of the south" are titles, they can refer to any ruling entity, including a king, a queen, or a bloc of nations.

16, 17. (a) Who took on the role of the king of the north referred to at Daniel 11:25? (b) Who came to occupy the position of the king of the south, and how did this occur?

rene army occupied Egypt in 269 C.E. under the pretext of making it secure for Rome. Zenobia wanted to make Palmyra the dominant city in the east and wanted to rule over Rome's eastern provinces. Alarmed by her ambition, Aurelian aroused "his power and his heart" to proceed against Zenobia.

[18] As the ruling entity headed by Zenobia, the king of the south 'excited himself' for warfare against the king of the north "with an exceedingly great and mighty military force" under two generals, Zabdas and Zabbai. But Aurelian took Egypt and then launched an expedition into Asia Minor and Syria. Zenobia was defeated at Emesa (now Homs), whereupon she retreated to Palmyra. When Aurelian besieged that city, Zenobia valiantly defended it but without success. She and her son fled toward Persia, only to be captured by the Romans at the Euphrates River. The Palmyrenes surrendered their city in 272 C.E. Aurelian spared Zenobia, making her the prize feature in his triumphal procession through Rome in 274 C.E. She spent the rest of her life as a Roman matron.

[19] Aurelian himself 'did not stand because of schemes against him.' In 275 C.E., he set out on an expedition against the Persians. While he was waiting in Thrace for the opportunity to cross the straits into Asia Minor, those who 'ate his food' carried out schemes against him and brought about his "breakdown." He was going to call his secretary Eros to account for irregularities. Eros, however, forged a list of names of certain officers marked for death. The sight of this list moved the officers to plot Aurelian's assassination and to murder him.

---

18. What was the outcome of the conflict between Emperor Aurelian, the king of the north, and Queen Zenobia, the king of the south?
19. How did Aurelian fall 'because of schemes against him'?

²⁰ The career of the king of the north did not end with the death of Emperor Aurelian. Other Roman rulers followed. For a time, there was an emperor of the west and one of the east. Under these men the "military force" of the king of the north was "flooded away," or "scattered,"* and many 'fell down slain' because of the invasions of the Germanic tribes from the north. Goths broke through the Roman frontiers in the fourth century C.E. Invasions continued, one after the other. In 476 C.E., German leader Odoacer removed the last emperor ruling from Rome. By the beginning of the sixth century, the Roman Empire in the west had been shattered, and German kings ruled in Britannia, Gaul, Italy, North Africa, and Spain. The eastern part of the empire lasted into the 15th century.

A GREAT EMPIRE IS DIVIDED

²¹ Without giving unnecessary details about the breakdown of the Roman Empire, which stretched over centuries, Jehovah's angel went on to foretell further exploits of the king of the north and the king of the south. However, a brief review of certain developments in the Roman Empire will help us to identify the two rival kings in later times.

²² In the fourth century, Roman Emperor Constantine gave State recognition to apostate Christianity. He even called and personally presided over a church council at Nicaea, Asia Minor, in 325 C.E. Later, Constantine moved the imperial residence from Rome to Byzantium, or Con-

---

* See the footnote on Daniel 11:26 in the *New World Translation of the Holy Scriptures—With References,* published by the Watchtower Bible and Tract Society of New York, Inc.

---

20. How was the "military force" of the king of the north "flooded away"?
21, 22. What changes did Constantine bring about in the fourth century C.E.?

stantinople, making that city his new capital. The Roman Empire continued under the rulership of a single emperor until the death of Emperor Theodosius I, on January 17, 395 C.E.

[23] Following the death of Theodosius, the Roman Empire was divided between his sons. Honorius received the western part, and Arcadius the eastern, with Constantinople as his capital. Britannia, Gaul, Italy, Spain, and North Africa were among the provinces of the western division. Macedonia, Thrace, Asia Minor, Syria, and Egypt were provinces of the eastern division. In 642 C.E., the Egyptian capital, Alexandria, fell to the Saracens (Arabs), and Egypt became a province of the caliphs. In January 1449, Constantine XI became the last emperor of the east. Ottoman Turks under Sultan Mehmed II took Constantinople on May 29, 1453, ending the Eastern Roman Empire. The year 1517 saw Egypt become a Turkish province. In time, though, this land of the ancient king of the south would come under the control of another empire from the western sector.

[24] In the western wing of the Roman Empire arose the Catholic bishop of Rome, notably Pope Leo I, who was renowned for asserting papal authority in the fifth century C.E. In time, the pope took it upon himself to crown the emperor of the western section. This occurred in Rome on Christmas day of 800 C.E., when Pope Leo III crowned Frankish King Charles (Charlemagne) emperor of the new Western Roman Empire. This coronation revived the emperorship in Rome and, according to some

---

23. (a) What division of the Roman Empire took place after the death of Theodosius? (b) When did the Eastern Empire come to an end? (c) Who ruled Egypt by 1517?

24, 25. (a) According to some historians, what marked the beginning of the Holy Roman Empire? (b) What finally happened to the title of "emperor" of the Holy Roman Empire?

historians, marked the beginning of the Holy Roman Empire. From then on there existed the Eastern Empire and the Holy Roman Empire to the west, both claiming to be Christian.

[25] As time passed, the successors of Charlemagne proved to be ineffectual rulers. The office of the emperor even lay vacant for a time. Meanwhile, German King Otto I had gained control of much of northern and central Italy. He proclaimed himself king of Italy. On February 2, 962 C.E., Pope John XII crowned Otto I emperor of the Holy Roman Empire. Its capital was in Germany, and the emperors were Germans, as were most of their subjects. Five centuries later the Austrian house of Hapsburg obtained the title of "emperor" and held it for most of the remaining years of the Holy Roman Empire.

THE TWO KINGS AGAIN IN CLEAR FOCUS

[26] Napoléon I delivered a deathblow to the Holy Roman Empire when he refused to recognize its existence following his victories in Germany during the year 1805. Unable to defend the crown, Emperor Francis II resigned from Roman imperial status on August 6, 1806, and withdrew to his national government as emperor of Austria. After 1,006 years, the Holy Roman Empire—founded by Leo III, a Roman Catholic pope, and Charlemagne, a Frankish king—came to an end. In 1870, Rome became the capital of the kingdom of Italy, independent of the Vatican. The following year, a Germanic empire began with Wilhelm I being named caesar, or kaiser. Thus the modern-day king of the north—Germany—was on the world scene.

---

26. (a) What can be said about the end of the Holy Roman Empire? (b) Who emerged as the king of the north?

1. Charlemagne   2. Napoléon I   3. Wilhelm I
4. German soldiers, World War I

KINGS IN DANIEL 11:20-26

	The King of the North	The King of the South
Daniel 11:20	Augustus	
Daniel 11:21-24	Tiberius	
Daniel 11:25, 26	Aurelian	Queen Zenobia
The foretold breakdown of the Roman Empire leads to the formation of	The Germanic Empire	Britain, followed by the Anglo-American World Power

Tiberius

Aurelian

Statuette of Charlemagne

17th-century British warship

Augustus

²⁷ But what was the identity of the modern-day king of the south? History shows that Great Britain took on imperial power in the 17th century. Wanting to disrupt British trade routes, Napoléon I conquered Egypt in 1798. War ensued, and a British-Ottoman alliance forced the French to withdraw from Egypt, identified as the king of the south at the onset of the conflict. During the following century, British influence in Egypt increased. After 1882, Egypt was actually a British dependency. When World War I broke out in 1914, Egypt belonged to Turkey and was ruled by a khedive, or viceroy. After Turkey sided with Germany in that war, however, Britain deposed the khedive and declared Egypt a British protectorate. Gradually forming close ties, Britain and the United States of America became the Anglo-American World Power. Together, they came into the position of the king of the south.

---

27. (a) How did Egypt become a British protectorate? (b) Who came into the position of the king of the south?

WHAT DID YOU DISCERN?

- Which Roman emperor first stood up as the king of the north, and when did he send out "an exactor"?

- Who took the position of the king of the north after Augustus, and how was 'the Leader of the covenant broken'?

- What was the outcome of the conflict between Aurelian as the king of the north and Zenobia as the king of the south?

- What became of the Roman Empire, and which powers occupied the positions of the two kings by the end of the 19th century?

ONE HONORED,
THE OTHER DESPISED
◆

ONE transformed a strife-ridden republic into a world empire. The other increased its wealth twentyfold in 23 years. One was honored when he died, but the other was despised. The reigns of these two emperors of Rome spanned Jesus' life and ministry. Who were they? And why was one honored, whereas the other was not?

HE "FOUND ROME BRICK AND LEFT IT MARBLE"

In 44 B.C.E. when Julius Caesar was assassinated, his sister's grandson Gaius Octavian was only 18 years of age. Being an adopted son of Julius Caesar and his chief personal heir, young Octavian immediately set out for Rome to claim his inheritance. There he encountered a formidable opponent—Caesar's chief lieutenant, Mark Antony, who expected to be the principal heir. The political intrigue and power struggle that followed lasted 13 years.

Only after defeating the combined forces of Egyptian Queen Cleopatra and her lover Mark Antony (in 31 B.C.E.) did Octavian emerge as the undisputed ruler of the Roman Empire. The following year Antony and Cleopatra committed suicide, and Octavian annexed Egypt. The last vestige of the Grecian Empire was thus removed, and Rome became the world power.

Remembering that Julius Caesar's exercise of despotic power had led to his assassination, Octavian was careful not to repeat the mistake. So as not to offend Roman sentiments favoring a republic, he disguised his monarchy under a republican garment. He declined the titles "king" and "dictator." Going a step further, he announced his intention to turn over the control of all provinces to the Roman Senate and offered to resign from the offices he held. This tactic worked. The appreciative Senate urged Octavian to retain his positions and keep control of some of the provinces.

Additionally, on January 16, 27 B.C.E., the Senate bestowed upon Octavian the title "Augustus," meaning "Exalted, Sacred." Octavian not only accepted the title but also renamed a month for himself and borrowed a day from February so that August would have as many days as July, the month named after Julius Caesar. Octavian thus became the first emperor of Rome and was thereafter known as Caesar Augustus or "August One." Later he also assumed the title "pontifex maximus" (high priest), and in 2 B.C.E.—the year of Jesus' birth—the Senate gave him the title *Pater Patriae*, "Father of His Country."

In that same year, "a decree went forth from Caesar Augustus for all the inhabited earth to be registered; . . . and all people went traveling to be registered, each one to his own city." (Luke 2:1-3) As a result of this decree, Jesus was born in Bethlehem in fulfillment of Bible prophecy.—Daniel 11:20; Micah 5:2.

The government under Augustus was marked by a measure of honesty and a sound currency. Augustus also established an effective postal system and constructed roads and bridges. He reorganized the army, created a permanent navy, and established an elite band of imperial bodyguards known as the Praetorian Guard. (Philippians 1:13) Under his patronage, such writers as Virgil and Horace flourished and sculptors created beautiful works in what is now called the classical style. Augustus completed buildings left unfinished by Julius Caesar and restored many temples. The *Pax Romana* ("Roman Peace") that he introduced lasted more than 200 years. On August 19, 14 C.E., at the age of 76, Augustus died and was deified thereafter.

Augustus boasted that he had "found Rome brick and left it marble." Not wanting Rome to revert to the strife-filled days of the former republic, he intended to groom the next emperor. But he had little choice regarding a successor. His nephew, two grandsons, a son-in-law, and a stepson had all died, leaving only his stepson Tiberius to take over.

THE "ONE WHO IS TO BE DESPISED"

Less than a month after Augustus' death, the Roman Senate named 54-year-old Tiberius emperor. Tiberius lived and ruled until March 37 C.E. Hence, he was the emperor of Rome for the duration of Jesus' public ministry.

As an emperor, Tiberius had both virtues and vices. Among his virtues was a reluctance to spend money on luxuries. As a result, the empire prospered and he had funds to assist in recovery from disasters and bad times. To his credit, Tiberius viewed himself as but a man, declined many honorary titles, and generally directed emperor worship to Augustus rather than to himself. He did not name a calendar month after himself as Augustus and Julius Caesar had done for themselves, nor did he allow others to honor him in that way.

Tiberius' vices, however, exceeded his virtues. He was extremely suspicious and hypocritical in his dealings with others, and his reign abounded with ordered killings —many of his former friends being counted among the victims. He extended the law of lèse-majesté (injured majesty) to include, in addition to seditious acts, merely libelous words against his own person. Presumably on the strength of this law, the Jews pressured Roman Governor Pontius Pilate to have Jesus killed. —John 19:12-16.

Tiberius

Tiberius concentrated the Praetorian Guard in the proximity of Rome by constructing fortified barracks north of the walls of the city. The Guard's presence intimidated the Roman Senate, which was a threat to his power, and kept any unruliness of the people in check. Tiberius also encouraged the informer system, and terror marked the latter part of his rule.

At the time of his death, Tiberius was considered to be a tyrant. When he died, the Romans rejoiced and the Senate refused to deify him. For these reasons and others, we see in Tiberius a fulfillment of the prophecy saying that "one who is to be despised" would arise as "the king of the north."—Daniel 11:15, 21.

WHAT DID YOU DISCERN?

- How did Octavian come to be the first emperor of Rome?
- What can be said about the accomplishments of the government of Augustus?
- What were the virtues and vices of Tiberius?
- How was the prophecy concerning the "one who is to be despised" fulfilled in Tiberius?

ZENOBIA—THE WARRIOR
QUEEN OF PALMYRA
◆

"SHE was of a dark complexion . . . Her teeth were of a pearly whiteness, and her large black eyes sparkled with uncommon fire, tempered by the most attractive sweetness. Her voice was strong and harmonious. Her manly understanding was strengthened and adorned by study. She was not ignorant of the Latin tongue, but possessed in equal perfection the Greek, the Syriac, and the Egyptian languages." Such were the praises that historian Edward Gibbon bestowed upon Zenobia—the warrior queen of the Syrian city of Palmyra.

Zenobia's husband was the Palmyrene noble Odaenathus, who was awarded the rank of consul of Rome in 258 C.E. because he had successfully campaigned against Persia on behalf of the Roman Empire. Two years later, Odaenathus received from Roman Emperor Gallienus the title *corrector totius Orientis* (governor of all the East). This was in recognition of his victory over King Shāpūr I of Persia. Odaenathus eventually gave himself the title "king of kings." These successes of Odaenathus may to a large extent be attributed to Zenobia's courage and prudence.

ZENOBIA ASPIRES TO CREATE AN EMPIRE
In 267 C.E., at the height of his career, Odaenathus and his heir were assassinated. Zenobia took over her husband's position, since her son was too young to do so. Beautiful, ambitious, capable as an administrator, accustomed to campaigning with her husband, and fluent in several languages, she managed to command the respect and support of her subjects. Zenobia had a love for learn-

Queen Zenobia addressing her soldiers

ing and surrounded herself with intellectuals. One of her advisers was philosopher and rhetorician Cassius Longinus —said to have been "a living library and a walking museum." In the book *Palmyra and Its Empire—Zenobia's Revolt Against Rome,* author Richard Stoneman notes: "During the five years after the death of Odenathus . . . , Zenobia had established herself in the minds of her people as mistress of the East."

On one side of Zenobia's domain was Persia, which she and her husband had crippled, and on the other was foundering Rome. Regarding conditions in the Roman Empire at that time, historian J. M. Roberts says: "The third century was . . . a terrible time for Rome on the frontiers east and west alike, while at home a new period of civil war and disputed successions had begun. Twenty-two emperors (excluding pretenders) came and went." The Syrian mistress, on the other hand, was a well-established absolute monarch in her realm. "Controlling the balance of two empires [Persian and Roman]," observes Stoneman, "she could aspire to create a third that would dominate them both."

An opportunity for Zenobia to expand her regal powers came in 269 C.E. when a pretender disputing Roman rulership appeared in Egypt. Zenobia's army swiftly marched into Egypt, crushed the rebel, and took possession of the country. Proclaiming herself queen of Egypt, she minted coins in her own name. Her kingdom now stretched from the river Nile to the river Euphrates. It was at this point in her life that Zenobia came to occupy the position of "the king of the south."—Daniel 11:25, 26.

ZENOBIA'S CAPITAL CITY

Zenobia strengthened and embellished her capital, Palmyra, to such an extent that it ranked with the larger cities of the Roman world. Its estimated population reached over 150,000. Splendid public buildings, temples, gardens, pillars, and monuments filled Palmyra, a city encircled by walls said to be 13 miles in circumference. A colonnade of Corinthian pillars over 50 feet high—some 1,500 of them—lined the principal avenue. Statues and busts of heroes and wealthy benefactors abounded in the city. In 271 C.E., Zenobia erected statues of herself and her late husband.

The Temple of the Sun was one of the finest structures in Palmyra and no doubt dominated the religious scene in the city. Zenobia herself may have worshiped a deity associated with the sun-god. Syria of the third century, however, was a land of many religions. In Zenobia's domain there were professing Christians, Jews, and worshipers of the sun and moon. What was her attitude toward these various forms of worship? Author Stoneman observes: "A wise ruler will not neglect any customs that seem appropriate to her people. . . . The gods, it was . . . hoped, had been marshaled on Palmyra's side." Apparently, Zenobia was religiously tolerant.

With her colorful personality, Zenobia won the admiration of many. Of greatest significance was her role in representing a political entity foretold in Daniel's prophecy. Her reign, however, lasted no more than five years. Roman Emperor Aurelian defeated Zenobia in 272 C.E. and subsequently sacked Palmyra beyond repair. Zenobia was granted clemency. She is said to have married a Roman senator and presumably spent the rest of her life in retirement.

WHAT DID YOU DISCERN?

- How has Zenobia's personality been described?
- What were some of the exploits of Zenobia?
- What was Zenobia's attitude toward religion?

CHAPTER FIFTEEN

THE RIVAL KINGS ENTER THE 20TH CENTURY

"THERE is a dynamism about nineteenth-century Europe that far exceeds anything previously known," writes historian Norman Davies. He adds: "Europe vibrated with power as never before: with technical power, economic power, cultural power, intercontinental power." The leaders of "Europe's triumphant 'power century,'" says Davies, "were in the first instance Great Britain . . . and in the later decades Germany."

"INCLINED TO DOING WHAT IS BAD"

² As the 19th century neared its end, the German Empire was "the king of the north" and Britain stood in the position of "the king of the south." (Daniel 11:14, 15) "As regards these two kings," said Jehovah's angel, "their heart will be inclined to doing what is bad, and at one table a lie is what they will keep speaking." He continued: "But nothing will succeed, because the end is yet for the time appointed."—Daniel 11:27.

---

1. Who does one historian say were the leaders of 19th-century Europe?
2. As the 19th century ended, what powers filled the roles of "the king of the north" and "the king of the south"?

At Yalta in 1945, British Prime Minister Winston Churchill, U.S. President Franklin D. Roosevelt, and Soviet Premier Joseph Stalin agreed on plans to occupy Germany, form a new government in Poland, and hold a conference to set up the United Nations

[3] On January 18, 1871, Wilhelm I became the first emperor of the German Reich, or Empire. He appointed Otto von Bismarck as chancellor. With his focus on developing the new empire, Bismarck avoided conflicts with other nations and formed an alliance with Austria-Hungary and Italy, known as the Triple Alliance. But the interests of this new king of the north soon clashed with those of the king of the south.

[4] After Wilhelm I and his successor, Frederick III, died in 1888, 29-year-old Wilhelm II ascended the throne. Wilhelm II, or Kaiser Wilhelm, forced Bismarck to resign and followed a policy of expanding Germany's influence throughout the world. "Under Wilhelm II," says one historian, "[Germany] assumed an arrogant and a truculent air."

[5] When Czar Nicholas II of Russia called a peace conference in The Hague, Netherlands, on August 24, 1898, the atmosphere was one of international tension. This conference and the one that followed it in 1907 established the Permanent Court of Arbitration at The Hague. By becoming members of this court, the German Reich as well as Great Britain gave the appearance that they favored peace. They sat "at one table," appearing to be friendly, but 'their hearts were inclined to do what was bad.' The diplomatic tactic of 'speaking a lie at one table' could not promote real peace. As to their political, commercial, and military ambitions, 'nothing could succeed'

3, 4. (a) Who became the first emperor of the German Reich, and what alliance was formed? (b) What policy did Kaiser Wilhelm follow? 5. How did the two kings sit "at one table," and what did they speak there?

1. Archduke Ferdinand   2. German navy   3. British navy
4. Lusitania   5. U.S. declaration of war

because the end of the two kings "is yet for the time appointed" by Jehovah God.

"AGAINST THE HOLY COVENANT"

⁶ Continuing on, God's angel said: "And he [the king of the north] will go back to his land with a great amount of goods, and his heart will be against the holy covenant. And he will act effectively and certainly go back to his land."—Daniel 11:28.

⁷ Kaiser Wilhelm went back to the "land," or earthly condition, of the ancient king of the north. How? By building up an imperial rule designed to expand the German Reich and extend its influence. Wilhelm II pursued colonial goals in Africa and other places. Wanting to challenge British supremacy at sea, he proceeded to build a powerful navy. "Germany's naval power went from being negligible to being second only to Britain's in little more than a decade," says *The New Encyclopædia Britannica.* In order to maintain its supremacy, Britain actually had to expand its own naval program. Britain also negotiated the entente cordiale (cordial understanding) with France and a similar agreement with Russia, forming the Triple Entente. Europe was now divided into two military camps—the Triple Alliance on one side and the Triple Entente on the other.

⁸ The German Empire followed an aggressive policy, resulting in "a great amount of goods" for Germany because it was the chief part of the Triple Alliance. Austria-Hungary and Italy were Roman Catholic. There-

6, 7. (a) In what way did the king of the north "go back to his land"? (b) How did the king of the south respond to the expanding influence of the king of the north?
8. How did the German Empire come to have "a great amount of goods"?

fore, the Triple Alliance also enjoyed papal favor, whereas the king of the south, with his largely non-Catholic Triple Entente, did not.

9 What about Jehovah's people? They had long declared that "the appointed times of the nations" would end in 1914.* (Luke 21:24) In that year, God's Kingdom in the hands of King David's Heir, Jesus Christ, was established in the heavens. (2 Samuel 7:12-16; Luke 22:28, 29) As far back as March 1880, the *Watch Tower* magazine linked the rule of God's Kingdom with the ending of "the appointed times of the nations," or "the times of the Gentiles." (*King James Version*) But the heart of the Germanic king of the north was 'against the holy Kingdom covenant.' Instead of acknowledging Kingdom rule, Kaiser Wilhelm 'acted effectively' by promoting his schemes for world domination. In so doing, though, he sowed the seeds for World War I.

THE KING BECOMES "DEJECTED" IN A WAR

10 "At the time appointed he [the king of the north] will go back," the angel foretold, "and he will actually come against the south; but it will not prove to be at the last the same as at the first." (Daniel 11:29) God's "time appointed" to end Gentile domination of the earth came in 1914 when he set up the heavenly Kingdom. On June 28 of that year, Austrian Archduke Francis Ferdinand and his wife were assassinated by a Serbian terrorist in Sarajevo, Bosnia. That was the spark that touched off World War I.

---

* See Chapter 6 of this book.

---

9. How was the king of the north "against the holy covenant" at heart?
10, 11. How did World War I start, and how was this "at the time appointed"?

¹¹ Kaiser Wilhelm urged Austria-Hungary to retaliate against Serbia. Assured of German support, Austria-Hungary declared war on Serbia on July 28, 1914. But Russia came to Serbia's aid. When Germany declared war on Russia, France (an ally in the Triple Entente) gave support to Russia. Germany then declared war on France. To make Paris more readily accessible, Germany invaded Belgium, whose neutrality had been guaranteed by Britain. So Britain declared war on Germany. Other nations became involved, and Italy switched sides. During the war, Britain made Egypt her protectorate in order to prevent the king of the north from cutting off the Suez Canal and invading Egypt, the ancient land of the king of the south.

¹² "Despite the size and strength of the Allies," says *The World Book Encyclopedia,* "Germany seemed close to winning the war." In previous conflicts between the two kings, the Roman Empire, as king of the north, had consistently been victorious. But this time, 'things were not the same as at the first.' The king of the north lost the war. Giving the reason for this, the angel said: "There will certainly come against him the ships of Kittim, and he will have to become dejected." (Daniel 11:30a) What were "the ships of Kittim"?

¹³ In Daniel's time Kittim was Cyprus. Early in the first world war, Cyprus was annexed by Britain. Moreover, according to *The Zondervan Pictorial Encyclopedia of the Bible,* the name Kittim "is extended to include the W[est]

---

12. During the first world war, in what way did things not turn out "the same as at the first"?

13, 14. (a) What mainly were "the ships of Kittim" that came up against the king of the north? (b) How did more ships of Kittim come as the first world war continued?

Adolf Hitler felt confident of victory
after Germany's wartime ally Japan bombed Pearl Harbor

in general, but esp[ecially] the seafaring W[est]." The *New International Version* renders the expression "ships of Kittim" as "ships of the western coastlands." During the first world war, the ships of Kittim proved to be mainly the ships of Britain, lying off the western coast of Europe.

¹⁴ As the war dragged on, the British Navy was strengthened by more ships of Kittim. On May 7, 1915, the German submarine *U-20* sank the civilian liner *Lusitania* off the southern coast of Ireland. Among the dead were 128 Americans. Later, Germany extended submarine warfare into the Atlantic. Subsequently, on April 6, 1917, U.S. President Woodrow Wilson declared war on Germany. Augmented by U.S. warships and troops, the king of the south—now the Anglo-American World Power—was fully at war with its rival king.

¹⁵ Under assault by the Anglo-American World Power, the king of the north became "dejected" and conceded defeat in November 1918. Wilhelm II fled into exile in the Netherlands, and Germany became a republic. But the king of the north was not yet finished.

THE KING ACTS "EFFECTIVELY"

¹⁶ "He [the king of the north] will actually go back and hurl denunciations against the holy covenant and act effectively; and he will have to go back and will give consideration to those leaving the holy covenant." (Daniel 11:30b) So prophesied the angel, and so it proved to be.

¹⁷ After the war ended, in 1918, the victorious Allies imposed a punitive peace treaty on Germany. The German people found the terms of the treaty harsh, and the new

---

15. When did the king of the north become "dejected"?
16. According to the prophecy, how would the king of the north react to his defeat?
17. What led to the rise of Adolf Hitler?

republic was weak from the start. Germany staggered for some years in extreme distress and experienced the Great Depression that ultimately left six million unemployed. By the early 1930's, conditions were ripe for the rise of Adolf Hitler. He became chancellor in January 1933 and the following year assumed the presidency of what the Nazis called the Third Reich.*

¹⁸ Immediately after coming to power, Hitler launched a vicious attack against "the holy covenant," represented by the anointed brothers of Jesus Christ. (Matthew 25:40) In this he acted "effectively" against these loyal Christians, cruelly persecuting many of them. Hitler enjoyed economic and diplomatic successes, acting "effectively" in those fields also. In a few years, he made Germany a power to be reckoned with on the world scene.

¹⁹ Hitler gave "consideration to those leaving the holy covenant." Who were these? Evidently, the leaders of Christendom, who claimed to have a covenant relationship with God but had ceased to be disciples of Jesus Christ. Hitler successfully called on "those leaving the holy covenant" for their support. For example, he made a concordat with the pope in Rome. In 1935, Hitler created the Ministry for Church Affairs. One of his goals was to bring Evangelical churches under state control.

THE "ARMS" PROCEED FROM THE KING

²⁰ Hitler soon went to war, as the angel had correctly

---

* The Holy Roman Empire was the first reich, and the German Empire, the second.

---

18. How did Hitler "act effectively"?
19. Seeking support, Hitler courted whom?
20. What "arms" did the king of the north utilize, and against whom?

foretold: "There will be arms that will stand up, proceeding from him; and they will actually profane the sanctuary, the fortress, and remove the constant feature." (Daniel 11:31a) The "arms" were the military forces that the king of the north used in order to fight the king of the south in World War II. On September 1, 1939, Nazi "arms" invaded Poland. Two days later, Britain and France declared war on Germany in order to help Poland. Thus began World War II. Poland collapsed quickly, and soon thereafter, German forces occupied Denmark, Norway, the Netherlands, Belgium, Luxembourg, and France. "At the end of 1941," says *The World Book Encyclopedia,* "Nazi Germany dominated the continent."

[21] Even though Germany and the Soviet Union had signed a Treaty of Friendship, Co-operation, and Demarcation, Hitler proceeded to invade Soviet territory on June 22, 1941. This action brought the Soviet Union to the side of Britain. The Soviet army put up strong resistance despite spectacular early advances of the German forces. On December 6, 1941, the German army actually suffered defeat at Moscow. The following day, Germany's ally Japan bombed Pearl Harbor, Hawaii. Learning of this, Hitler told his aides: "Now it is impossible for us to lose the war." On December 11 he rashly declared war on the United States. But he underestimated the strength of both the Soviet Union and the United States. With the Soviet army attacking from the east and British and American forces closing in from the west, the tide soon turned against Hitler. German forces began losing territory after territory. Following Hitler's suicide, Germany surrendered to the Allies, on May 7, 1945.

---

21. How did the tide turn against the king of the north during World War II, resulting in what outcome?

[22] "They [Nazi arms] will actually profane the sanctuary, the fortress, and remove the constant feature," said the angel. In ancient Judah the sanctuary was part of the temple in Jerusalem. However, when the Jews rejected Jesus, Jehovah rejected them and their temple. (Matthew 23:37–24:2) Since the first century C.E., Jehovah's temple has actually been a spiritual one, with its holy of holies in the heavens and with a spiritual courtyard on earth, in which the anointed brothers of Jesus, the High Priest, serve. From the 1930's onward, the "great crowd" have worshiped in association with the anointed remnant and are therefore said to serve 'in God's temple.' (Revelation 7:9, 15; 11:1, 2; Hebrews 9:11, 12, 24) In lands under his control, the king of the north profaned the earthly courtyard of the temple by relentlessly persecuting the anointed remnant and their companions. So severe was the persecution that "the constant feature"—the public sacrifice of praise to Jehovah's name—was removed. (Hebrews 13:15) Despite horrible suffering, however, faithful anointed Christians together with the "other sheep" kept on preaching during World War II.—John 10:16.

'THE DISGUSTING THING IS PUT IN PLACE'

[23] When the end of the second world war was in sight, another development occurred, just as God's angel had foretold. "They will certainly put in place the disgusting thing that is causing desolation." (Daniel 11:31b) Jesus had also spoken of "the disgusting thing." In the first century, it proved to be the Roman army that came to Jerusalem in 66 C.E. to put down Jewish rebellion.*
—Matthew 24:15; Daniel 9:27.

---

* See Chapter 11 of this book.

---

22. How did the king of the north 'profane the sanctuary and remove the constant feature'?
23. What was "the disgusting thing" in the first century?

KINGS IN DANIEL 11:27-31

	The King of the North	The King of the South
Daniel 11:27-30a	German Empire (World War I)	Britain, followed by the Anglo-American World Power
Daniel 11:30b, 31	Hitler's Third Reich (World War II)	Anglo-American World Power

President Woodrow Wilson with King George V

Many Christians were persecuted in concentration camps

Leaders in Christendom supported Hitler

Automobile in which Archduke Ferdinand was assassinated

German soldiers, World War I

[24] What "disgusting thing" has been "put in place" in modern times? Apparently, it is a "disgusting" counterfeit of God's Kingdom. This was the League of Nations, the scarlet-colored wild beast that went into the abyss, or ceased to exist as a world-peace organization, when World War II erupted. (Revelation 17:8) "The wild beast," however, was "to ascend out of the abyss." This it did when the United Nations, with 50 member nations including the former Soviet Union, was established on October 24, 1945. Thus "the disgusting thing" foretold by the angel—the United Nations—was put in place.

[25] Germany had been a leading enemy of the king of the south during both world wars and had occupied the position of the king of the north. Who would be next in that position?

24, 25. (a) What is "the disgusting thing" in modern times? (b) When and how was 'the disgusting thing put in place'?

WHAT DID YOU DISCERN?

- At the end of the 19th century, what powers filled the roles of the king of the north and the king of the south?

- During World War I, how did the outcome of the conflict "not prove to be at the last the same as at the first" for the king of the north?

- Following World War I, how did Hitler make Germany a power to be reckoned with on the world scene?

- What was the outcome of the rivalry between the king of the north and the king of the south during World War II?

CHAPTER SIXTEEN

THE CONTENDING KINGS NEAR THEIR END

REFLECTING on the political climate of the United States and Russia, the French philosopher and historian Alexis de Tocqueville wrote in 1835: "One has freedom as the principal means of action; the other has servitude. Their . . . paths [are] diverse; nevertheless, each seems called by some secret design of Providence one day to hold in its hands the destinies of half the world." How did this prediction fare in the wake of World War II? Historian J. M. Roberts writes: "At the end of a second World War the destinies of the world did, indeed, at last appear to be likely to be dominated by two great and very differing systems of power, one based in what had been Russia, one in the United States of America."

[2] During the two world wars, Germany had been the chief enemy of the king of the south—the Anglo-American World Power—and had occupied the position of the king of the north. After World War II, however, that nation stood divided. West Germany became an ally of the king of the south, and East Germany aligned itself with another powerful entity—the Communist bloc of nations headed by the Soviet Union. This bloc, or political entity, stood up as the king of the north, in strong opposition to the Anglo-American alliance. And the rivalry between the two kings became a Cold War that lasted from 1948 to 1989. Previously, the German king of the

1, 2. How did the identity of the king of the north change after the second world war?

north had acted "against the holy covenant." (Daniel 11: 28, 30) How would the Communist bloc act with regard to the covenant?

TRUE CHRISTIANS STUMBLE BUT PREVAIL

3 "Those who are acting wickedly against the covenant," said God's angel, "he [the king of the north] will lead into apostasy by means of smooth words." The angel added: "But as regards the people who are knowing their God, they will prevail and act effectively. And as regards those having insight among the people, they will impart understanding to the many. And they will certainly be made to stumble by sword and by flame, by captivity and by plundering, for some days."—Daniel 11:32, 33.

4 The ones "acting wickedly against the covenant" can only be the leaders of Christendom, who claim to be Christian but by their actions profane the very name of Christianity. In his book *Religion in the Soviet Union,* Walter Kolarz says: "[During the second world war] the Soviet Government made an effort to enlist the material and moral assistance of the Churches for the defence of the motherland." After the war church leaders tried to maintain that friendship, despite the atheistic policy of the power that was now the king of the north. Thus, Christendom became more than ever a part of this world —a disgusting apostasy in Jehovah's eyes.—John 17:16; James 4:4.

5 What of genuine Christians—"the people who are knowing their God" and "those having insight"? Although they were properly "in subjection to the superior

---

3, 4. Who are those "acting wickedly against the covenant," and what relationship have they had with the king of the north?
5, 6. Who were 'the people knowing their God,' and how did they fare under the king of the north?

authorities," Christians living under the rulership of the king of the north were not a part of this world. (Romans 13:1; John 18:36) Careful to pay back "Caesar's things to Caesar," they also gave "God's things to God." (Matthew 22:21) Because of this, their integrity was challenged.—2 Timothy 3:12.

⁶ As a result, true Christians both 'stumbled' and 'prevailed.' They stumbled in that they suffered intense persecution, some even being killed. But they prevailed in that the vast majority remained faithful. They conquered the world, just as Jesus did. (John 16:33) Moreover, they never stopped preaching, even if they found themselves in prison or in concentration camps. In so doing, they 'imparted understanding to the many.' Despite persecution in most lands ruled over by the king of the north, the number of Jehovah's Witnesses increased. Thanks to the faithfulness of "those having insight," an ever-expanding part of the "great crowd" has appeared in those lands.—Revelation 7:9-14.

JEHOVAH'S PEOPLE ARE REFINED

⁷ "When they [God's people] are made to stumble they will be helped with a little help," said the angel. (Daniel 11:34a) The triumph of the king of the south in the second world war had resulted in some relief for Christians living under the rival king. (Compare Revelation 12:15, 16.) Similarly, those who were persecuted by the

---

7. What "little help" did the anointed Christians living under the king of the north receive?

successor king experienced relief from time to time. As the Cold War wound down, many leaders came to realize that faithful Christians are no threat and thus granted them legal recognition. Help came, too, from the swelling numbers of the great crowd, who responded to the faithful preaching of the anointed ones and helped them.—Matthew 25:34-40.

⁸ Not all who professed to have an interest in serving God during the Cold War years had good motives. The angel had warned: "Many will certainly join themselves to them by means of smoothness." (Daniel 11:34b) A considerable number showed an interest in the truth but were not willing to make a dedication to God. Yet others who seemed to accept the good news were really spies for the authorities. A report from one land reads: "Some of these unscrupulous characters were avowed Communists who had crept into the Lord's organization, made a great display of zeal, and had even been appointed to high positions of service."

⁹ The angel continued: "And some of those having insight will be made to stumble, in order to do a refining work because of them and to do a cleansing and to do a whitening, until the time of the end; because it is yet for the time appointed." (Daniel 11:35) The infiltrators caused some faithful ones to fall into the hands of the authorities. Jehovah allowed such things to happen for a refining and a cleansing of his people. Just as Jesus "learned obedience from the things he suffered," so these faithful ones learned endurance from the testing of

8. How did some join themselves to God's people "by means of smoothness"?
9. Why did Jehovah allow some faithful Christians "to stumble" because of infiltrators?

their faith. (Hebrews 5:8; James 1:2, 3; compare Malachi 3:3.) They are thus 'refined, cleansed, and whitened.'

¹⁰ Jehovah's people were to experience stumbling and refining "until the time of the end." Of course, they expect to be persecuted until the end of this wicked system of things. However, the cleansing and whitening of God's people as a result of the intrusion from the king of the north was "for the time appointed." Hence, at Daniel 11:35, "the time of the end" must relate to the end of the period of time needed for God's people to be refined while enduring the assault of the king of the north. The stumbling evidently ended at the time appointed by Jehovah.

THE KING MAGNIFIES HIMSELF

¹¹ Regarding the king of the north, the angel added: "The king will actually do according to his own will, and he will exalt himself and magnify himself above every god; and [refusing to acknowledge Jehovah's sovereignty] against the God of gods he will speak marvelous things. And he will certainly prove successful until the denunciation will have come to a finish; because the thing decided upon must be done. And to the God of his fathers he will give no consideration; and to the desire of women and to every other god he will give no consideration, but over everyone he will magnify himself." —Daniel 11:36, 37.

¹² Fulfilling these prophetic words, the king of the

---

10. What is meant by the expression "until the time of the end"?
11. What did the angel say about the attitude of the king of the north toward Jehovah's sovereignty?
12, 13. (a) In what way did the king of the north reject "the God of his fathers"? (b) Who were the "women" whose "desire" the king of the north did not consider? (c) To which "god" did the king of the north give glory?

north rejected "the God of his fathers," such as the Trinitarian divinity of Christendom. The Communist bloc promoted outright atheism. Thus the king of the north made a god of himself, 'magnifying himself over everyone.' Giving no consideration "to the desire of women" —subservient lands, such as North Vietnam, that served as handmaids of his regime—the king acted "according to his own will."

¹³ Continuing with the prophecy, the angel said: "To the god of fortresses, in his position he will give glory; and to a god that his fathers did not know he will give glory by means of gold and by means of silver and by means of precious stone and by means of desirable things." (Daniel 11:38) In fact, the king of the north placed his trust in modern scientific militarism, "the god of fortresses." He sought salvation through this "god," sacrificing enormous wealth on its altar.

¹⁴ "He will act effectively against the most fortified strongholds, along with a foreign god. Whoever has given him recognition he will make abound with glory, and he will actually make them rule among many; and the ground he will apportion out for a price." (Daniel 11: 39) Trusting in his militaristic "foreign god," the king of the north acted most "effectively," proving to be a formidable military power in "the last days." (2 Timothy 3:1) Those who supported his ideology were rewarded with political, financial, and sometimes military support.

"A PUSHING" IN THE TIME OF THE END

¹⁵ "In the time of the end the king of the south will

14. How did the king of the north "act effectively"?
15. How did the king of the south engage with the king of the north in "a pushing"?

engage with him in a pushing," the angel told Daniel. (Daniel 11:40a) Has the king of the south 'pushed' the king of the north during "the time of the end"? (Daniel 12:4, 9) Yes, indeed. After the first world war, the punitive peace treaty imposed upon the then king of the north —Germany—was surely "a pushing," an incitement to retaliation. After his victory in the second world war, the king of the south targeted fearsome nuclear weapons on his rival and organized against him a powerful military alliance, the North Atlantic Treaty Organization (NATO). Concerning NATO's function, a British historian says: "It was the prime instrument for the 'containment' of the USSR, which was now perceived as the principal threat to European peace. Its mission lasted for 40 years, and was carried out with indisputable success." As the years of the Cold War went by, the "pushing" by the king of the south included high-tech espionage as well as diplomatic and military offensives.

[16] How did the king of the north react? "Against him the king of the north will storm with chariots and with horsemen and with many ships; and he will certainly enter into the lands and flood over and pass through." (Daniel 11:40b) The history of the last days has featured the expansionism of the king of the north. During the second world war, the Nazi "king" flooded over his borders into the surrounding lands. At the end of that war, the successor "king" built a powerful empire. During the Cold War, the king of the north fought his rival in proxy wars and insurgencies in Africa, Asia, and Latin America. He persecuted genuine Christians, hindering—but by no means stopping—their activity. And his military and

---

16. How did the king of the north react to the pushing by the king of the south?

political offensives brought a number of lands under his control. This is exactly what the angel had prophesied: "He will also actually enter into the land of the Decoration [the spiritual estate of Jehovah's people], and there will be many lands that will be made to stumble."—Daniel 11:41a.

¹⁷ Nevertheless, the king of the north did not achieve world conquest. The angel foretold: "These are the ones that will escape out of his hand, Edom and Moab and the main part of the sons of Ammon." (Daniel 11:41b) In ancient times, Edom, Moab, and Ammon were situated between the domains of the Egyptian king of the south and the Syrian king of the north. In modern times they represent nations and organizations that the king of the north targeted but was unable to bring under his influence.

EGYPT DOES NOT ESCAPE

¹⁸ Jehovah's angel continued: "He [the king of the north] will keep thrusting out his hand against the lands; and as regards the land of Egypt, she will not prove to be an escapee. And he will actually rule over the hidden treasures of the gold and the silver and over all the desirable things of Egypt. And the Libyans and the Ethiopians will be at his steps." (Daniel 11:42, 43) Even the king of the south, "Egypt," did not escape the effects of the expansionist policies of the king of the north. For example, the king of the south suffered a notable defeat in

17. What limits were there to the expansionism of the king of the north?
18, 19. In what ways did the king of the south feel the influence of his rival?

"Pushing" by the king of the south has included high-tech espionage and the threat of military action

Vietnam. And what of "the Libyans and the Ethiopians"? These neighbors of ancient Egypt might well foreshadow nations that are, geographically speaking, neighbors of modern "Egypt" (the king of the south). At times, they have been followers of—'at the steps of'—the king of the north.

[19] Has the king of the north ruled over 'the hidden treasures of Egypt'? He has indeed had a powerful influence on the way that the king of the south has used his financial resources. Because of fear of his rival, the king of the south has devoted huge sums to maintaining a formidable army, navy, and air force. To this extent, the king of the north 'ruled over,' or controlled, the disposition of the wealth of the king of the south.

THE FINAL CAMPAIGN

[20] The rivalry between the king of the north and the king of the south—whether by military, economic, or other means—is nearing its end. Revealing the details of a conflict yet to come, Jehovah's angel said: "There will be reports that will disturb him [the king of the north], out of the sunrising and out of the north, and he will certainly go forth in a great rage in order to annihilate and to devote many to destruction. And he will plant his palatial tents between the grand sea and the holy mountain of Decoration; and he will have to come all the way to his end, and there will be no helper for him."—Daniel 11:44, 45.

[21] With the disbanding of the Soviet Union in December 1991, the king of the north suffered a serious setback.

---

20. How does the angel describe the final campaign of the king of the north?
21. What is there yet to learn about the king of the north?

Who will be this king when Daniel 11:44, 45 is fulfilled? Will he be identified with one of the countries that were part of the former Soviet Union? Or will he change identity completely, as he has done a number of times before? Will the development of nuclear weapons by additional nations result in a new arms race and have a bearing on the identity of that king? Only time will provide answers to these questions. We are wise not to speculate. When the king of the north embarks on his final campaign, the fulfillment of prophecy will be clearly discerned by all who have Bible-based insight.—See "Kings in Daniel Chapter 11," on page 284.

22 However, we do know what action the king of the north will soon take. Moved by the reports "out of the sunrising and out of the north," he will conduct a campaign 'in order to annihilate many.' Against whom is this campaign directed? And what "reports" trigger such an attack?

ALARMED BY DISTURBING REPORTS

23 Consider what the book of Revelation has to say about the end of Babylon the Great, the world empire of false religion. Before "the war of the great day of God the Almighty," Armageddon, this great enemy of true worship "will be completely burned with fire." (Revelation 16:14, 16; 18:2-8) Her destruction is foreshadowed by the pouring out of the sixth bowl of God's wrath on the symbolic river Euphrates. The river is dried up so that "the way might be prepared for the kings from the rising of

---

22. What questions arise about the final attack by the king of the north?
23. (a) What outstanding event must take place before Armageddon? (b) Who are "the kings from the rising of the sun"?

the sun." (Revelation 16:12) Who are these kings? None other than Jehovah God and Jesus Christ!—Compare Isaiah 41:2; 46:10, 11.

²⁴ The destruction of Babylon the Great is graphically described in the book of Revelation, which states: "The ten horns that you saw [the kings ruling in the time of the end], and the wild beast [the United Nations], these will hate the harlot and will make her devastated and naked, and will eat up her fleshy parts and will completely burn her with fire." (Revelation 17:16) Why will the rulers destroy Babylon the Great? Because 'God puts it into their hearts to carry out his thought.' (Revelation 17: 17) Included among these rulers is the king of the north. What he hears "out of the sunrising" may well refer to this act of Jehovah, when he puts it into the hearts of human leaders to annihilate the great religious harlot.

²⁵ But there is a special target for the wrath of the king of the north. He will "plant his palatial tents between the grand sea and the holy mountain of Decoration," says the angel. In Daniel's time the grand sea was the Mediterranean and the holy mountain was Zion, once the site of God's temple. Hence, in the prophecy's fulfillment, the enraged king of the north conducts a campaign against God's people. In a spiritual sense, the location "between the grand sea and the holy mountain" represents the spiritual estate of Jehovah's anointed servants. They have come out of "the sea" of mankind alienated from God and have the hope of ruling on heavenly Mount Zion with Jesus Christ.—Isaiah 57:20; Hebrews 12:22; Revelation 14:1.

---

24. What act of Jehovah may disturb the king of the north?
25. (a) What special target does the king of the north have? (b) Where does the king of the north "plant his palatial tents"?

26 Ezekiel, a contemporary of Daniel, also prophesied an attack on God's people "in the final part of the days." He said that the hostilities would be initiated by Gog of Magog, that is, by Satan the Devil. (Ezekiel 38:14, 16) Symbolically, from which direction does Gog come? "From the remotest parts of the north," says Jehovah, through Ezekiel. (Ezekiel 38:15) However vicious this assault, it will not destroy Jehovah's people. This dramatic encounter will result from a strategic move on Jehovah's part to annihilate Gog's forces. Thus, Jehovah says to Satan: "I shall certainly . . . put hooks in your jaws and bring you forth." "I will . . . cause you to come up from the remotest parts of the north and bring you in upon the mountains of Israel." (Ezekiel 38:4; 39:2) The news "out of the north" that enrages the king of the north, therefore, must originate with Jehovah. But just what the reports "out of the sunrising and out of the north" will finally contain, only God will determine and time will tell.

27 As for Gog, he organizes his all-out assault because of the prosperity of "the Israel of God," who, along with the "great crowd" of "other sheep," are no longer part of his world. (Galatians 6:16; Revelation 7:9; John 10:16; 17: 15, 16; 1 John 5:19) Gog looks askance upon "a people gathered together out of the nations, one that is accumulating [spiritual] wealth and property." (Ezekiel 38:12) Viewing the Christian spiritual estate as "open rural country" ripe for the taking, Gog makes a supreme effort

---

26. As indicated by Ezekiel's prophecy, what may be the origin of the news "out of the north"?

27. (a) Why will Gog incite the nations, including the king of the north, to attack Jehovah's people? (b) How will Gog's attack turn out?

KINGS IN DANIEL CHAPTER 11

	The King of the North	The King of the South
Daniel 11:5	Seleucus I Nicator	Ptolemy I
Daniel 11:6	Antiochus II (wife Laodice)	Ptolemy II (daughter Berenice)
Daniel 11:7-9	Seleucus II	Ptolemy III
Daniel 11:10-12	Antiochus III	Ptolemy IV
Daniel 11:13-19	Antiochus III (daughter Cleopatra I) Successors: Seleucus IV and Antiochus IV	Ptolemy V Successor: Ptolemy VI
Daniel 11:20	Augustus	
Daniel 11:21-24	Tiberius	
Daniel 11:25, 26	Aurelian The Roman Empire breaks down	Queen Zenobia
Daniel 11:27-30a	German Empire (World War I)	Britain, followed by the Anglo-American World Power
Daniel 11:30b, 31	Hitler's Third Reich (World War II)	Anglo-American World Power
Daniel 11:32-43	Communist bloc (Cold War)	Anglo-American World Power
Daniel 11:44, 45	Yet to rise*	Anglo-American World Power

* The prophecy in Daniel chapter 11 does not fore-tell the names of the political entities that occupy the positions of the king of the north and the king of the south at various times. Their identities become known only after the events start to occur. Moreover, since the conflict occurs in episodes, there are intervals of no conflict—one king holds sway while the other remains inactive.

to wipe out this obstacle to his total control of mankind. But he fails. (Ezekiel 38:11, 18; 39:4) When the kings of the earth, including the king of the north, attack Jehovah's people, they will 'come all the way to their end.'

'THE KING WILL COME TO HIS END'

28 The final campaign of the king of the north is not directed against the king of the south. Therefore, the king of the north does not come to his end at the hands of his great rival. Similarly, the king of the south is not destroyed by the king of the north. The king of the south is destroyed, "without [human] hand," by God's Kingdom.* (Daniel 8:25) In fact, at the battle of Armageddon, all earthly kings are to be removed by God's Kingdom, and this evidently is what happens to the king of the north. (Daniel 2:44) Daniel 11:44, 45 describes events leading up to that final battle. No wonder "there will be no helper" when the king of the north meets his end!

---

* See Chapter 10 of this book.

---

28. What do we know about the future of the king of the north and the king of the south?

WHAT DID YOU DISCERN?

- How did the identity of the king of the north change after the second world war?

- What will finally happen to the king of the north and the king of the south?

- How have you benefited from paying attention to Daniel's prophecy about the rivalry between the two kings?

CHAPTER SEVENTEEN

IDENTIFYING TRUE WORSHIPERS IN THE TIME OF THE END

A TINY, defenseless group of people come under vicious attack by a mighty world power. They survive intact and even experience a renewal—not as a result of their own strength but because Jehovah God values them. Daniel chapter 7 foretold these events, which occurred in the early part of the 20th century. Who, though, were these people? The same chapter of Daniel referred to them as "the holy ones of the Supreme One," Jehovah God. It also revealed that these individuals will ultimately be corulers in the Messianic Kingdom!—Daniel 7:13, 14, 18, 21, 22, 25-27.

² As we learned in Daniel chapter 11, the king of the north will meet his final end after threatening the secure spiritual land of these faithful people. (Daniel 11:45; compare Ezekiel 38:18-23.) Yes, Jehovah is very protective of his faithful anointed ones. Psalm 105:14, 15 tells us: "On their account [Jehovah] reproved kings, saying: 'Do not you men touch my anointed ones, and to my prophets do nothing bad.'" Would you not agree, then, that in these turbulent times, it would be wise for the expanding

---

1. According to Daniel chapter 7, what extraordinary experiences were to befall a small, defenseless group of people in our day?
2. (a) How does Jehovah feel about his anointed servants? (b) What would be a wise course to follow during these times?

Prominent servants of Jehovah were unjustly sent to the federal penitentiary in Atlanta, Georgia, U.S.A. From left to right: (seated) A. H. Macmillan, J. F. Rutherford, W. E. Van Amburgh; (standing) G. H. Fisher, R. J. Martin, G. DeCecca, F. H. Robison, and C. J. Woodworth

"great crowd" to associate as closely as possible with these holy ones? (Revelation 7:9; Zechariah 8:23) Jesus Christ recommended that sheeplike people do exactly that—associate with his anointed spiritual brothers by supporting them in their work.—Matthew 25:31-46; Galatians 3:29.

³ However, God's Adversary, Satan, has been waging an all-out war against the anointed. He has promoted false religion, effectively filling the world with counterfeit Christians. As a result, many people have been misled. Others simply despair of ever finding those who represent the true religion. (Matthew 7:15, 21-23; Revelation 12:9, 17) Even those who do find the "little flock" and associate with them must fight to maintain faith, for this world constantly seeks to erode faith. (Luke 12:32) What about you? Have you found "the holy ones of the Supreme One," and are you associating with them? Are you aware of the solid evidence proving that those you have found are indeed the ones God has chosen? Such evidence can bolster your faith. It can also equip you to help others see through the religious confusion of today's world. Daniel chapter 12 contains a wealth of this lifesaving knowledge.

THE GREAT PRINCE GOES INTO ACTION

⁴ Daniel 12:1 reads: "During that time Michael will stand up, the great prince who is standing in behalf of the sons of your people." This verse foretells these two distinct things regarding Michael: one, that he "is standing," suggesting a state of affairs that extends over a period of time; two, that he "will stand up," suggesting an *event* during that period of time. First, we want to know the period when Michael is "standing in behalf of the sons of

---

3. (a) Why is it not easy to find Jesus' anointed followers and remain close to them? (b) How will Daniel chapter 12 help in this regard?
4. (a) Daniel 12:1 foretells what two distinct things regarding Michael? (b) In Daniel, what is often meant by a monarch's "standing"?

[Daniel's] people." Recall that Michael is a name given to Jesus in his role as a heavenly Ruler. The reference to his "standing" reminds us of the way that this term is used elsewhere in the book of Daniel. It often refers to the action of a king, such as his taking up royal power.—Daniel 11:2-4, 7, 20, 21.

⁵ It is evident that the angel was here pointing to a period of time specified elsewhere in Bible prophecy. Jesus called it his "presence" (Greek, *pa·rou·si′a*), when he would rule as King in heaven. (Matthew 24:37-39) This time period is also called "the last days" and "the time of the end." (2 Timothy 3:1; Daniel 12:4, 9) Ever since that period began in 1914, Michael has been standing as King in heaven.—Compare Isaiah 11:10; Revelation 12:7-9.

⁶ When, though, does Michael "stand up"? When he rises up to take special action. This, Jesus will do in the future. Revelation 19:11-16 prophetically describes Jesus as the mighty Messianic King riding at the head of an angelic army and bringing destruction upon enemies of God. Daniel 12:1 continues: "And there will certainly occur a time of distress such as has not been made to occur since there came to be a nation until that time." As Jehovah's Chief Executioner, Christ will bring an end to the entire wicked system of things during the foretold "great tribulation."—Matthew 24:21; Jeremiah 25:33; 2 Thessalonians 1:6-8; Revelation 7:14; 16:14, 16.

⁷ How will people who exercise faith fare during this dark time? Daniel was further told: "During that time your people will escape, every one who is found written

---

5, 6. (a) During what time period is Michael standing? (b) When and how does Michael "stand up," and with what results?

7. (a) What hope is there for all faithful ones during the coming "time of distress"? (b) What is Jehovah's book, and why is it vital to be found therein?

down in the book." (Compare Luke 21:34-36.) What is this book? In essence, it represents Jehovah God's remembrance of those who do his will. (Malachi 3:16; Hebrews 6:10) Those who are written down in this book of life are the most secure people in the world, for they enjoy divine protection. Whatever harm may come to them, it can and will be undone. Even if death should overtake them before this coming "time of distress," they remain safe in Jehovah's limitless memory. He will remember them and resurrect them during the Thousand Year Reign of Jesus Christ.—Acts 24:15; Revelation 20:4-6.

HOLY ONES "WAKE UP"

⁸ Comforting indeed is the hope of the resurrection. Daniel 12:2 touches on it, saying: "There will be many of those asleep in the ground of dust who will wake up, these to indefinitely lasting life and those to reproaches and to indefinitely lasting abhorrence." (Compare Isaiah 26:19.) These words may well remind us of Jesus Christ's moving promise of a general resurrection. (John 5:28, 29) What a thrilling hope! Just think of beloved friends and family—now dead—given a chance to live again in the future! But this promise in the book of Daniel refers primarily to another kind of resurrection—one that has already occurred. How could that be?

⁹ Consider the context. The first verse of chapter 12 applies, as we have seen, not only to the end of this system of things but also to the entire period of the last days. In fact, the bulk of the chapter finds fulfillment, not in the coming earthly paradise, but during the time of the

---

8. Daniel 12:2 offers what delightful prospect?
9. (a) Why is it reasonable to expect that Daniel 12:2 would find fulfillment during the last days? (b) To what kind of resurrection does the prophecy refer, and how do we know?

end. Has there been a resurrection during this period? The apostle Paul wrote of the resurrection of "those who belong to the Christ" as occurring *"during his presence."* However, those who are resurrected to life in heaven are raised "incorruptible." (1 Corinthians 15:23, 52) None of them are raised "to reproaches and to indefinitely lasting abhorrence" foretold at Daniel 12:2. Is there another kind of resurrection? In the Bible, resurrection sometimes has a spiritual significance. For example, both Ezekiel and Revelation contain prophetic passages that apply to a spiritual revival, or resurrection.—Ezekiel 37:1-14; Revelation 11:3, 7, 11.

[10] Has there been such a spiritual revival of God's anointed servants in the time of the end? Yes! It is a historical reality that in 1918 a small remnant of faithful Christians were subjected to an extraordinary attack that disrupted their organized public ministry. Then, against all likelihood, in 1919 they returned to life in a spiritual sense. These facts fit the description of the resurrection foretold at Daniel 12:2. Some did "wake up" spiritually at that time and thereafter. Sadly, though, not all remained in a spiritually alive state. Those who after being awakened chose to reject the Messianic King and who left God's service earned for themselves the 'reproaches and indefinitely lasting abhorrence' described at Daniel 12:2. (Hebrews 6:4-6) However, the faithful anointed ones, making good use of their spiritually revived state, loyally supported the Messianic King. Ultimately, their faithfulness leads, as the prophecy states, to "indefinitely lasting life." Today, their spiritual vitality in the face of opposition helps us to identify them.

---

10. (a) In what sense were the anointed remnant resurrected during the time of the end? (b) How did some of the anointed who were revived nonetheless awaken "to reproaches and to indefinitely lasting abhorrence"?

THEY 'SHINE LIKE THE STARS'

[11] The next two verses of Daniel chapter 12 do even more to help us identify "the holy ones of the Supreme One." In verse 3 the angel tells Daniel: "The ones having insight will shine like the brightness of the expanse; and those who are bringing the many to righteousness, like the stars to time indefinite, even forever." Who are "the ones having insight" today? Again, the evidence points to the same "holy ones of the Supreme One." After all, who but the faithful anointed remnant had the insight to discern that Michael, the Great Prince, began standing as King in 1914? By preaching such truths as this—as well as by maintaining Christian conduct—they have been "shining as illuminators" in this spiritually bedarkened world. (Philippians 2:15; John 8:12) Concerning them, Jesus prophesied: "At that time the righteous ones will shine as brightly as the sun in the kingdom of their Father."—Matthew 13:43.

[12] Daniel 12:3 even tells us what work would occupy these anointed Christians in the time of the end. They would be "bringing the many to righteousness." The anointed remnant set about gathering the remaining number of the 144,000 joint heirs of Christ. (Romans 8:16, 17; Revelation 7:3, 4) When that work was completed—evidently by the mid-1930's—they began gathering the "great crowd" of "other sheep." (Revelation 7:9; John 10:16) These too exercise faith in the ransom sacrifice of Jesus Christ. Therefore, they have a clean standing before

---

11. Who are "the ones having insight" today, and in what sense do they shine like the stars?

12. (a) During the time of the end, how have the anointed been involved in "bringing the many to righteousness"? (b) How will the anointed bring many to righteousness and 'shine like the stars' during the Thousand Year Reign of Christ?

Jehovah. Numbering into the millions today, they cherish the hope of surviving the coming destruction of this wicked world. During Christ's Thousand Year Reign, Jesus and his 144,000 fellow kings and priests will apply to obedient mankind on earth the full benefits of the ransom, thereby helping all of those exercising faith to shed every last trace of sin inherited from Adam. (2 Peter 3:13; Revelation 7:13, 14; 20:5, 6) In the fullest sense, the anointed will then share in "bringing the many to righteousness" and will 'shine like the stars' in heaven. Do you value the hope of living on earth under the glorious heavenly government of Christ and his corulers? What a privilege it is to share with "the holy ones" in preaching this good news of God's Kingdom!—Matthew 24:14.

THEY "ROVE ABOUT"

¹³ The angel's declaration to Daniel, which began back at Daniel 10:20, now concludes with these heartwarming words: "And as for you, O Daniel, make secret the words and seal up the book, until the time of the end. Many will rove about, and the true knowledge will become abundant." (Daniel 12:4) Much of what Daniel was inspired to write was indeed made secret and sealed up to human understanding. Why, Daniel himself later wrote: "Now as for me, I heard, but I could not understand." (Daniel 12:8) In this sense Daniel's book remained sealed for centuries. What about today?

¹⁴ We are privileged to live in "the time of the end" foretold in the book of Daniel. As prophesied, many faithful

---

13. In what sense were the words of Daniel's book sealed and made secret?
14. (a) During "the time of the end," who have 'roved about,' and where? (b) What evidence is there that Jehovah has blessed this 'roving about'?

ones have 'roved about' in the pages of God's Word. The result? With Jehovah's blessing, true knowledge has become abundant. The faithful anointed Witnesses of Jehovah have been blessed with insight enabling them to understand that the Son of man became King in 1914, to identify the beasts of Daniel's prophecy, to warn against "the disgusting thing that is causing desolation"—and these are just a few examples. (Daniel 11:31) This abundance of knowledge, then, is yet another identifying mark of "the holy ones of the Supreme One." But Daniel received further evidence.

THEY ARE 'DASHED TO PIECES'

15 Daniel, we recall, received these angelic messages on the bank of "the great river" Hiddekel, also known as the Tigris. (Daniel 10:4) Here he now sees three angelic creatures and says: "I saw, I Daniel, and, look! there were two others standing, one on the bank here of the stream and the other on the bank there of the stream. Then one said to the man clothed with the linen, who was up above the waters of the stream: 'How long will it be to the end of the wonderful things?' " (Daniel 12:5, 6) The question the angel raised here may again remind us of "the holy ones of the Supreme One." At the beginning of "the time of the end," in 1914, they were greatly concerned with the question of how long it would be until God's promises were fulfilled. That they are the focus of this prophecy becomes apparent in the answer to this question.

16 Daniel's account continues: "And I began to hear the man clothed with the linen, who was up above the waters

---

15. What question is now raised by an angel, and of whom might this question remind us?
16. What prophecy does the angel utter, and how does he emphasize the certainty of its fulfillment?

of the stream, as he proceeded to raise his right hand and his left hand to the heavens and to swear by the One who is alive for time indefinite: 'It will be for an appointed time, appointed times and a half. And as soon as there will have been a finishing of the dashing of the power of the holy people to pieces, all these things will come to their finish.' " (Daniel 12:7) This is a solemn matter. The angel raises both hands in an oath, perhaps so that this gesture is visible to the two angels on opposite sides of the broad river. He thereby emphasizes the absolute certainty of the fulfillment of this prophecy. When, though, are these appointed times? The answer is not as difficult to find as you might think it is.

¹⁷ This prophecy is remarkably similar to two other prophecies. One, which we considered in Chapter 9 of this publication, is found at Daniel 7:25; the other, at Revelation 11:3, 7, 9. Note some of the parallels. Each is set during the time of the end. Both prophecies concern holy servants of God, showing them to be persecuted and even temporarily unable to carry out their public preaching activity. Each prophecy shows that God's servants revive and then resume their work, foiling their persecutors. And each prophecy mentions the duration of this time of hardship for the holy ones. Both prophecies in Daniel (7:25 and 12:7) refer to 'a time, times, and half a time.' Scholars generally recognize this to mean three and a half times. Revelation refers to the same period as 42 months, or 1,260 days. (Revelation 11:2, 3) This confirms that the three and a half times in Daniel refer to three and a half years of 360 days each. But when did these 1,260 days begin?

---

17. (a) What parallels are to be found in the prophecies recorded at Daniel 7:25, Daniel 12:7, and Revelation 11:3, 7, 9? (b) How long are the three and a half times?

¹⁸ The prophecy is quite explicit as to when the 1,260 days would *end*—when there is "a finishing of the dashing of the power of the holy people to pieces." In the middle of 1918, leading members of the Watch Tower Bible and Tract Society, including its president, J. F. Rutherford, were convicted on false charges, sentenced to long terms of confinement, and imprisoned. God's holy ones did indeed see their work 'dashed to pieces,' their power broken. Counting back three and a half years from mid-1918 brings us to the end of 1914. At that time the little band of anointed ones were bracing themselves for the onslaught of persecution. World War I had broken out, and opposition to their work was mounting. For the year 1915, they even based their yeartext on this question that Christ asked his followers: "Are ye able to drink of my cup?" (Matthew 20:22, *King James Version*) As predicted at Revelation 11:3, the 1,260-day period that ensued was a mournful time for the anointed—it was as if they were prophesying in sackcloth. Persecution worsened. Some of them were imprisoned, others were mobbed, and still others were tortured. Many were disheartened by the death of the Society's first president, C. T. Russell, in 1916. What, though, was to happen after this dark time concluded with the killing of these holy ones as a preaching organization?

¹⁹ The parallel prophecy found at Revelation 11:3, 9, 11 shows that after the "two witnesses" are killed, they lie dead for only a short period of time—three and a half days—until they are revived. Similarly, the prophecy in

---

18. (a) According to Daniel 12:7, what would mark the end of the 1,260 days? (b) When was "the power of the holy people" finally dashed to pieces, and how did this happen? (c) When did the 1,260 days begin, and how did the anointed 'prophesy in sackcloth' during that period?
19. How does the prophecy in Revelation chapter 11 assure us that the anointed ones were not to be silenced for long?

Daniel chapter 12 shows that the holy ones would not remain silent but had more work ahead of them.

THEY ARE 'CLEANSED, WHITENED, AND REFINED'

²⁰ As noted earlier, Daniel wrote these things down but could not understand them. Still, he must have wondered if the holy ones would actually be finished off at the hands of their persecutors, for he asked, "What will be the final part of these things?" The angel answered: "Go, Daniel, because the words are made secret and sealed up until the time of the end. Many will cleanse themselves and whiten themselves and will be refined. And the wicked ones will certainly act wickedly, and no wicked ones at all will understand; but the ones having insight will understand." (Daniel 12:8-10) There was a sure hope for the holy ones! Rather than being destroyed, they would be whitened, blessed with a clean standing before Jehovah God. (Malachi 3:1-3) Their insight into spiritual matters would enable them to keep clean in God's eyes. In contrast, the wicked would refuse to understand spiritual things. But when would all of this occur?

²¹ Daniel was told: "From the time that the constant feature has been removed and there has been a placing of the disgusting thing that is causing desolation, there will be one thousand two hundred and ninety days." So this time period would begin when certain conditions had been brought about. "The constant feature"—or "the continual sacrifice"*—had to be removed. (Daniel 12:11, footnote) What sacrifice did the angel mean? Not the

---

* Translated simply as "the sacrifice" in the Greek *Septuagint*.

---

20. According to Daniel 12:10, what blessings would come upon the anointed after their hard experiences?
21. (a) The time period foretold at Daniel 12:11 would begin when what conditions had been brought about? (b) What was "the constant feature," and when was it removed? (See box on page 298.)

REMOVAL OF THE CONSTANT FEATURE

In the book of Daniel, the term "constant feature" occurs five times. It refers to a sacrifice of praise—"the fruit of lips"—regularly offered to Jehovah God by his servants. (Hebrews 13:15) Its foretold removal is referred to at Daniel 8:11, 11:31, and 12:11.

During both world wars, Jehovah's people were severely persecuted in the realms of "the king of the north" and "the king of the south." (Daniel 11:14, 15) The removal of "the constant feature" took place toward the end of World War I when the preaching work was all but suspended in mid-1918. (Daniel 12:7) During World War II, "the constant feature" was similarly "taken away" for 2,300 days by the Anglo-American World Power. (Daniel 8:11-14; see Chapter 10 of this book.) It was also removed by Nazi "arms" for a period of time unspecified in the Scriptures. —Daniel 11:31; see Chapter 15 of this book.

animal sacrifices offered at any earthly temple. Why, even the temple that once stood in Jerusalem was a mere "copy of the reality"—Jehovah's great spiritual temple, which went into operation when Christ became its High Priest in 29 C.E.! In this spiritual temple, representing God's arrangement for pure worship, there is no need of continual sin offerings, for "Christ was offered once for all time to bear the sins of many." (Hebrews 9:24-28) Yet, all true Christians do offer sacrifices at this temple. The apostle Paul wrote: "Through [Christ] let us always offer to God a sacrifice of praise, that is, the fruit of lips which make public declaration to his name." (Hebrews 13:15) So this first condition of the prophecy—the removing of "the constant feature"—was brought about in mid-1918 when the preaching work was virtually suspended.

Landmark conventions were held at
Cedar Point, Ohio, U.S.A., in 1919 (above) and 1922 (below)

²² What, though, about the second condition—the "placing," or installation, of "the disgusting thing that is causing desolation"? As we saw in our discussion of Daniel 11:31, this disgusting thing was first the League of Nations and reemerged later as the United Nations. Both are disgusting in that they have been heralded as the only hope for peace on earth. Thus, in the hearts of many, these institutions actually take the place of God's Kingdom! The League was officially proposed in January 1919. At that time, then, both conditions of Daniel 12:11 were met. So the 1,290 days began in early 1919 and ran until the autumn (Northern Hemisphere) of 1922.

²³ During that time, did the holy ones make progress toward becoming whitened and cleansed in God's eyes? They certainly did! In March 1919 the president of the Watch Tower Society and his close associates were released from prison. They were later exonerated of the false charges against them. Aware that their work was far from over, they got busy immediately, organizing a convention for September 1919. In the same year, a companion magazine to *The Watch Tower* was first published. Originally called *The Golden Age* (now *Awake!*), it has always supported *The Watchtower* in fearlessly exposing the corruption of this world and in helping God's people to remain clean. By the end of the foretold 1,290 days, the holy ones were well on the way to a cleansed and restored standing. In September 1922, right about the time when this period ended, they held a landmark convention at Cedar Point, Ohio, U.S.A. It gave tremendous

---

22. (a) What is the desolating "disgusting thing," and when was it installed? (b) When did the time period foretold at Daniel 12:11 begin, and when did it end?
23. How did God's holy ones progress toward a cleansed standing during the 1,290 days foretold in Daniel chapter 12?

PROPHETIC TIME PERIODS IN DANIEL

Seven times (2,520 years): Daniel 4:16, 25	October 607 B.C.E. to October 1914 C.E. (Messianic Kingdom established. See Chapter 6 of this book.)
Three and a half times (1,260 days): Daniel 7:25; 12:7	December 1914 to June 1918 (Anointed Christians harassed. See Chapter 9 of this book.)
2,300 evenings and mornings: Daniel 8:14	June 1 or 15, 1938, to October 8 or 22, 1944 ("Great crowd" emerge, multiply. See Chapter 10 of this book.)
70 weeks (490 years): Daniel 9:24-27	455 B.C.E. to 36 C.E. (Messiah's coming and his earthly ministry. See Chapter 11 of this book.)
1,290 days: Daniel 12:11	January 1919 to September 1922 (Anointed Christians awaken and progress spiritually.)
1,335 days: Daniel 12:12	September 1922 to May 1926 (Anointed Christians attain a happy state.)

impetus to the preaching work. However, there was still a need for making more progress. That remained for the next marked period.

HAPPINESS FOR THE HOLY ONES

²⁴ Jehovah's angel concludes his prophecy regarding the holy ones with these words: "Happy is the one who is keeping in expectation and who arrives at the one thousand three hundred and thirty-five days!" (Daniel 12:12) The angel gives no clues as to when this period begins or ends. History suggests that it simply follows on the heels of the preceding period. In that case it would run from the autumn of 1922 to the late spring of 1926 (Northern Hemisphere). Did the holy ones come to a state of happiness by the end of that period? Yes, in important spiritual ways.

²⁵ Even after the convention in 1922 (shown on page 302), some of God's holy ones were still looking longingly to the past. The basic study material for their meetings was still the Bible and the volumes of *Studies in the Scriptures,* by C. T. Russell. At that time, there was a widely held view that pointed to 1925 as the year for the resurrection to begin and for Paradise to be restored to the earth. Thus, many were serving with a fixed date in mind. Some proudly refused to share in the work of preaching to the public. This was not a happy state of affairs.

²⁶ As the 1,335 days progressed, however, all of this began to change. Preaching came to the fore, as regular arrangements for everyone to participate in the field ministry were established. Meetings were scheduled to

---

24, 25. (a) What time period is foretold at Daniel 12:12, and when did it evidently begin and end? (b) What was the spiritual condition of the anointed remnant at the outset of the 1,335 days?
26. As the 1,335 days progressed, how did the spiritual condition of the anointed change?

study *The Watch Tower* each week. The issue of March 1, 1925, carried the historic article "Birth of the Nation," giving God's people a full understanding of what had happened in the 1914-19 period. After 1925 passed, the holy ones no longer served God with an immediate, explicit deadline in view. Rather, the sanctification of Jehovah's name was paramount. This vital truth was highlighted, as never before, in the January 1, 1926, *Watch Tower* article "Who Will Honor Jehovah?" At the convention in May 1926, the book *Deliverance* was released. (See page 302.) This was one of a series of new books designed to replace *Studies in the Scriptures.* No longer were the holy ones looking to the past. They were looking confidently to the future and the work ahead. As prophesied, the 1,335 days therefore ended with the holy ones in a happy state.

²⁷ Of course, not all endured through this tumultuous era. No doubt that is why the angel had emphasized the importance of "keeping in expectation." Those who endured and kept in expectation were greatly blessed. An overview of Daniel chapter 12 makes this clear. As foretold, the anointed were revived, or resurrected, in a spiritual sense. They were given outstanding insight into God's Word, being empowered to "rove about" in it and, guided by holy spirit, to unlock age-old mysteries. Jehovah cleansed them and made them shine spiritually, as brightly as stars. Consequently, they brought many into a righteous standing with Jehovah God.

²⁸ With all these prophetic marks to identify "the holy ones of the Supreme One," what excuse can there be

27. How does an overview of Daniel chapter 12 help us to make a conclusive identification of Jehovah's anointed ones?
28, 29. What should be our resolve as "the time of the end" nears its conclusion?

for failure to recognize them and associate with them? Wonderful blessings await the great crowd, who join this dwindling anointed class in serving Jehovah. All of us must keep in expectation of the fulfillment of God's promises. (Habakkuk 2:3) In our day Michael, the Great Prince, has been standing in behalf of God's people for decades. Soon now he will go into action as the divinely appointed executioner of this system of things. When he does so, where will we stand?

²⁹ The answer to that question will depend on whether we choose to live a life of integrity now. To strengthen our resolve to do so as "the time of the end" draws to a close, let us consider the final verse of Daniel's book. Our discussion of it in the next chapter will help us to see how Daniel stood before his God and how he will stand before Him in the future.

WHAT DID YOU DISCERN?

- During what time period is Michael "standing," and how and when will he "stand up"?

- To what kind of resurrection does Daniel 12:2 refer?

- What dates mark the beginning and the end of the

  three and a half times mentioned at Daniel 12:7?

  1,290 days foretold at Daniel 12:11?

  1,335 days prophesied at Daniel 12:12?

- How does paying attention to Daniel chapter 12 help us identify Jehovah's true worshipers?

CHAPTER EIGHTEEN

JEHOVAH PROMISES DANIEL A WONDERFUL REWARD

A RUNNER stretches toward the finish line. He is nearly exhausted, but with his goal in sight, he pours every ounce of energy into those last few paces. Straining with every muscle, he crosses the line at last! His face registers relief and triumph. Enduring to the end has paid off.

² At the conclusion of Daniel chapter 12, we find the beloved prophet nearing the finish line of his own "race" —his life of service to Jehovah. After citing various examples of faith among Jehovah's pre-Christian servants, the apostle Paul wrote: "So, then, because we have so great a cloud of witnesses surrounding us, let us also put off every weight and the sin that easily entangles us, and let us run with endurance the race that is set before us, as we look intently at the Chief Agent and Perfecter of our faith, Jesus. For the joy that was set before him he endured a torture stake, despising shame, and has sat down at the right hand of the throne of God."—Hebrews 12:1, 2.

³ Among that 'great cloud of witnesses' was Daniel. He certainly was one who had to "run with endurance," and he was motivated to do so by deep love for God. Jehovah had revealed much to Daniel about the future of world governments, but now He sent him this personal encouragement: "As for you yourself, go toward the end; and you

---

1, 2. (a) What important quality does a runner need in order to succeed? (b) How did the apostle Paul compare a life of faithfulness in Jehovah's service to a race?
3. (a) What motivated Daniel to "run with endurance"? (b) What three distinct things did Jehovah's angel tell Daniel?

will rest, but you will stand up for your lot at the end of the days." (Daniel 12:13) Jehovah's angel was telling Daniel three distinct things: (1) that Daniel should "go toward the end," (2) that he would "rest," and (3) that he would "stand up" again at a future time. How can these words encourage Christians today to endure to the finish line in the race for life?

"GO TOWARD THE END"

⁴ What did the angel mean when he told Daniel: "As for you yourself, go toward the end"? The end of what? Well, since Daniel was almost 100 years old, apparently this was a reference to the end of his own life, which likely was quite near.* The angel was urging Daniel to endure faithfully until death. But doing so would not necessarily be easy. Daniel had lived to see Babylon overthrown and a remnant of the Jewish exiles return to Judah and Jerusalem. That must have brought the aged prophet much joy. There is no record, though, that he joined in that trek. He may well have been too old and frail by that time. Or perhaps it was Jehovah's will for him to remain in Babylon. In any case, one cannot help but wonder if Daniel felt somewhat wistful as his countrymen left for Judah.

⁵ Daniel no doubt gathered great strength from the angel's kind statement: "Go toward the end." We might be reminded of the words Jesus Christ spoke some six centuries later: "He that has endured to the end is the one that will be saved." (Matthew 24:13) No doubt that is what

---

* Daniel had been taken into exile in Babylon in 617 B.C.E., likely as a teenager. He received this vision in the third year of Cyrus, or 536 B.C.E.—Daniel 10:1.

---

4. What did Jehovah's angel mean by saying "go toward the end," and why might that have presented a challenge to Daniel?
5. What indication is there that Daniel endured to the end?

Daniel did. He endured to the end, faithfully running the race for life to its very finish. That could be one reason why he is favorably referred to later in God's Word. (Hebrews 11:32, 33) What enabled Daniel to endure to the end? The record of his life helps us with the answer.

ENDURING AS A STUDENT OF GOD'S WORD

⁶ For Daniel, enduring to the end involved continuing to study and ponder deeply the thrilling promises of God. We know that Daniel was a devout student of God's Word. Otherwise, how would he have known of Jehovah's promise to Jeremiah that the exile would be 70 years in duration? Daniel himself wrote: "I . . . discerned by the books the number of the years." (Daniel 9:2; Jeremiah 25: 11, 12) Without question, Daniel sought out the books of God's Word then extant. The writings of Moses, David, Solomon, Isaiah, Jeremiah, Ezekiel—whatever was available to him—surely provided Daniel with many pleasant hours of reading and meditation.

⁷ Studying God's Word, being absorbed in it, is vital in order for us to cultivate endurance today. (Romans 15: 4-6; 1 Timothy 4:15) And we have the complete Bible, which includes the written record of how some of Daniel's prophecies were fulfilled centuries later. Further, we are blessed to live during "the time of the end," foretold at Daniel 12:4. In our own day, the anointed have been blessed with spiritual insight, shining as beacons of truth in this bedarkened world. As a result, many of the deep prophecies in the book of Daniel, some of which mystified him, are rich in meaning for us today. Therefore, let

6. How do we know that Daniel was a diligent student of God's Word?
7. When we compare our time with Daniel's day, what advantages do we have in studying God's Word?

us continue to study God's Word daily, never taking these things for granted. Doing so will help us to endure.

DANIEL PERSEVERED IN PRAYER

[8] Prayer also helped Daniel to endure to the end. Daily he turned to Jehovah God and spoke openly to him with a heart full of faith and confidence. He knew Jehovah to be the "Hearer of prayer." (Psalm 65:2; compare Hebrews 11:6.) When Daniel's heart was burdened with grief over Israel's rebellious course, he poured out his feelings to Jehovah. (Daniel 9:4-19) Even when Darius decreed that he alone be petitioned for 30 days, Daniel did not let that stop him from praying to Jehovah God. (Daniel 6:10) Does it not touch our hearts to visualize that faithful old man braving a pit full of lions rather than relinquishing the precious privilege of prayer? There can be no doubt that Daniel faithfully went to his end, praying fervently to Jehovah every day.

[9] Prayer is a simple act. We can pray virtually anytime, anywhere, aloud or silently. Never, though, should we take this precious privilege lightly. The Bible links prayer with endurance, perseverance, and staying awake spiritually. (Luke 18:1; Romans 12:12; Ephesians 6:18; Colossians 4:2) Is it not remarkable that we have a free and open channel of communication with the highest personage in the universe? And he listens! Recall the occasion when Daniel prayed, and Jehovah sent an angel in response. The angel arrived *while Daniel was yet praying!* (Daniel 9:20, 21) Ours may not be the era for such angelic visits, but Jehovah has not changed. (Malachi 3:6) Just as he heard Daniel's prayer, he will listen to ours. And as we pray, we

---

8. What example did Daniel set in the matter of prayer?
9. Why should we never take the privilege of prayer for granted?

will draw closer to Jehovah, forming a bond that will help us to endure to the end, as Daniel did.

ENDURING AS A TEACHER OF GOD'S WORD

[10] Daniel had to "go toward the end" in another sense. He had to endure as a teacher of the truth. He never forgot that he was one of the chosen people of whom the Scriptures had said: " 'You are my witnesses,' is the utterance of Jehovah, 'even my servant whom I have chosen.' " (Isaiah 43:10) Daniel did all he could to live up to that commission. Likely his work included teaching his own people who were exiled in Babylon. We know little of his dealings with his fellow Jews except for his connection to the three referred to as "his companions"—Hananiah, Mishael, and Azariah. (Daniel 1:7; 2:13, 17, 18) Their close friendship surely did much to help each one of them to endure. (Proverbs 17:17) Daniel, blessed by Jehovah with special insight, had much to teach his friends. (Daniel 1:17) But he had other teaching to do as well.

[11] More than any other prophet, Daniel had the work of witnessing to Gentile dignitaries. Although he often had to deliver unpopular messages, he did not treat these rulers as if they were abhorrent or in some way beneath him. He spoke to them respectfully and skillfully. There were some—such as those jealous, scheming satraps—who wanted to destroy Daniel. Yet, other dignitaries came to respect him. Because Jehovah enabled Daniel to explain secrets that mystified kings and wise men, the prophet gained great prominence. (Daniel 2:47, 48; 5:29) True, as he aged, he could not be as active as in his youth. But he surely went to his end still faithfully seeking any way in which he could serve as a witness of his beloved God.

---

10. Why was teaching the truth of God's Word important to Daniel?
11. (a) What was unique about Daniel's work? (b) How effective was Daniel in carrying out his unusual assignment?

¹² In the Christian congregation today, we may find faithful companions who will help us to endure, just as Daniel and his three associates helped one another. We also teach one another, providing "an interchange of encouragement." (Romans 1:11, 12) Like Daniel, we have a commission to witness to unbelievers. (Matthew 24:14; 28:19, 20) We therefore need to hone our skills so that we 'handle the word of the truth aright' in talking to people about Jehovah. (2 Timothy 2:15) And it will help if we obey the apostle Paul's counsel: "Go on walking in wisdom toward those on the outside." (Colossians 4:5) Such wisdom includes a balanced view of those who do not share our faith. We do not look down on such people, viewing ourselves as superior. (1 Peter 3:15) Rather, we seek to attract them to the truth, using God's Word tactfully and skillfully so as to reach their hearts. When we succeed in reaching someone, what joy this gives us! Such joy certainly helps us to endure to the end, as Daniel did.

"YOU WILL REST"

¹³ The angel next assured Daniel: "You will rest." (Daniel 12:13) What did those words mean? Well, Daniel knew that death lay ahead of him. Death has been the inescapable end for all humans, from Adam's day until our own. The Bible aptly calls death an "enemy." (1 Corinthians 15:26) To Daniel, however, the prospect of dying meant something quite different from what it meant to the Babylonians all around him. For them, steeped in the complex worship of some 4,000 false deities, death held

---

12. (a) What teaching activities do we as Christians engage in today? (b) How can we follow Paul's counsel to "go on walking in wisdom toward those on the outside"?
13, 14. Why did the prospect of dying terrify many Babylonians, and how was Daniel's view different?

all manner of terrors. They believed that after death, those who had lived unhappily or had died violently became vengeful spirits who haunted the living. The Babylonians also believed in a terrifying netherworld, populated by hideous monsters in human and animal forms.

¹⁴ For Daniel, death meant none of those things. Hundreds of years before Daniel's day, King Solomon had been divinely inspired to say: "As for the dead, they are conscious of nothing at all." (Ecclesiastes 9:5) And concerning one who dies, the psalmist had sung: "His spirit goes out, he goes back to his ground; in that day his thoughts do perish." (Psalm 146:4) So Daniel knew that the angel's words to him would prove true. Death meant rest. No thoughts, no bitter regrets, no torment—and certainly no monsters. Jesus Christ expressed matters similarly when Lazarus died. He said: "Lazarus our friend has gone to rest."—John 11:11.

¹⁵ Consider another reason why the prospect of dying held no terrors for Daniel. God's Word says: "A name is better than good oil, and the day of death than the day of one's being born." (Ecclesiastes 7:1) How could the day of death, a mournful time if ever there was one, be better than the joyful day of birth? The key is in the "name." "Good oil" could be enormously costly. Lazarus' sister Mary once greased Jesus' feet with perfumed oil that cost nearly a year's wages! (John 12:1-7) How could a mere name be so precious? At Ecclesiastes 7:1, the Greek *Septuagint* says, "a good name." It is not merely the name but what it stands for that is so valuable. At his birth, there is no reputation, no record of fine works, no treasured memory of the name bearer's personality and qualities. But at life's end, the name signifies all these things. And

---

15. How can the day of death be better than the day of birth?

if it is a good name from God's standpoint, it is far more precious than any material possessions could ever be.

¹⁶ Throughout his life, Daniel did everything in his power to make a good name with God, and Jehovah overlooked none of this. He watched Daniel and examined his heart. God had done as much for King David, who sang: "O Jehovah, you have searched through me, and you know me. You yourself have come to know my sitting down and my rising up. You have considered my thought from far off." (Psalm 139:1, 2) Granted, Daniel was not perfect. He was a descendant of the sinner Adam and was a member of a sinful nation. (Romans 3:23) But Daniel repented of his sinfulness and kept trying to walk with his God in an upright way. The faithful prophet could therefore be confident that Jehovah would forgive his sins and would never hold them against him. (Psalm 103:10-14; Isaiah 1:18) Jehovah chooses to remember the good works of his faithful servants. (Hebrews 6:10) Thus, Jehovah's angel twice called Daniel a "very desirable man." (Daniel 10:11, 19) This meant that Daniel was beloved of God. Daniel could go to rest satisfied, knowing that he had made a good name with Jehovah.

¹⁷ Each of us may well ask, 'Have I made a good name with Jehovah?' We live in troubled times. It is not morbid but simply realistic to recognize that death may overtake any of us at any time. (Ecclesiastes 9:11) How vital it is, then, that each of us resolves to make a good name with God right now, without delay. If we do so, we need not fear death. It is a mere rest—like sleep. And like sleep, it is followed by an awakening!

---

16. (a) How did Daniel endeavor to make a good name with God? (b) Why could Daniel go to rest with full confidence that he had succeeded in making a good name with Jehovah?
17. Why is it urgent that we make a good name with Jehovah today?

"YOU WILL STAND UP"

¹⁸ The book of Daniel closes with one of the most beautiful promises God has ever made to a human. Jehovah's angel told Daniel: "You will stand up for your lot at the end of the days." What did the angel mean? Well, since the "rest" he had just referred to was death, the promise that Daniel would "stand up" at some later time could mean only one thing—resurrection!* In fact, some scholars have asserted that Daniel chapter 12 contains the first explicit reference to resurrection to be found in the Hebrew Scriptures. (Daniel 12:2) In this, though, they are wrong. Daniel was very familiar with the resurrection hope.

¹⁹ For example, Daniel no doubt knew these words that Isaiah had recorded two centuries earlier: "Your dead ones will live. A corpse of mine—they will rise up. Awake and cry out joyfully, you residents in the dust! For . . . the earth itself will let even those impotent in death drop in birth." (Isaiah 26:19) Long before that, Elijah and Elisha were empowered by Jehovah to perform actual resurrections. (1 Kings 17:17-24; 2 Kings 4:32-37) Even earlier, Hannah, the mother of the prophet Samuel, acknowledged that Jehovah is able to raise people up from Sheol, the grave. (1 Samuel 2:6) Earlier still, faithful Job expressed his own hope with these words: "If an able-bodied man dies can he live again? All the days of my compulsory service I shall wait, until my relief comes. You will call, and I myself shall answer you. For the work of your hands you will have a yearning."—Job 14:14, 15.

---

* According to *The Brown-Driver-Briggs Hebrew and English Lexicon,* the Hebrew word for "stand" used here refers to "revival after death."

18, 19. (a) What did the angel mean when he foretold that Daniel would "stand up" in the future? (b) Why would Daniel have been familiar with the resurrection hope?

²⁰ Like Job, Daniel had reason to be confident that Jehovah would actually yearn to bring him back to life one day in the future. Still, it must have been deeply comforting to hear a mighty spirit creature confirm that hope. Yes, Daniel will stand up in "the resurrection of the righteous ones," which will occur during Christ's Millennial Reign. (Luke 14:14) What will that be like for Daniel? God's Word tells us much about it.

²¹ Jehovah is "a God, not of disorder, but of peace." (1 Corinthians 14:33) It is evident, then, that the resurrection in Paradise will take place in an orderly way. Perhaps some time will have passed since Armageddon. (Revelation 16:14, 16) All vestiges of the old system of things will have been cleared away, and preparations will no doubt have been made to welcome back the dead. As to the order in which the dead will return, the Bible offers this precedent: "Each one in his own rank." (1 Corinthians 15:23) It seems likely that when it comes to 'the resurrection of the righteous and the unrighteous,' the righteous will be brought back first. (Acts 24:15) In that way, faithful men of old, such as Daniel, will be able to help in the administration of earthly affairs, including the instructing of billions of "unrighteous" ones brought back to life. —Psalm 45:16.

²² Before Daniel is ready to take on such responsibilities, he will surely have some questions to ask. After all, regarding some of the deep prophecies entrusted to him, he said: "I heard, but I could not understand." (Daniel 12:8) How thrilled he will be to understand these divine mysteries at last! No doubt he will want to hear all about the Messiah. Daniel will learn with fascination about the

---

20, 21. (a) Of what resurrection is Daniel sure to be a part? (b) In what way is the resurrection in Paradise likely to take place?
22. What are some questions that Daniel will no doubt be eager to have answered?

march of world powers from his day down to our own, about the identity of the faithful "holy ones of the Supreme One"—who persevered despite persecution during "the time of the end"—and about the final destruction of all human kingdoms by God's Messianic Kingdom. —Daniel 2:44; 7:22; 12:4.

DANIEL'S LOT IN PARADISE—AND YOURS!

²³ Daniel will want to know about the world in which he will find himself at that time—a world so unlike that of his day. Gone will be every trace of the wars and oppression that marred the world he knew. There will be no sorrow, no sickness, no death. (Isaiah 25:8; 33:24) But there will be an abundance of food, plentiful housing, and fulfilling work for all. (Psalm 72:16; Isaiah 65:21, 22) Mankind will be one united, happy family.

²⁴ Daniel will definitely have a place in that world. "You will stand up for *your lot*," the angel told him. The Hebrew word here translated "lot" is the same as that used for literal plots of land.* Daniel may have been familiar with Ezekiel's prophecy on the apportioning of the restored land of Israel. (Ezekiel 47:13–48:35) In its Paradise fulfillment, what does Ezekiel's prophecy suggest? That all of God's people will have a place in Paradise, even the land itself being apportioned in an orderly and just manner. Of course, Daniel's lot in Paradise will involve more than mere land. It will include his place in God's purpose there. Daniel's promised reward is guaranteed.

---

* The Hebrew word is related to the word for "pebble," as small stones were used for casting lots. Land was sometimes apportioned in this way. (Numbers 26:55, 56) *A Handbook on the Book of Daniel* says that here the word means "that which is set aside (by God) for a person."

23, 24. (a) How will the world in which Daniel finds himself resurrected differ from the one he knew? (b) Will Daniel have a place in Paradise, and how do we know?

Like Daniel, do you pay attention to God's prophetic word?

²⁵ What, though, about your lot? The same promises can apply to you. Jehovah wants obedient humans to "stand up" for their lot, to have a place in Paradise. Just think! Surely, it will be a thrill to meet Daniel in person, along with other faithful men and women of Bible times. Then there will be countless others returning from the dead, needing instruction so as to know and love Jehovah God. Picture yourself caring for our earthly home and helping to turn it into a paradise of infinite variety and undying beauty. Think of being taught by Jehovah, learning how to live the way he meant mankind to live. (Isaiah 11:9; John 6:45) Yes, there is a place for you in Paradise. Strange though Paradise may sound to some today, remember that Jehovah originally designed mankind to live in such a place. (Genesis 2:7-9) In that sense, Paradise is the natural habitat of earth's billions. It is where they belong. Reaching it will be like going home.

---

25. (a) What are some prospects of life in Paradise that appeal to you? (b) Why can it be said that humans belong in Paradise?

²⁶ Our hearts burn with appreciation when we think of all of this, do they not? Do you yourself not yearn to be there? No wonder, then, that Jehovah's Witnesses are eager to know when the end of this system of things will come! Waiting is not easy. Jehovah acknowledges as much, for he urges us to "keep in expectation" of the end "even if it should delay." He means that it may seem to delay from our point of view, for in the same scripture, we are assured: "It will not be late." (Habakkuk 2:3; compare Proverbs 13:12.) Yes, the end will come right on time.

²⁷ What should you do as the end nears? Like Jehovah's beloved prophet Daniel, endure faithfully. Study God's Word diligently. Pray fervently. Lovingly associate with fellow believers. Zealously teach the truth to others. With the end of this wicked system of things drawing closer every day, remain determined to be a loyal servant of the Most High and a staunch advocate of his Word. By all means, pay attention to Daniel's prophecy! And may the Sovereign Lord Jehovah grant you the privilege of standing before him joyfully throughout all eternity!

---

26. How does Jehovah acknowledge that waiting for the end of this system is not easy for us?
27. What must you do in order to stand before God throughout eternity?

WHAT DID YOU DISCERN?

- What helped Daniel to endure to the end?
- Why did the prospect of dying hold no terrors for Daniel?
- How will the angel's promise that Daniel 'will stand up for his lot' be fulfilled?
- How have you personally benefited by paying attention to Daniel's prophecy?

Would you welcome more information?
Write Watch Tower at appropriate address below.

ALASKA 99507: 2552 East 48th Ave., Anchorage. **ALBANIA:** Kutia Postare 118, Tiranë. **ANGOLA:** Caixa Postal 6877, Luanda. **ANTIGUA:** Box 119, St. Johns. **ARGENTINA:** Casilla de Correo 83 (Suc. 27B), 1427 Buenos Aires. **AUSTRALIA:** Box 280, Ingleburn, N.S.W. 2565. **AUSTRIA:** Postfach 67, A-1134 Vienna. **BAHAMAS:** Box N-1247, Nassau, N.P. **BARBADOS:** Fontabelle Rd., Bridgetown. **BELGIUM:** rue d'Argile–Potaardestraat 60, B-1950 Kraainem. **BELIZE:** Box 257, Belize City. **BENIN, REP. OF:** 06 B.P. 1131, Akpakpa pk3, Cotonou. **BOLIVIA:** Casilla 6397, Santa Cruz. **BRAZIL:** Caixa Postal 92, 18270-970 Tatuí, SP. **BRITAIN:** The Ridgeway, London NW7 1RN. **CAMEROON:** B.P. 889, Douala. **CANADA:** Box 4100, Halton Hills (Georgetown), Ontario L7G 4Y4. **CENTRAL AFRICAN REPUBLIC:** B.P. 662, Bangui. **CHILE:** Casilla 267, Puente Alto. **COLOMBIA:** Apartado Aéreo 85058, Santa Fe de Bogotá 8, D.C. **CONGO, DEMOCRATIC REPUBLIC OF:** B.P. 634, Limete, Kinshasa. **COSTA RICA:** Apartado 10043, San José. **CÔTE D'IVOIRE (IVORY COAST), WEST AFRICA:** 06 B P 393, Abidjan 06. **CROATIA:** p.p. 6058, HR-10090 Zagreb. **CURAÇAO, NETHERLANDS ANTILLES:** P.O. Box 4708, Willemstad. **CYPRUS:** P.O. Box 33, CY-2550 Dhali. **CZECH REPUBLIC:** P.O. Box 90, 198 21 Prague 9. **DENMARK:** Stenhusvej 28, DK-4300 Holbæk. **DOMINICAN REPUBLIC:** Apartado 1742, Santo Domingo. **ECUADOR:** Casilla 09-01-1334, Guayaquil. **EL SALVADOR:** Apartado Postal 401, San Salvador. **ESTONIA:** Postbox 73, 10502 Tallinn. **ETHIOPIA:** P.O. Box 5522, Addis Ababa. **FIJI:** Box 23, Suva. **FINLAND:** Postbox 68, FIN-01301 Vantaa 30. **FRANCE:** B.P. 625, F-27406 Louviers cedex. **GERMANY:** Niederselters, Am Steinfels, D-65618 Selters. **GHANA:** P. O. Box GP 760, Accra. **GREECE:** 77 Kifisias Ave., GR-151 24, Marousi, Athens. **GUADELOUPE:** Monmain, 97180 Sainte Anne. **GUAM 96913:** 143 Jehovah St., Barrigada. **GUATEMALA:** Apartado postal 711, 01901 Guatemala. **GUYANA:** 50 Brickdam, Georgetown 16. **GUYANE FRANÇAISE (FRENCH GUIANA):** CD 2, Route du Tigre, 97300 Cayenne. **HAITI:** Post Box 185, Port-au-Prince. **HAWAII 96819:** 2055 Kam IV Rd., Honolulu. **HONDURAS:** Apartado 147, Tegucigalpa. **HONG KONG:** 4 Kent Road, Kowloon Tong. **HUNGARY:** Cserkút u. 13, H-1162 Budapest. **ICELAND:** P. O. Box 8496, IS-128 Reykjavík. **INDIA:** Post Bag 10, Lonavla, Pune Dis., Mah. 410 401. **IRELAND:** Newcastle, Greystones, Co. Wicklow. **ISRAEL:** P. O. Box 961, 61-009 Tel Aviv. **ITALY:** Via della Bufalotta 1281, I-00138 Rome RM. **JAMAICA:** Box 103, Old Harbour P.O., St. Catherine. **JAPAN:** 1271 Nakashinden, Ebina City, Kanagawa Pref., 243-0496. **KENYA:** Box 47788, Nairobi. **KOREA, REPUBLIC OF:** Box 33 Pyungtaek P. O., Kyunggido, 450-600. **LIBERIA:** P. O. Box 10-0380, 1000 Monrovia 10. **LUXEMBOURG:** B. P. 2186, L-1021 Luxembourg, G. D. **MACEDONIA, REPUBLIC OF:** P.f. 800, 91000 Skopje. **MADAGASCAR:** B.P. 116, 105 Ivato. **MALAWI:** Box 30749, Lilongwe 3. **MALAYSIA:** Peti Surat No. 580, 75760 Melaka. **MARTINIQUE:** 20, Cour Campêche, 97200 Fort de France. **MAURITIUS:** Rue Baissac, Petit Verger, Pointe aux Sables. **MEXICO:** Apartado Postal 896, 06002 Mexico, D. F. **MOLDOVA, REPUBLIC OF:** Căsuţa poştală 3263, MD-2044 Chişinău. **MOZAMBIQUE:** Caixa Postal 2600, Maputo. **MYANMAR:** P.O. Box 62, Yangon. **NETHERLANDS:** Noordbargerstraat 77, NL-7812 AA Emmen. **NEW CALEDONIA:** BP 1741, 98810 Mont Dore. **NEW ZEALAND:** P. O. Box 142, Manurewa. **NICARAGUA:** Apartado 3587, Managua. **NIGERIA:** P.M.B. 1090, Benin City, Edo State. **NORWAY:** Gaupeveien 24, N-1914 Ytre Enebakk. **PAKISTAN:** P.O. Box 3883, Karachi 75600. **PANAMA:** Apartado 6-2671, Zona 6A, El Dorado. **PAPUA NEW GUINEA:** Box 636, Boroko, NCD 111. **PARAGUAY:** Casilla de Correo 482, 1209 Asunción. **PERU:** Apartado 18-1055, Lima 18. **PHILIPPINES, REPUBLIC OF:** P. O. Box 2044, 1060 Manila. **POLAND:** Skr. Poczt. 13, PL-05-830 Nadarzyn. **PORTUGAL:** Apartado 91, P-2766 Estoril Codex. **PUERTO RICO 00970:** P.O. Box 3980, Guaynabo. **ROMANIA:** Căsuţa Poştală nr. 132, O.P. 39 Bucureşti. **RUSSIA:** Srednyaya 6, Solnechnoye, 189649 St. Petersburg. **SAMOA:** P. O. Box 673, Apia. **SENEGAL:** B.P. 3107, Dakar. **SIERRA LEONE, WEST AFRICA:** P. O. Box 136, Freetown. **SLOVAKIA:** P.O. Box 17, 810 00 Bratislava 1. **SLOVENIA:** Poljanska cesta 77 A, p.p. 2019, SI-1001 Ljubljana. **SOLOMON ISLANDS:** P.O. Box 166, Honiara. **SOUTH AFRICA:** Private Bag X2067, Krugersdorp, 1740. **SPAIN:** Apartado postal 132, 28850 Torrejón de Ardoz (Madrid). **SRI LANKA, REP. OF:** 711 Station Road, Wattala 11300. **SURINAME:** P.O. Box 2914, Paramaribo. **SWEDEN:** Box 5, SE-732 21 Arboga. **SWITZERLAND:** P.O. Box 225, CH-3602 Thun. **TAHITI:** B.P. 7715, 98719 Taravao. **TAIWAN:** No. 3-12, 10 Lin, Shetze, Hsinwu, Taoyuan, 327. **THAILAND:** 69/1 Soi Phasuk, Sukhumwit Rd., Soi 2, Bangkok 10110. **TOGO:** B.P. 4460, Lome. **TRINIDAD AND TOBAGO, REP. OF:** Lower Rapsey Street & Laxmi Lane, Curepe. **UKRAINE:** P.O. Box 246, 290000 Lviv. **UNITED STATES OF AMERICA:** 25 Columbia Heights, Brooklyn, NY 11201-2483. **URUGUAY:** Francisco Bauzá 3372, Casilla de Correo 16006, 11600 Montevideo. **VENEZUELA:** Apartado 20.364, Caracas, DF 1020A. **YUGOSLAVIA, F.R.:** p. fah 173, YU-11080 Beograd, Serbia. **ZAMBIA:** Box 33459, Lusaka 10101. **ZIMBABWE:** P. Bag A-6113, Avondale.